Meeting of the Minds

Meeting
of
the Minds

CREATING THE MARKET-BASED
ENTERPRISE

Vincent P. Barabba

Harvard Business School Press
Boston, Massachusetts

JAN 10 1997

Library of Congress Cataloging-in-Publication Data

Barabba, Vincent P., 1934–
    Meeting of the minds : creating the market-based enterprise /
Vincent P. Barabba.
        p.   cm.
    Includes bibliographical references and index.
    ISBN 0-87584-577-0
    1. Marketing research.   2. Marketing—Decision making.   3. New
products.   4. Consumer satisfaction.   I. Title.
HF5415.2.B333   1995
658.8'3—dc20   95-13342
                                                                                          CIP

The paper used in this publication meets the requirements of the American National
Standard for Permanence of Paper for Printed Library Materials Z39.49-1984.

To my wife, Sheryl . . . a mind worth meeting

CONTENTS

PREFACE

Woodworking is my hobby. I deeply enjoy the hours spent "making chips" in the shop and rummaging in musty antique stores and barn corners in search of the old tools that created the handmade things I have come to cherish. To my surprise—and delight—I recently came upon two stories from the lore of woodworking that have helped me to understand the connection between my hobby and my livelihood—showing how both have benefited enormously from "systems thinking."

In *The American Cabinetmaker's Plow Plane,* John A. Moody imagines "a dirt floored cabinet maker's shop. The tools are primitive, but the Joiner knows them well, and knows as the Pharaoh's carpenter he enjoys special privileges."[1] The Pharaoh wants this carpenter to build him a perfect chest to take into the afterlife—one that will be tightly built and yet remain free of cracks through eternity.

The Pharaoh's request creates a dilemma for our carpenter. He knows from observation to expect wood to shrink in dry weather and expand in dampness. Shrinkage and expansion are not problems when the wood stands in the workshop, but if bound tightly into a chest, the wood will surely crack. The carpenter could avoid this problem by joining the wood panels in a way that leaves room between them for expansion, but then the Pharaoh's requirement for a tightly built chest would not be met and the carpenter could find himself joining not wood but the Pharaoh in the afterlife. So how can our carpenter satisfy this demanding customer?

Moody describes the synthesis of observation, experience, and a desire to succeed that leads to the resolution of this dilemma: "Then, one day . . . the Joiner thought—'What if I make the ends of chest panels, with their edges in grooves, free to shrink or expand?' So he slipped the edges of the panels into grooved posts and rails. The panels were thus free to expand and contract within the grooves allowing the chest to remain tight *and* free of cracks forever."[2]

Modern decision makers face similar dilemmas. Like Pharaoh's carpenter, they have ways of doing things, but the old ways are often insufficient to meet the more stringent demands of today's customers, whose requirements, like those of the Pharaoh, often seem mutually exclusive—at least at first glance. High quality at low prices. Products that are environmentally safe *and* highly effective. High value for customers *and* profits for shareholders. And on and on. The carpenter solved what had appeared to be an unsolvable dilemma by viewing his product (the chest) in a new way—not as the sum of its parts but as a system of interdependent parts. In so doing, he discovered that the solution lay not in fixing any one of the parts but in fixing the way they interact—a classic example of systems thinking.

Thomas Levenson offers another example of systems thinking in his article "How Not to Make a Stradivarius." After stating a core principle of experimental science—that "what one person can discover any other can find again"—he wonders why it is that for more than three centuries no one has been able to rediscover the secret of the great instrument maker or "build an instrument that reproduces the range, power and expressiveness of the Stradivari sound." It is clear to Levenson that Stradivari had mastered his physics, "for while one great instrument might be an accident, hundreds cannot be, which certainly suggests that Stradivari knew what he was doing."[3] But why is it that others—who also know their physics—cannot find again what Stradivari understood and practiced?

Levenson's conclusion is that modern sleuths, using the methods of modern science, analyze the parts of the instrument in a search for a single solution to the Stradivarius puzzle. But "the answer, most simple, is that the cello, any cello, is more than the sum of its parts."[4] The real secret of the Stradivarius is that it represents a system that combines the physics of materials and vibrating strings with the unique understanding and vision that Stradivari developed over years of making stringed instruments. Science can tell us a great deal about the former (theory), but little about the latter (practice). Stradivari had both, and this combined understanding, melded by his passion and vision, created a sound of unparalleled quality.

Just as those who have attempted to duplicate the Stradivarius have failed, those who describe marketing as a function and those who do marketing for a living have failed to bring theory and practice together in a way that produces a harmonious enterprise that works for the customer, the community, and the enterprise itself. This book uses understanding gained from theory and experience gained from practice to paint a picture of an enterprise designed to interact with customers and community. The result of this interaction generates greater value than the sum of the individual parts of the extended enterprise. It involves moving from marketing as a way of doing things (a component function of a system) to marketing as a state of mind that seeks improved customer and enterprise value by optimizing the interactions of all the components of the extended enterprise. It attempts to fulfill a challenge set forth by Wroe Alderson many years ago when he wrote, "In the longer view, theory should facilitate the accumulation and integration of a body of knowledge, so that what is learned through coping with one set of problems can be brought to bear on others."[5]

During a long career in business and government, I have had the opportunity to learn from many sets of problems with dozens of talented people. Many were academics who had temporarily migrated from the ivory tower to apply their theories to practical problems—often with exceptional results. The most enduring of these relationships were with Russ Ackoff, James Bonnen, John Henderson, Ron Howard, Bill Kruskal, John Little, Richard Mason, Ian Mitroff, Everett Rogers, Glen Urban, Gerald Zaltman, and the late W. Edwards Deming. These individuals, particularly Russ Ackoff, introduced me to the theory, the tools, and the importance of systems thinking.

Academics carry forward the scientific approach to making sense of the world around us. This approach is based on observation and experimentation in which environmental variables are controlled. From these controlled experiments, it is reasoned, the laws of nature can be determined and cause-and-effect relationships understood. The outcome of such work takes the form of *formal* theory. My own university education was based on this approach.

My on-the-job education, however, has followed another method entirely and has produced insights, intuitions, and understandings better described as *informal* theory. Gerald Zaltman, now a professor at the Harvard Business School, helped me to understand the differences between formal theory and the informal theories that many of us develop over years of problem-solving experience. Formal theory, by his definition, is a model consisting of concepts connected to form hypotheses under carefully controlled experimental conditions. In other words, if it can't be measured or controlled—hold it constant. Informal theory, on the other hand, is based on everyday observations, having less than precise concepts. The elements of informal theory are intuitively related; its development seldom relies on a controlled experiment.

This book is a synthesis of both forms of theory. The formal theories come from the scholars just mentioned as well as from the writings of Wroe Alderson, Chris Argyris, C. West Churchman, James G. March, Abraham Maslow, and Peter Senge, to name only a few. The informal theories are drawn from years of creating and developing ideas, programs, and products in political campaigns, in government, and in small and large businesses. The range of applications from which these theories derive is both wide and deep: voter research, two appointments as director of the U.S. Census Bureau, and market research and decision analysis with Xerox, Eastman Kodak, and General Motors. By synthesizing these two very different forms of understanding, I hope to avoid the following errors so often associated with "scientific" inquiry:

- What one person can discover any other can find again.
- There is a single right answer.
- Understanding the elements of a system is sufficient to understanding the system itself.
- The role of personal vision and passion can be ignored.

In discussing different approaches to improving the enterprise, I have tried to present them as viable alternatives—not competing ideas. Though differences in each approach are identified and appreciated, the book tries not to set up competition between them; there is limited whipping of straw men to make one idea appear superior to another (for example, both the strengths and limitations of consumer research are presented). This contrivance of creating an easily defeated straw man merely distracts the reader from the basic value that can be learned from the differences.

Nor is the reader offered a silver bullet that purports to solve every business problem. Business is far too complex for one-shot remedies. Indeed, the ideas offered here are necessary to but not sufficient for the creation of a successful enterprise.

Throughout, this book adheres to the notion of the *extended enterprise*—a notion that will become the norm in the years ahead. Stakeholders in this enterprise are all those individuals or entities that can either affect or be affected by decisions of the enterprise.[6] Though the list of stakeholders is diverse, this book collapses them into three groups:

- the customer, which includes any individual or entity in the distribution system that accepts a product or service from the enterprise;
- the community, which is made up of customers and noncustomers in a societal context, the governments that represent them, the special-interest groups that carry strong views on specific issues, and competitors for customer and community attention and resources; and
- the enterprise, which in addition to its employees includes everyone who contributes to the creation, production, or delivery of its products and services (suppliers, investors, engineers, etc.).

As a system, the extended enterprise must simultaneously deal with the interests of each group, seeking synergy in the systematic relationship. If the total value of that relationship is greater than the sum of the individual contributions, the relationship will flourish; if not, the relationship will and should fail. The synergy of the extended enterprise system is greatest when there is a meeting of the minds of the customers, the community, and the enterprise.

ACKNOWLEDGMENTS

In addition to the aforementioned colleagues, I would like to acknowledge the cooperation, criticism, and patience of the following, without whom my development of informal theory would not have occurred: Ken Baker, J. T. Battenberg III, Donald K. Brown, Wayne Cherry, Wendy Coles, Jerry Collins, Tom Davis, George Day, Robert Dorn, Mike DiGiovanni, Michael Grimaldi, Don Hackworth, Steve Haeckel, Jeff Hartley, Patricia Hawkins, Alice Hayes, Bob Hendry, George Humphreys, Ralph Kilmann, Rob Kleinbaum, Michael Kusnic, Robert Macon, Richard Mason, Joe D. Miller, Arv Mueller, Bob O'Connell, Jack Osborn, Dan Owen, Barbara Richardson, Sheila Ronis, Don Runkle, J. Philip Samper,

John Smale, Richard Smallwood, Stu Spencer, Carl Spetzler, Joe Spielman, Vince Vacarelli, Steve Weiss, and my first partner, Richard Wirthlin. Those who made specific contributions are acknowledged within the book itself. Deep appreciation is offered to Chris Guerrini for her patience in keeping the stacks of papers in reasonable order while I continued to perform my regular job and to Mary Frances Mullin for helping me find my way through the GM archives and for assisting in documenting the notes.

Special acknowledgment is made of Richard Luecke, who through his experience in writing books and his deep understanding of the publishing business helped to clarify many of my opaque thoughts and to make *Meeting of the Minds* a more interesting and readable book.

NOTES

1. John A. Moody, *The American Cabinetmaker's Plow Plane: Its Design and Improvement, 1700–1900* (Evansville, Ind.: The Tool Box, 1981), 3.

2. Ibid.

3. Thomas Levenson, "How Not to Make a Stradivarius," *American Scholar* (summer 1994): 351.

4. Ibid., 369.

5. Wroe Alderson, *Marketing Behavior and Executive Action* (Homewood, Ill.: Richard D. Irwin, Inc., 1957), 7.

6. For elaboration on stakeholders, see Russell L. Ackoff, *The Democratic Corporation: A Radical Prescription for Recreating Corporate America and Rediscovering Success* (New York: Oxford University Press, 1994), 38, and Ian I. Mitroff, Ralph H. Kilmann, and Vincent P. Barabba, "Management Information versus Misinformation Systems," *Management Principles for Nonprofit Agencies and Organizations*, ed. Gerald Zaltman (New York: American Management Association, 1979), 401–429.

Meeting of the Minds

INTRODUCTION

Winning isn't everything—it's the only thing!
Vince Lombardi
Knowledge is power.
Sir Francis Bacon
What's good for General Motors is good for the Country.
Charles E. Wilson

Sir Francis Bacon, Vince Lombardi, and Charles E. Wilson had at least one thing in common. All three were misquoted. Coaches and motivational speakers by the hundreds assert that Lombardi said, "Winning isn't everything—it's the only thing!" What he actually said was, "Winning isn't everything. The desire to win is everything. In fact, it's the only thing!"

The phrase "Knowledge is power" attributed to Bacon is usually used in the sense that controlling knowledge is controlling power. Bacon, however, in a statement on the relationship of knowledge of God to God's power, actually said, "For Knowledge itself is Power." His remark reflects the sixteenth-century view that knowledge is the power through which humankind could create a better life here on earth. For Bacon and his contemporaries, knowledge was a resource that made it possible for other good things to happen.

During his U.S. Senate confirmation hearing to become secretary of defense, former GM president Charles E. Wilson was asked, "if a situation did arise where you had to make a decision which was extremely adverse to the interests of your stock and General Motors Corporation . . . , in the interest of the United States Government, could you make that decision?" Wilson replied, "Yes, sir; I could. I cannot conceive of [a conflict] because for years I thought what was good for our country was good for General Motors and vice versa."[1]

If they were alive and in a position to apply their values and beliefs to the current state of affairs in modern business, all three of these misquoted men would probably uphold the notion that knowledge of the enterprise and the markets it serves is a power through which the enterprise can cause good things to happen to customers, to the community, and, by extension, to itself. Their actual views—Bacon's understanding of the power of knowledge to cause good things to happen, Vince Lombardi's value of the desire to be successful (the process) over the success itself (the outcome), and Charles E. Wilson's recognition of the interdependence of the enterprise and its community—are consistent with what experienced managers and business scholars agree on: that a passion for understanding and creating customers and serving their individual needs and wants as well as those of the community is the whole point of being in business.

Meeting of the Minds is based on the following premise: If you provide customers with innovative solutions to what they want and need, keep your costs below what your customers are willing to pay, and make sure your employees are healthy, motivated, and informed, all else should follow—profits, growth, a sense of accomplishment and service, and favorable recognition by the communities within which you exist.

Peter Drucker may have been the first to say in print what many highly successful managers have said through their actions over the years, that "There is only one valid definition of business purpose: to create a customer."[2] Making good on Drucker's simple rule for action, however, is anything but simple. Doing so presumes an intimate knowledge of the customer that is difficult to come by. How customers can be created is never certain. What customers want and need isn't always obvious— even to them. Sony Corporation has sold millions of Walkman radio and tape players over the past decade. But how many people had any inkling that they wanted—much less needed—a device like the Walkman before joggers and subway commuters by the millions began wearing them? Knowing what customers *don't* want and *don't* need is also less than obvious. It was the same Sony Corporation, after all, that hitched its fortunes to the beta-format VCR when the VHS format was on its way to becoming the established standard.

Even when customer needs (what they require) are fairly certain, customer wants (what they desire or aspire to) can surprise you. Simple household demographics can tell you how many families need a motor vehicle capable of accommodating five people, their cargo, and the family dog. To automakers, the facts almost shout the words *minivan* . . .

station wagon! But when some car shoppers walk into the showroom, a few of these same "family" people—children in tow—head directly and glassy-eyed to the sporty convertible with bucket seats and enough cargo space for a briefcase and airplane bag. This may not be what these customers need, but it is certainly what some of them want.

Understanding the customer is rarely easy, perhaps because people are so complex. Nor is success permanent. The customer keeps changing. Henry Ford was a genius in developing and mass-producing a simple and affordable automobile. The Model T was just what a lot of people needed at the time, and it made Ford the richest man in America. But Ford committed the cardinal sin of thinking that his standard black Model T represented the culmination of the auto transportation needs of the American public, which it was—for a while—but not forever. The market changed, moving away from Ford to the greater product variety and annual model changes that Alfred Sloan and General Motors were willing to provide. The fortunes of the Ford Motor Company declined almost to the point of failure, while those of GM rose. Half a century later, all U.S. automakers felt the tides of consumer sentiment shift yet again—this time away from their chromed-outfitted powerhouses to the smaller, more efficient, higher-quality vehicles that foreign car companies had learned to produce. Even the demand for these smaller and more efficient cars has turned out to be somewhat fickle.

Understanding customers and acting to satisfy their needs and wants is—just as it always has been—the ultimate challenge of modern business organizations. Over the years, these businesses have created marketing and market research departments to meet this challenge, investing them with "ownership" of the customer. This seemed logical enough. After all, manufacturing "owned" the factory, finance owned the books, human resources controlled staffing and employment, and so forth. As in the medieval universe, there was a place for everything, and everything was in its place. Senior management could hover overhead, pulling the strings that led to each department, making the organization dance like a marionette to whichever tune seemed most timely.

Ownership of the customer by the marketing organization, however, has proven to be an idea whose time has passed. Customers are too complex and the signals they send about their needs and wants are too varied, too subtle for marketing alone to detect in their entirety. Every day, customers indicate their preferences, their likes and dislikes of current products and services, their innovative ways of using or improving off-the-shelf products. A marketing organization will pick up some of these signals, but not others. Product developers and service engineers often pick up different signals in dealing with "lead users" (pioneering adopters of newly developed products); they learn how the company's new products are being used or adapted. Service departments and repair facilities see a side of the customer that market researchers seldom see. Credit departments are privy to important information about the buying power of individual customers and dealers. But how many of these signals actually find their way to the marketing department, the sanctioned owner of the customer?

Each of us sees the world through a unique set of lenses that is determined by our personal experiences, our responsibilities, and our singular interests. The result is that none of us, either as an individual or as part of a functional group, sees reality in its entirety. This is sometimes referred to as the *silo problem*. The silo problem is one of particularism versus globalism. In the typical business organization, employees have particular interests, particular tasks, and particular responsibilities, and these are organized into narrow, vertically structured functions. Those who manage the business, on the other hand, have broader interests and more general tasks and responsibilities.

My first encounter with the silo problem occurred during my senior year as an undergraduate student. One of my professors had developed a business simulation in which students were organized into teams that competed in making and selling a product. One year, instead of assigning students to a particular team at random, the professor organized the students according to major. This led to strikingly different outcomes. The marketing majors spent most of their time and money on sales and promotion. They acquired an impressive share of the total market, but at high cost, and were bankrupt before the game ended. The accounting majors aimed at maximizing profits by minimizing investments in products and promotion. With no new products and only meager promotion of existing ones, the eyeshade brigade lost market share and slipped by degrees into bankruptcy. The production majors spent all their money on product development and manufacturing processes. They ended up with great products at the right prices, but with no money to tell customers about them, they too went out of business. To the consternation of all concerned, the personnel majors won. The marketing majors ran out of money, the accountants ran out of products, and the production majors ran out of customers. The personnel types occupied themselves with endless changes to the organization chart. Having spent no money, they simply ran out of time and won the game by default.

Unfortunately, our corporate organizations too often fail to bring together cross-functional teams. In the traditional organization, market data acquired by different functions of the business generally fall into separate silos, where the data do little to enrich what the enterprise knows. Marketing knows what it knows, engineers know what they know, and so forth. By themselves, these isolated bits of information are often meaningless, but when combined with other information from other sources, they can take on great importance. Like threads in a tapestry, single threads of information are of little value; when woven together properly, however, they form a coherent image of greater value.

The failure of organizations to bring together bits of information already captured in separate functional areas can be catastrophic. My generation, which grew up in the shadows of World War II, was schooled to remember the American disaster of Pearl Harbor. One of the great lessons of that event—and a shocking revelation to many even today—came from the discovery of how many indications the U.S. government and its military establishment had had of the impending Japanese attack in the weeks, days, and hours before the first enemy aircraft struck. As Gordon Prange, the leading historical authority on the event, writes: "Pearl Harbor was less a failure of intelligence than a failure to use the excellent data available."[3] Even if all the data had been brought together, the attack on December 7, 1941, would have occurred, but it would not have been a surprise. Japanese radio messages hinting at imminent operations were intercepted and decoded by naval intelligence, but these warnings were never passed on to Adm. Husband E. Kimmel, commander of the U.S. Pacific Fleet on Oahu. Valuable data obtained through "Magic," the War Department's secret code-breaking operation, were confined to a small group of cryptographers and technical officers. It was known in

Washington, for instance, that Japanese consular officials in Honolulu had been ordered to step up their observations of U.S. naval preparedness at Pearl Harbor and to report ship and defensive positions, but this knowledge was not passed on to local commanders.

On Oahu, lack of information coordination played a part in the disaster. The U.S. Army's commanding general, William Short, had been ordered by the War Department to provide reconnaissance because of growing tensions with Japan. He complied by intensifying radar surveillance, but radar personnel were never informed of the gravity of the situation and viewed their activities as normal training. So when two privates observed a large blip on the radar screen indicating incoming planes to Oahu, their lieutenant assumed it to be a flight of U.S. B-17 bombers and told the privates, "Well, don't worry about it." Even the fact that Oahu's combat intelligence unit had lost track of six Japanese carriers failed to connect with other pertinent facts available to the island's defenders.

Prange viewed the greatest lesson of Pearl Harbor as "the need for a centralized pool of intelligence" in which data were not merely available but properly evaluated and disseminated.[4] Henry Clausen, a special investigator appointed by the secretary of the War Department to determine the cause or causes of the disaster, also concluded that the United States had all the intelligence data required to accurately predict the attack on Pearl Harbor. Clausen found that lack of teamwork, turf issues, interservice rivalries, and lack of a sense of urgency explained why that intelligence data failed to come together in a clear warning to the U.S. fleet.[5]

Lack of teamwork. Turf issues. Interfunctional rivalries. Just as these factors caused American armed forces to fail to acknowledge and act on the warnings of an impending air attack in 1941, they stand in the way of enterprises as they try to listen to the voice of the market and to respond appropriately.[6]

Unfortunately, most large enterprises, like my professor's teams, are organized in ways that prevent the signals of the marketplace from forming a rich and vivid picture of what customers need and/or want. Organized by functions, or silos, knowledge and market information captured by one function tends to be trapped within that function, never enriching the market understanding of the others. By the same token, the tradition of organizing by functional activities makes it difficult for people to form a co-herent picture of what the enterprise as a whole is capable of delivering.

If the enterprise is to fulfill its purpose as creator and servant of cus-tomers, management must mold it to the form of its chosen customers and the competitive environment in which it exists. In nature, species that survive do so because they are formed to meet the challenges of their environments. Humpback whales survive because their mouths have ba-leen, fibrous strainers that catch the tiny krill and plankton that fill vast parts of the sea. Hawks survive because their combination of vision, soar-ing wings, and talons help them prey upon the small birds and mammals that live in open fields and meadows. These animals have evolved in a way that allows them to respond to the challenges they face every day. If their environments change faster than they can biologically evolve, however, they are out of luck. Few animal species have the capacity to adapt to this type of change.

Human beings and their organizations are quite different. To some de-gree they too must form themselves to the environment. But they also have the capacity to change the environment. Jacob Bronowski describes this difference between human beings and other animals quite simply: "Man is a single creature. He has a set of gifts which make him unique among the animals: so that, unlike them, he is not a figure in the land-scape—he is a shaper of the landscape. In body and in mind he is the explorer of nature, the ubiquitous animal, who did not find but has made his home in every continent."[7]

As we will see later, many business organizations have failed on both counts: adaptation and creation. Their market environments have changed, but they have not changed with them. Nor have they shaped their markets in ways that ensure their own success and survival. Many enterprises remain relics of the factory age and a long-vanished seller's market in which companies sold what they made and customers bought what they were offered, the Model-T age of the mass market and mass communication. The environment has changed, but leaders have not re-formed their enterprises. Nor do they have the luxury of "evolutionary time" in which to change. If corporate leaders do not cause the changes to occur, their enterprises, like other endangered species, will be replaced by better, more adaptive competitors.

All sloganeering about being "market-driven" notwithstanding, many managers are still struggling to fulfill Drucker's injunction to address the customer in a satisfactory way. If managers limit the change to organizational adaptations to fit the current competitive environment, they will observe some improvement, but not a solution. The environment keeps changing. What is needed is a mechanism that allows managers to do what they are uniquely capable of doing: keep the enterprise on the same evolutionary trajectory as its markets and customers by altering both to the extent possible. What is needed is a systematic approach. Russell Ackoff defines a system as "any entity, conceptual or physical, which consists of interdependent parts." Conversely, "a system is a whole that cannot be divided into independent parts."[8]

What this means for the market-based enterprise is that each element of the organization must rely on and interact with the rest of the organization if the organization as a whole is to succeed. Problems are best solved not by breaking them up into functional bites but by carrying them into the next larger system and solving them through integrative mechanisms.

Using knowledge about the customer to develop products and services that meet customer requirements is not a new idea. It's talked about a great deal, but it doesn't get done very well very often. This book explains why. And it provides a framework for and a vision of the enterprise as a system in which all functional units—including the marketing organization—work as a team to develop knowledge about the market and use that knowledge to make decisions that create satisfied customers—no matter what external changes take place. To make this vision a reality, the enterprise must tap its most valuable and least-accessed resource— the knowledge base held in the minds of its experienced and creative employees, its external associates, its customers, and the community in which it exists. This book provides a plan of action, showing managers how to learn about customers and about their own capabilities. It also discusses approaches to capturing that learning in a bank of knowledge to which all can contribute and from which all can draw. That knowledge bank becomes the memory, the mind, and the nervous system of the enterprise, cutting through all the artificial boundaries created by labels such as "finance," "engineering," "product development," and "marketing." It is the repository of everything the enterprise has learned, and it is available for all to share in serving customers.

Knowledge for its own sake, as Bacon surely understood, is sterile. It must serve a purpose to have real value. The power of knowledge lies in its role as a basis for action. For the enterprise, knowledge must serve as a basis for decision making and the allocation of resources that follow from those decisions. Indeed, knowledge forms the basis for a network of decisions within the enterprise: decisions on the creation of products and services, on the allocation of resources in ways that best satisfy customers, and on future strategy. The network of decisions based on market knowledge integrates the functional activities of the enterprise, allowing people, as Charles Savage says, to "reach out to one another to work on whole sets of challenges in teams and clusters of teams in distributed environments across functional and organizational boundaries."[9] Russell Ackoff reinforces this point by stating, "The performance of a system is not the sum of the performance of its parts taken separately, but the product of their interactions."[10]

Creating and using knowledge requires managing the balance and interactions between the three most challenging activities any successful organization engages in: listening, learning, and leading. We listen to acquire information about the market and other parts of the enterprise. We learn by processing and sharing that information. And we lead when we establish a decision-making process through which people can act. The extent to which an enterprise can listen, learn, and lead generally determines the dimensions of business success or failure.

In 1988, Peter Drucker observed that

> we are entering a third period of change: a shift from the command-and-control organization, the organization of departments and divisions, to the information-based organization, the organization of knowledge specialists. . . . But the job of actually building the information-based organization is still ahead of us—it is the managerial challenge of the future.[11]

The chapters that follow address this managerial challenge. They describe practical ways in which organizations can be transformed from the nineteenth-century command-and-control model that still dominates commercial enterprise into a twenty-first-century contextual model that coordinates the enterprise's use of resources with its use of knowledge and a network of market-based decisions. We will see how cross-functional and integrated processes have already reshaped a number of successful enterprises, providing them with the means to capture and use market information to serve customers. This is shown to be an important step, but only one step, on the road to building a market-based enterprise. This new-style enterprise knows how to listen to the market, to learn from what it hears and experiences, and, from this learning, to develop the capacity to lead with products and services that create and satisfy customers.

This is not a book about organizational theory or about the technicalities of market research. Nor is the idea of the market-based enterprise some "blue sky" notion of how enterprises will operate in the era of Jean Luc Picard (or even Captain Kirk). Many contemporary corporations— large and small—are working (or have worked) through these challenges successfully, and some of these are described where appropriate. The role of management in making the transition to the market-based enterprise is explained. Dealing with change is a big part of the manager's job, and the last chapter of this book describes the "knowledge use network" as the instrument of change in moving from a corporation driven by functions to one driven by people empowered with knowledge of the market and of their own capabilities. Many examples of the knowledge use network in action are drawn from General Motors, where such new approaches for decision making are a key part of the revitalization now in process. Equally valuable examples are drawn from other sources.

The concepts described in this book have important meaning for customers, for product developers, for researchers, and for general managers. No one, however, is more affected by these concepts than are the marketer and members of what I describe as the information priesthood (e.g., market researchers, forecasters, data base managers, and so forth). As Chapter 2 points out, corporations that truly adopt the marketing concept as defined in these pages have no further need for marketing as a distinct entity within the organization. Logically, it should disappear as a separate entity.

It is doubtful that the idea mentioned earlier of how marketing "owns the customer" has ever been formally advocated. Few scholars or managers have gone on record as supporting it. Yet marketing departments believe they own the customer in many business organizations today. This book calls for a shift from marketing as a function to marketing as a state of mind (systems thinking).[12] In the market-based enterprise, marketing is everyone's business. Marketing activities will surely persist; there will still be a need for sales, distribution, advertising, and service. But marketing as a separate function will no longer be necessary because creating and satisfying customers will be a priority for everyone everywhere in the organization. Likewise, the collectors and keepers of market information will find a new and higher purpose in the enterprise.

As a student of the process of developing useful knowledge, I became interested in the integrative power of market and societal knowledge years ago while working at the U.S. Census Bureau, Xerox, and Eastman Kodak, and my interest continued when I joined General Motors in 1985 as executive director of market research and planning. In 1992, the enterprise took a formal step in adopting this concept of looking at customers (market) in the context of their community (society) when it set up the General Motors Business Decision Center (now called the Strategic Decision Center). It was a humbling experience, therefore, when I discovered that many of the ideas I espoused, ideas that GM and other enterprises were experimenting with, had been intuitively understood by those who managed the company during its initial glory days.

My excursions into the GM archives have produced a number of interesting discoveries, some of which find their way into subsequent chapters. This letter from Alfred Sloan to GM stockholders on September 11, 1933, seems apropos here:

To Stockholders:

It so happens that the enclosed dividend check will reach you shortly before the twenty-fifth anniversary of General Motors. In a general way the past twenty-five years might be described as an era of broad technological development bearing vitally upon the country's growth. In this field the automobile industry has played a leading part—and General Motors, through its laboratories, its proving ground facilities and its engineering staffs has contributed in no small way to the progress of that great key industry. . . .

To me, however, the present seems an especially appropriate time to briefly discuss another phase of General Motors fact-finding, which, although in no sense new to the Corporation, is peculiarly deserving of our intensified study and attention in line with the spirit and philosophy of the times. *I refer to fact-finding in its application to the tastes and desires of the great consuming public—or what is generally described as Consumer Research* [emphasis added]. Modern manufacturing methods have brought about tremendous savings to the consumer. Through modern technique, products undreamed of by our forefathers have been brought into being, and placed within reach of everybody. But as a result of large scale operations and world-wide distribution, producer and consumer have become more and more widely separated, so that the matter of keeping a business sensitively in tune with the requirements of the ultimate consumer becomes a matter of increasing importance.

Through Consumer Research General Motors aims to bridge this gap and provide guidance not only with reference to details of design but as regards public relations, advertising, sales, service—in fact, everything affecting our customer relations, directly and indirectly [emphasis added]. . . .

The activities of the Customer Research Staff involve sending out questionnaires, calling on owners, and digesting customer reactions flowing into the Corporation through miscellaneous channels. During the past year well over 1,000,000 motorists have been invited "to pool their practical experience with the technical skill of General Motors engineers and production experts." But it would be a mistake to think of Consumer Research as an isolated department. Sending out questionnaires, calling on people and compiling statistics—these are only incidents, or tools; very important tools, to be sure, but tools nevertheless.

To discuss consumer research as a functional activity would give an erroneous impression. In its broad implications it is more in the nature of an OPERATING PHILOSOPHY, which, to be fully effective, must extend through all phases of a business—weighing every action from the standpoint of how it affects the goodwill of the institution, recognizing that *the quickest way to profits—and the permanent assurance of such profits—is to serve the customer in ways in which the customer wants to be served* [emphasis added].

Of course there is nothing really new in this. It is the fundamental basis upon which all successful business is founded, but as stated above, modern industry with its large scale operations tends to create a gulf between the customer and those responsible for guiding the destiny of the institution. We can no longer depend upon casual contacts and personal impressions—our business is too big; our operations too far-flung.

Furthermore, we are passing through a kaleidoscopic era characterized by swift movements—social as well as economic—and such conditions cannot fail to bring more rapid changes in the tastes, desires and buying habits of the consuming public. So it becomes increasingly important that we provide the means for keeping our products and our policies sensitively attuned to these changing conditions.

And irrespective of what these changes may be—regardless of what the new economic and social order may hold—I am confident that a more intimate, detailed and systematic knowledge of the consumer's desires will afford the Corporation a sound and progressive basis upon which to meet the new conditions as they unfold.[13]

Sloan's message is remarkably close to what Drucker advocated decades later and to what so many of today's business thinkers describe as the key to success in our time. Not surprisingly, what mattered sixty years ago matters today. Sloan's identification of "a more intimate, detailed and systematic knowledge of the consumer's desires" as a requirement for business success is as timely as it is timeless. It represents not an activity but an operating philosophy. Today's fragmented markets and greater numbers of competitors may complicate the business of creating systematic knowledge, and they may make the need for formal knowledge-use centers more compelling, but the goal remains the same: *relating knowledge of what the enterprise can do to knowledge of what the market and the customer want and need in the development of satisfying products and services.*

In any age, knowledge by itself is not power. Instead, knowledge is an enabling force that makes it possible for good things to happen. Business decisions based on knowledge, gleaned from the process of listening, learning, and leading, give a competitive advantage to the enterprise whose purpose is to create long-term relationships with customers. Therefore, achieving market leadership means acquiring the best information possible (listening), relating it to what the enterprise knows it is capable of doing (learning), and making sure that all functions within the enterprise use that listening and learning to make quality decisions (leading).

PLAN FOR THE BOOK

Chapter 1 considers the traditional command-and-control organization—the historic paradigm that most big corporations continue to live with. Its origins and its vertical structure, with control at the top and activities organized by particular functions, are described. While this form of organization continues to have unique strengths, it clearly has its defects with respect to developing knowledge of the marketplace and disseminating that knowledge broadly throughout the organization, where it could be used for decision making.

Chapter 2 describes the *marketing concept,* a philosophy that identifies customer creation and innovation as the end-all of corporate activities. In its operating form, this philosophy supports a decision-making network that brings together all relevant knowledge, understandings, and activities. The marketing concept has enjoyed a checkered history in recent decades, but is again receiving much attention. Its precepts suggest a framework for decision making that integrates the voice of the market with the voice of the enterprise as a system.

While the marketing concept enjoys wide support, its implementation in modern business has been meager. Chapter 3 presents a framework for action and practical tools for *putting the marketing concept to work.* These include enterprise business and process models, the influence diagram, the strategy table, and the scenario table. These tools help to clarify the linkages shared by the parts of the enterprise, its strategy, and the markets it hopes to serve.

Management scholars argue endlessly about the merits of this or that form of organizational structure. Chapter 4 moves beyond these arguments to a vision of the *market-based enterprise.* It suggests that the important business of creating unity between customer and enterprise probably has less to do with organizational structure and more to do with the ways in which the organization's knowledge and competencies are brought together to reach market-based decisions.

Chapter 5 is on the *listening* component of the listen, learn, and lead triad—the activities that market-based enterprises do well. The ability to listen actively, to listen to understand, and to listen to the right voices is a precondition for creating market knowledge in the enterprise. For the business enterprise, listening has a definite purpose with respect to building a foundation of knowledge on which market-based decisions can be made. This chapter describes both focused and "broad-band" modes of listening. It contains sections on who should listen and who should be listened to. The recent case of GM's initial market research for its electric vehicle program offers insights into the special benefits of listening to lead users, opinion leaders, and "market mavens."

Chapter 6 is on *learning*, particularly on organizational learning and the development and sharing of knowledge within the enterprise. It is the sharing of knowledge that enables any enterprise to create customers and to innovate.

Chapter 7 is on *leading*—through market-based decision making. This chapter develops the dialogue decision process that is proving to be a powerful and effective tool for bringing together and sharing the specialized knowledge scattered throughout every large (and sometimes the not so large) enterprise.

Finally, Chapter 8 looks at the *role of management* in creating a market-based enterprise.

A Visualization of the Book

During the late stages of developing this book, I had the good fortune to be asked by my friend Gerry Zaltman of the Harvard Business School to participate in a pilot interview using his pioneering method of understanding people's beliefs and values by having them select and then discuss their choice of visual symbols representing a particular subject. The method itself is described in Chapter 5.

Gerry asked me to bring some visual material of my choosing that would represent how I would go about dealing with "messy problems." Gerry and I, along with Ian Mitroff of the University of Southern California, had been thinking about messy problems for some time and had described them as problems that are generally poorly defined, ambiguous, and complex. A high degree of uncertainty surrounds their solutions, and there are usually multiple solutions to one such problem. Russ Ackoff reminds us of his understanding of these problems in *The Democratic Corporation:*

> Problems are abstractions extracted from experience by analysis. They are related to experience as atoms are to tables. Tables are experienced, not atoms. Managers are not confronted with separate problems but with situations that consist of complex systems of strongly interacting problems. I call such situations messes.[14]

In any case, dealing with messy situations was on my mind as I gathered visual images for my interview with Gerry Zaltman. As we went through the interview process, which involved in-depth discussion of each visual, it became clear that, in a serendipitous way, Gerry had asked me a question that went to the heart of this book. As he probed deeper and deeper into my understanding and experience in dealing with messy situations, it became clear that the essence of this book was really driven by my experience with messy situations in private enterprises, public agencies, and political campaign management.

At the end of the discussion of the individual images, Gerry and his staff supported me in scanning several images into a collage, which is shown in Figure I-1. The graphic in the upper-left corner represents the exact opposite of what this book is about. This book rejects the notion that decision making takes place in an enterprise represented as a simple mechanical cog wheel with a single decision maker. It also rejects the notion that the decision maker and the enterprise are enclosed by impermeable boundaries.

The image in the upper-right corner captures the idea that the resolution of messy situations requires two groups of people: the decision makers—the people at the top who ultimately make the decisions as to how resources will be allocated—and those who aid them with ideas, analysis, and feedback. Between the two groups is a dynamic "process" that connects them. In the book, we call this the dialogue decision process. This process makes certain that the organization describes (or frames) its messy situations correctly, that it considers alternative solutions based on a fair appraisal of their merits, that appropriate analysis is conducted, and

Figure I-1. *Messy Situation Collage*

that there is a connection between the decision at hand and the other initiatives of the enterprise.

In the upper-middle portion of the collage is a map, a symbolic reminder that there are usually alternative routes to objectives. In messy situations there is seldom a single solution. The loosely arranged pile of books is meant to suggest that knowledge, the ultimate asset of the enterprise, cannot be neatly packaged or stacked like books on library shelves. Instead, knowledge resides in the nooks and crannies of organizations and our own minds; these fragments of knowledge must be brought together in a way that truly informs us as we make decisions and take actions. Superimposed across the lower portion of the collage is an image of distant lines of trees. The fact that the trees form a pattern tells us that we are standing far back, taking them all in. But we do so at the expense of seeing the rich detail of branches or leaves that could be seen were we to move in closer. Of course, by moving closer we could get lost in the details and fail to appreciate the broader view—"missing the forest for the trees," as the saying goes. This is a serious issue that must be addressed by decision makers at all levels of an enterprise. Which do we need more, the larger picture or the details? Can we have both?

Finally, in the lower-right corner and the center we have the images of a group of people and a music conductor's hands and baton. The people represent the many voices that exist in every organization. Often, these people represent the enterprise's different functional areas. Like the strings section, percussionists, horns, and so forth, people in finance, marketing, engineering, and other functional areas of the enterprise need a conductor to bring out their best—to bring them together in a harmonious union in which all play from the same score with the shared goal of pleasing the audience.

The conductor is the ideal executive. He or she recognizes and respects the unique capabilities of each function. The ideal executive encourages the development of each employee's capabilities—just as the conductor encourages greater skill in each member of the orchestra. Without the specialized skills of the orchestra members, the score cannot be executed. But the conductor also recognizes that these skills are not an end in themselves—their purpose is to contribute to an audience-pleasing performance. Notice also that the light, or energy, is reflected onto the hands of the conductor from the direction of the people. The energy comes from the skills of the people, not from the conductor.

This collage should give you a sense of where we are going in this book. The following chapters offer further insights into the "messy situations" executives must deal with and a practical set of tools for addressing them.

NOTES

1. U.S. Senate Nomination Hearing, Charles E. Wilson, January 15, 1953 (Washington, D.C.: GPO, 1953). Abraham Maslow, in the daily journal of experiences he kept while observing an enterprise, mused about this same subject (interestingly, not being aware of what Charles E. Wilson actually said):

> what's good for the world is good for the country, which is good for the state, which is good for the community, which is good for the enterprise, which is good for the managers, which is good for the workers, which is good for the product. This comes close to the statement that roused so much fuss that "what's good for General Motors is good for the country," and yet the fact that in an ideally holistic or organismic or integrated world situation exactly this would be true and should be true.

See Abraham H. Maslow, *Eupsychian Management: A Journal* (Homewood, Ill.: Richard D. Irwin and the Dorsey Press, 1965), 111. An additional perspective on the famous quote is presented by Robert A. Nitschke:

> [Wilson] responded that "What's good for the country is good for GM" and then added "and vice versa." The newspapers reported the "vice versa" as meaning "What's good for GM is good for the country" and published only this interpretation as a direct quote. Wilson told Power [GM general counsel] that what he had meant by his "vice versa" was "and what is bad for the country is bad for GM."

See Robert A. Nitschke, *The General Motors Legal Staff, 1920–1947* (Detroit, Mich., 1989), 41.

2. Peter F. Drucker, *Management: Tasks, Responsibilities, Practices* (New York: Harper & Row, 1973), 61.

3. Gordon W. Prange, *Pearl Harbor: The Verdict of History* (New York: Penguin Books, 1991), 290.

4. Ibid., 555.

5. Henry Clausen and Bruce Lee, *Pearl Harbor: The Final Judgment* (New York: Crown Publishing Group, 1992).

6. The issue of particularism and the way people see the world is, of course, not limited to the military. The issue has arisen time and again in the way information systems have been developed—with many re-

sulting in associated "silo" data bases. Efforts to legislate common data definitions by the organization's information technology department instead of by senior business managers often result in a significant information problem—not a solution.

As Tom Davenport writes,

> There will always be a healthy tension between *information globalism*, which seeks to create meanings that apply to an entire organization, and *information particularism*, in which individuals and small groups define information in ways that make sense to them. . . . Operating with multiple meanings also requires basic changes in behavior—not only for information providers, who categorize and collect the information, but also for users. The CEO who is annoyed when told there's no quick answer to how many customers (or employees, or products) the company has is just as guilty of oversimplifying information as the database designer who insists on one definition of customer.

See Thomas H. Davenport, "Saving IT's Soul: Human-Centered Information Management," *Harvard Business Review*, March–April 1994, 123–124.

7. Jacob Bronowski, *The Ascent of Man* (Boston: Little, Brown and Co., 1973), 19.

8. Russell L. Ackoff, *The Democratic Corporation: A Radical Prescription for Recreating Corporate America and Rediscovering Success* (New York: Oxford University Press, 1994), 21.

9. Charles M. Savage, *Fifth Generation Management* (Burlington, Mass.: Digital Press, 1990), 67.

10. Ackoff, *The Democratic Corporation*, 23.

11. Peter F. Drucker, "The Coming of the New Organization," *Harvard Business Review*, January–February 1988, 53.

12. The idea of shifting from marketing as a function to marketing as a state of mind came from Everett Rogers during a Future of Marketing Conference sponsored by Quest and Associates at the Offices of Strategic Decisions Group in Menlo Park, California, in September, 1991.

13. Alfred P. Sloan, Jr., *Quarterly Dividend Mailing to GM Common Stockholders* (Detroit, Mich.: General Motors Corp.), September 11, 1933.

14. Ackoff, *The Democratic Corporation*, 211.

1

The Late Great Age of Command and Control

We trained hard—but it seemed that every time we were beginning to form into teams, we would be reorganized. I was to learn later in life that we tend to meet any new situation by reorganizing; and what a wonderful method it can be for creating the illusion of progress while producing confusion, inefficiency, and demoralization.

Petronius Arbiter

Many of our corporate organizations are relics of the nineteenth and early twentieth centuries. They were not developed to support notions of the marketing concept and customer satisfaction but to support efficient production and distribution for the Industrial Age—an age that for many businesses has already faded away. Yet, while the times have changed, the nature of these organizations persists, much as the feudal aristocracy of Europe persisted in the use of armor for at least a century after the introduction of firearms had rendered it obsolete.

This chapter reviews the contributions and limitations of the traditional command-and-control organization, an organizational form that has its analogy in the Industrial Age machine, whose cog wheels and other parts are driven and controlled from a central power force. It is useful to understand the strengths and weaknesses of this type of organization as we move toward other ways of getting things done.

More often than not, traditional corporations are described as "functional organizations" in that they organize work into categories of related skills, such as finance, engineering, marketing, and research and development. The idea of dividing organizations into functional groups with hierarchies of authority has its origins in the armies of the ancient world, its highest expression being that of the Romans, who perfected the concept and made it their instrument in dominating the Mediterranean world. As individuals, Roman soldiers were neither better equipped nor more skillful than their adversaries. In most cases, they were outnumbered and had to operate far from home. Indeed, during the time of Augustus, Rome's 28 legions numbered only about 150,000 men, and these were posted thinly over most of what is modern-day Europe, the Middle East, and North Africa. The power of the Roman army rested not in its numbers, its weapons superiority, or the personal courage of its individual members. Its strength was its organization, which made it possible for Roman commanders to direct and control resources in achieving their objectives. Indeed, harnessing the energy and intellect of the many, then causing them to act as one, is how all big jobs are handled—by armies, by builders of cathedrals, and by business enterprises alike.

Command and control—or C² in military parlance—is the mind that directs the body of the hierarchical, functional organization. *Command* is strategic and concentrates on the "big picture"; it takes the form of deliberate direction of what to do. *Control* is described as tactical or operational; it is related to delegating or to restraining various functions. In an excellent primer on this subject, *Command and Control for War and Peace*, Thomas P. Coakley writes

> [c]ommand and control involves the complex collection of functions and systems an executive draws on to arrive at decisions and to see they're carried out. Thus, the acronym C² may be used to refer to anything from information to sophisticated communications and computer equipment, to the executive's own mind—the last involving education, training, experience, native intelligence, and other aspects of cognition.[1]

There is, as one might expect, a weakness in this highly structured system. The extent to which command and control is concentrated increases the vulnerability of the entire organization and thereby the imperative to protect it—or, in the case of an enemy, to destroy it or cut it off from its fighting and supporting forces. In business, the concentration of command and control at the top requires that top management take full responsibility for "sensing" the environment, interpreting what it senses, thinking through all potential responses, and directing the other parts of the organization to act. As we will see in later chapters, this is an overwhelming set of responsibilities, especially in the current business environment.

A FORM TO FIT THE TIMES

If a hierarchical structure managed by command-and-control processes is a legacy of military tradition, the organization of enterprises by specialized functions is more recent. In *The Wealth of Nations*, Adam Smith speaks of the benefits of labor specialization in the pin factory: "One man draws out the wire, another straightens it, a third cuts it, a fourth points, a fifth grinds it at the top for receiving the head." The specialization of management functions would have to wait until the age of mass production. The objective of management in that age was high-volume, low-cost production of standardized products, and the organization of activities into specialized functions served that objective well and for a long time. This attitude is exemplified in Peter Drucker's epilogue to the 1972 edition of the *Concept of the Corporation* (twenty-five years after its original publication). In 1946 Drucker had concluded that change rather than continuity was what GM needed. In 1972 he recalled GM management's concern regarding the publication:

> The first thing practically all of them said was: "You want us to reexamine our basic principles. Your book is full of suggestions for changes in specific policies. But above all, if I read you right, you believe that the time has come for GM again to think through carefully its basic objectives and its basic structure, and to attempt major constitutional reform. This is dead wrong. The validity and effectiveness of our objectives, our organization, and our policies are proven by their success. They not only enabled us to become the world's largest and most profitable manufacturing company. They enabled us successfully to compete in very different markets, such as those of Europe. They enabled us to switch from peace time production to war production and to do things none of us had ever done before; and you yourself point out that of all major producers in the American war effort, GM has by far the best record. And now you ask us to throw all this away, just as we are about to return to the very conditions of a peace time economy for which these policies were developed and in which they have proved themselves. This is not just folly. This is frivolous."[2]

This intransigency of GM management led to an automobile industry, the very industry that had spawned the age of mass production, that could in 1970 still be described as one in which the main output was "standardized, virtually a commodity distinguishable only in terms of cost."[3] The management structure that developed to accommodate that sort of high-volume, highly standardized production with the primary aim of controlling highly integrated production and vast distribution systems was still entrenched. Quick response to rapid changes in customer tastes was not an issue, as changes were slow in coming.

That same industry today is practically driven by product and process innovation. In a strange twist to the normal cycle of industrial innovation, the mature auto industry has entered a second childhood. Intense new competition and growing customer sophistication have stimulated a cornucopia of innovations. The number of features being added to new models today would amaze Alfred Sloan, the man who practically made automotive differentiation an art form. In just a few years, we have seen once-exotic features like fuel injection, microprocessor controls, four-wheel drive, air bags, and antilock brakes become commonplace. Far from being frivolous, most of these innovations have improved auto performance and reliability in fundamental ways. More important still are the proliferation of models coming to market in a given year and the much lower volume of per-model production.[4]

Henri Fayol (1840–1925) is often cited as the innovator of the functionally organized business, in which command and control was to play a key role. During the first decade of this century, Fayol devised the concepts of functional organization and applied them to the coal-mining business he owned and managed. Organization by related skills has proven to be an economical and effective way to break the work of an enterprise into its logical components, wherein personnel with specialized skills apply themselves to those different components. It fulfills the logic of Adam Smith's specialization of labor. What Smith had described in the specialization of physical labor, Fayol applied in the organizational structure of his coal mine.

Specialization by function has the great virtue of making each individual's responsibility clear: "This is the engineering department. Our personnel are trained in engineering. Engineering is what we do."

Figure 1-1. *The Functionally Organized Enterprise*

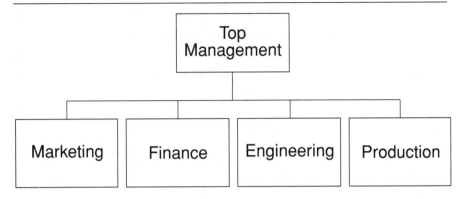

With the work of the enterprise broken into related activities, as in Figure 1-1, the job of top management becomes much simpler. Since each function is run by a submanager, the job of top management is to plan, control, direct, and motivate the whole through a handful of submanagers placed at the top of each function. Larry Hirschhorn and Thomas Gilmore make this observation very clear when they write:

> In the traditional company, boundaries were "hardwired" into the very structure of the organization. The hierarchy of occupational titles made manifest differences in power and authority. . . . This organizational structure was rigid, but . . . the roles of managers and employees within this structure were simple, clear, and relatively stable. Company boundaries functioned like markers on a map. By making clear who reported to whom and who was responsible for what, boundaries oriented and coordinated individual behavior and harnessed it to the purposes of the company as a whole.
>
> The problem is that this traditional organizational map describes a world that no longer exists.[5]

FUNCTIONAL TRIBALISM

Fayol's innovation, nevertheless, is still a popular and practical arrangement for businesses in which the individuals in each function remain in close contact with customers and with the work of their colleagues in other functions. This is typically the case in the small to medium-sized company. The engineering function in a small enterprise may represent less than a dozen people, and they may have close contact with customers and work in close physical proximity to everyone else in the enterprise. Communications between functions are likely to be plentiful and direct, without the need for special liaison or coordination. In this case, each function has a clear sense of its own responsibilities, yet also understands those of other functions and of the overall goals of the enterprise.

The great weakness of the functional organization becomes evident as the entire enterprise grows larger or becomes geographically dispersed. Suddenly, departments find themselves in separate buildings—perhaps in different towns. Each has specialized responsibilities, and the connections between these responsibilities become less and less clear to anyone operating inside the separate departments.

As if to prove that we are still tribal creatures under our button-down shirts, personnel in each function identify with their immediate group, viewing outsiders with suspicion. The interests of the immediate group command greater allegiance than do the interests of the enterprise as a whole. Peter Drucker may have described the worst features of the functional organization twenty-some years ago when he wrote:

> As soon as it approaches even a modest degree of size or complexity, "friction" builds up. It rapidly becomes an organization of misunderstandings, feuds, empires and Berlin Wall building. It soon requires elaborate, expensive, and clumsy management crutches—coordinators, committees, meetings, troubleshooters, special dispatchers—which waste everybody's time without, as a rule, solving much. . . . [U]sed beyond fairly narrow limits of size and complexity it creates emotional tensions, hostilities, and insecurities. People will then tend to see themselves and their functions belittled, besieged, attacked. They will come to see it as their first job to defend their function, to protect it against marauders in other functions.[6]

This description may sound extreme, yet anyone who has worked for an enterprise of even modest size can relate to it and add his or her own horror stories about interdepartmental turf battles or errors caused by lack of coordination. In some cases, the problems described by Drucker have become so pervasive that the greater part of the enterprise's energy is consumed in maintaining peace between warring departments. At some point, then, the benefits of specialization by function are outweighed by its disadvantages. Management efforts to maintain the organization eventually consume more energy than the organization itself produces. And important tasks can take forever to complete.

The hierarchical structure of authority in traditional organizations has also been observed to be dysfunctional in what many now call the age of the "empowered" worker. The industrial revolution disempowered the vast majority of workers. As a result, companies get only that small part of the worker's creativity, experience, and basic intelligence that they've paid for—and no more.

The extent to which some top managers recognize these problems may be evidenced by the number of development projects that are quite deliberately located geographically and organizationally outside the existing structure of the company. For example, when IBM in the late 1970s determined that it would enter the personal computer business, it set up an independent team of engineers and designers in Boca Raton, Florida—far away from the traditional center of its product development—and gave the team enough authority and resources to get the job done. Top management believed that the same project would have taken much more time had it been undertaken by IBM's mainframe division. GM's successful strategy in setting up the Saturn Corporation as an independent entity with the mission of designing and producing a vehicle development and delivery system that would satisfy customers throughout their entire ownership experience with a small car can be listed as another example.

The strengths of the functional organization, then, are associated with complementary weaknesses. Both are summarized in Table 1-1.

Notable evolutions of Fayol's functional structure occurred during the 1920s, when Pierre S. Du Pont and then Alfred Sloan reorganized their companies. Mindful of Du Pont's work, Sloan broke General Motors into a federated enterprise. He created an organization of many divisions with an elaborate headquarters staff of central services, budgets, and operational policies whose purpose was to manage the interactions among the divisions and to ensure that each division made trade-offs for the good of GM as a whole. Even though each division continued to follow a functional approach, Sloan's vision of GM gave it more value than the sum of its parts. A portion of an advertisement that appeared in an early 1920s campaign, titled "A Famous Family," elegantly describes the concept (see Figure 1-2 on pages 32–33).

Table 1-1. *Strengths and Weaknesses of the Functionally Organized Enterprise*

Strengths	Weaknesses
Stability	Inflexibility
Focused view	Myopia
Specialized expertise	No overarching vision; a lack of integrative learning
Many checks to reduce risk	Slow response to opportunities
Clear view of each personís and each functionís responsibility	Few people who understand how each function contributes to the whole

Since each function has its own narrow view and is naturally dedicated to its own tasks, the job of knowing what each of the functions does and how their activities can be related to the marketplace falls to top management. Perched above the busy functionaries and unencumbered by the details of their individual work, top management preserves a broader view of the marketplace and of the enterprise's potential to deliver. Like a commanding general and his headquarters staff, top management observes the competitive battleground and directs various units into the fray, each according to its special skills. This is a command-and-control organization, but one that has proven ill-suited to environments in which rapid change is the norm and in which flexibility of response is crucial. It is, in fact, better suited to a "make-to-sell" environment, in which enterprises produce and sell and consumers buy what they are offered. Unfortunately, few industries in the late twentieth century operate in such an environment.

A FRAGMENTED KNOWLEDGE BASE

In the command-and-control organization, knowledge accumulated within one silo tends to stay there, controlled by that function's "information keepers," who are driven by a "need-to-know" mentality. Knowledge and know-how do not cross-pollinate from one silo to another. Research questions are framed by the narrow perspective of the silo; responses to research are interpreted in light of the silo's prejudices. Each silo forms an enterprise in miniature: data are picked up through listening, a certain amount of learning takes place, and decisions are made on the basis of that learning. But too much of this activity takes place inside the silo, and that is where it often languishes. It does not enrich the learning or decision making taking place elsewhere. Figure 1-3 (on page 34) illustrates this phenomenon. At best, only a weak signal connects one silo to another (as indicated by the dashed arrows).

Like the blind men and the elephant, each silo develops a view of the market that makes sense in terms of what it knows, but what it knows is rarely a complete or accurate view of the world. To convince yourself of this, set up a focus meeting with a group of prospective buyers. Then send in teams of engineers, designers, and marketing people by turns. Debrief each team separately, and chances are that you will hear quite different versions of what the "market" wants. That's because each of these groups is disposed to ask certain questions (and not others) and to listen for certain answers (and not others). They are also more likely to ascribe different values to the information, based on what their "filters" allow them to "hear" or "see." Regis McKenna describes this silo mentality as a particular problem in large companies:

> These companies break various functional groups into different divisions, then make it difficult for those groups to interact. In small companies, people in engineering, marketing, and sales talk regularly and exchange ideas. This interaction is vital to creativity and innovation, but it is usually missing in large companies.[7]

Tradition often plays a part in maintaining silos. The case of GM's Fisher Body Division is an excellent example. Fisher Body started as a builder of horse-drawn carriages in the late nineteenth century, and its design concepts carried over to the automotive age. In horse-and-carriage days, the passenger vehicle was located directly behind its power source—the horse (see page 35, Figure 1-4, top). When the mechanical engine displaced the horse, this configuration was adopted intact (page 35, Figure 1-4, bottom); the engine was simply placed where the horse had been. We still refer to the horsepower rating of an engine.

The traditional separation of passenger compartment and power source was carried over to the organization of production as well. When

Figure 1-2. *The Initial Systems View of General Motors*

"But what does General Motors mean to me?"

Each of its cars brought to General Motors a record of achievement and a famous name. "But what," you ask, "does all this mean to me? In what respects am I benefited because General Motors unites in one family so many different members?"

Source: "A Famous Family," 1923, Archives, General Motors Corp., Detroit.

Fisher became a division of General Motors in 1926, the production of engine and body was reorganized with each function going to a separate silo. And "Body by Fisher" persisted as a functional silo until its dismemberment during the GM reorganization of 1984. During this entire period, Fisher worked on that part of the vehicle that ended at the engine cowl (at the windshield and fire wall). These boundaries were

The answer is four-fold.

1 By uniting the purchasing power of many companies, General Motors buys more economically, whether the material purchased be tiny lockwashers or tons of steel. You benefit by these economies in the price you pay for General Motors products.

2 Many minds are better than one. No American automobile company is more than 29 years old, but the car and truck divisions of General Motors have an aggregate experience of more than 100 years, which is available for each separate division in the development of its cars.

3 You can pay for a General Motors car out of income, just as you pay for a home. The General Motors Acceptance Corporation makes this possible, through resources which place it among the nation's principal banking institutions.

4 In Detroit and in Dayton, General Motors maintains the largest automotive laboratories in the world—two cooperating organizations of scientists and engineers, working constantly for progress in the automotive industry.

* * * * *

Thus General Motors, the family, is more than the sum of its members, for it adds a contribution of its own to the contributions made by each individual company. And these united contributions, crystallized in added value, find their way to you.

You recognize the trademarks on these two pages. They are the crests of manufacturing members of the General Motors family—symbols made valuable by years of public confidence.

"Product of General Motors" is your assurance that back of each company are the resources and strength of the whole family of which it is a part.

PRODUCT OF GENERAL MOTORS

reflected in service and repair manuals. There were manuals for the body and manuals for the front end of the vehicle. If you wanted to fix a door, for example, you consulted the Fisher Body manual. If you wanted to fix the engine or a front fender, you consulted the automotive manual.

There were many strengths in this separation. Fisher Body developed great expertise in creating the passenger compartment, the mechanisms

Figure 1-3. *The Isolated Activities of the Silo*

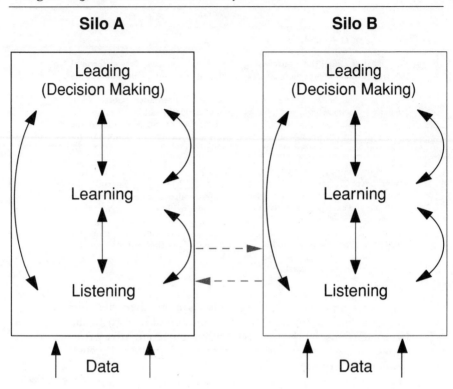

for effective and comfortable exit out of and entry into the vehicle, latches that were foolproof and reliable, and so forth. (The door is, in fact, a major focus of customer satisfaction or dissatisfaction.) Matters of coordination, however, were a significant problem.

The way in which we collect information about the market can also contribute to maintaining silos. Lorraine Scarpa provides an excellent example from the package goods business.

> Brand Management keeps on doing the same thing they've done for 50 years: pricing, product development, packaging, advertising, consumer promotion and forecasting. Brand by brand. Why is this so? Well for one thing, companies have brand managers run brands because they think that's all they can do—not as people, but as a system. This fact is largely attributable to the ingenuity of Arthur C. Nielsen, Sr., founder of A.C. Nielsen, who cleverly devised a measurement system that could be sold

Figure 1-4. *Tradition and Formation of Organizational Silos*

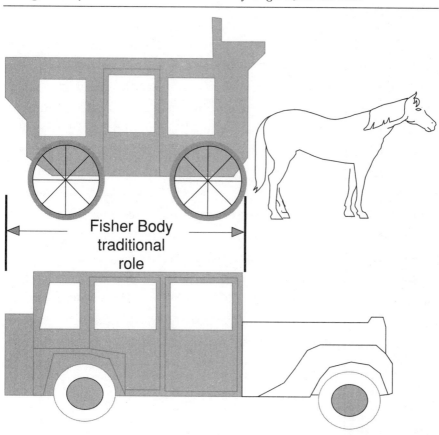

to a lot of people for a few very good reasons: he collected all the data brand by brand that reasonably and economically could be collected on an ongoing basis and he sold it by the slice (he called a category) to people who competed or so they thought brand by brand within that slice and therefore couldn't afford not to know what the other guy was doing. This is true customer focus. Regrettably, it is not true consumer focus. Nielsen sold what he *could* measure about consumption, not what was true. We marketers compounded the error by worshipping this measurement for its own sake and pronouncing dicta like "that which cannot be measured cannot be managed." We committed the logical error and cardinal sin of concluding that managing what we could measure was management with a capital M and we sauntered through the last 50 years. Now it's catching up with us.[8]

The Marketing Silo's Claim to Owning the Customer

In the traditional corporate structure, the marketing organization (silo) controls the communication channel to the customer and thus "owns" the customer. It conducts and analyzes market research, it interprets the "market" for the other functions, and it conducts test marketing of new products as well as subsequent advertising and promotion. But since marketing's understanding of the richness of the competitive environment, of the customer, of the technologies that support the company, and even of the capabilities of the enterprise as a whole is incomplete, the enterprise's ability to truly create and serve customers is impaired. Also, when there is a pickup in the "pace" of a given market, the organization must be able to respond quickly. In this environment, the benefits of a function that specializes in understanding the customer are offset by the time it takes to sequentially gather, analyze, and translate customer wants and needs into product characteristic terms that product designers and engineers can use in the performance of their function.

The New Business Environment

Even a decade ago, the handwriting on the wall indicated that the business environment of the 1990s and beyond would be different from what had gone before. In 1984, George P. Huber described a business environment that is becoming more and more familiar as we approach the end of the century. This environment, according to Huber, would be characterized by increasing diversity, knowledge richness, and greater turbulence.[9]

Increasing diversity of customer markets and variety of products have become the order of the day as the 1990s unfold. Easier communication and transportation and rising levels of international trade have opened markets to new producers. At the same time, advances in manufacturing technology have made it possible for these same producers to broaden the variety of their offerings without appreciable reductions in quality or additions to unit cost. The evolution from mass production to "mass customization" has produced a blizzard of product choices and raised the ante for all competitors.

It is clear that knowledge and information are displacing labor and capital as wealth-generating assets in many industries. One need look no further than the computer software industry to appreciate this fact. Microsoft, Lotus Development, and dozens of others have grown on a rich mixture of knowledge and creativity without the traditional legions of workers, teeming factories, and mountains of invested capital that characterized growth companies of the past.

Turbulence in the business environment can take many forms—a faster pace of technological change, shorter product life cycles, and so forth. In his award-winning book, *Mass Customization*, B. Joseph Pine II describes turbulence as being related to demand-based and structural factors. Demand-based factors—such as a change from homogeneous customer desires to heterogeneous customer desires—and structural factors—such as a change from a market environment of few substitutable products or services to one in which the customer is afforded many feasible alternatives—both contribute to greater turbulence in the current business environment.[10]

This "new environment" has not been friendly to enterprises in which activities are narrowly cast into functions controlled from the top. And a number of approaches have been used to minimize their weaknesses while retaining their strengths. Over the years, attempts to bridge business functions via matrix management and teams have enjoyed periodic success, and current efforts to re-create corporations as horizontal organizations are long overdue and are bound to lead to more lasting results. (More about these later.) Still, these efforts in themselves address neither the important issues of creating and using integrated functional knowledge within the company nor its role in decision making. The traditional organization of enterprises by function is not an entirely obsolete idea and still has important advantages. What's needed is a process through which cross-functional decisions can be made without giving up the benefits of strong functional management and information systems.

FINDING A WAY TO THE FUTURE

In its traditional form, the functionally organized enterprise, in which command and control emanates from the top, is ill-suited to the demands of the modern marketplace. It separates decision making (at the top) from doing (within the functions). It links decision makers and customers by means of a single, narrow, and inadequate channel—the marketing function. Worse still, it provides few opportunities to move knowledge and know-how between the functions, allowing the creation of what we call organizational knowledge.

We may find the best of both worlds if we redesign the decision-making process from the command-and-control tradition of the past so that it draws from and links the functional silos in which information and knowledge ultimately reside. This process will require trust between functions, the sharing of information and knowledge, and enterprise-wide knowledge creation. Just what that new decision-making process will look like and how we can design it—and the resulting organization—will be explained as we move ahead.

NOTES

1. Thomas P. Coakley, *Command and Control for War and Peace* (Washington, D.C.: National Defense University Press, 1991), 5.

2. Peter F. Drucker, *Concept of the Corporation* (New York: The John Day Co., 1972), 293–294.

3. William J. Abernathy, Kim B. Clark, and Alan M. Kantrow, *Industrial Renaissance: Producing a Competitive Future for America* (New York: Basic Books, 1983), 15.

4. James P. Womack, Daniel T. Jones, and Daniel Roos, *The Machine That Changed the World* (New York: Rawson Associates, 1990).

5. Larry Hirschhorn and Thomas Gilmore, "The New Boundaries of the 'Boundaryless Company,'" *Harvard Business Review*, May–June 1992, 105.

6. Peter F. Drucker, *Management: Tasks, Responsibilities, Practices* (New York: Harper & Row, 1973), 560.

7. Regis McKenna, *The Regis Touch* (Reading, Mass.: Addison Wesley, 1985), 142.

8. Lorraine C. Scarpa, "Brand Management as Dinosaur and Other Things We Can Learn from Ants," presented to Quest and Associates Annual Conference, Naples, Florida, April 6–7, 1995.

9. George P. Huber, "The Nature and Design of Post-Industrial Organizations," *Management Science* 30, no. 8 (August 1984): 928–951. For more discussion of Huber's "new business environment," see Ravi S. Achrol, "Evolution of the Marketing Organization: New Forms for Turbulent Environments," *Journal of Marketing* 55, no. 4 (October 1991): 78–80.

10. B. Joseph Pine II, *Mass Customization: The New Frontier in Business Competition* (Boston: Harvard Business School Press, 1993), 53–56.

2

THE MARKETING CONCEPT THEN AND NOW

Sense-and-respond firms will require a modular, fluid, organic organization to respond effectively to dynamic non-linear change. In most larger firms, this means networks of skills, assets, cross-functional processes, information, and knowledge that are linked into capabilities, which are in turn linked into processes for creating product and service responses to customer needs.
Stephan H. Haeckel

The command-and-control organization described in Chapter 1 was well-suited for the Industrial Age and ancient military bureaucracies. "Make the product, then go out and sell it." This statement guided many leading businesses during the nineteenth century and the early half of the twentieth. Today we recognize the philosophy underlying this statement as the *production concept*. What we need today is an organizational framework that serves the *marketing concept*—a philosophy that says to customers, "Help me to identify your needs and let's work together to satisfy them." In its operational form, this framework supports a market-based decision network that brings together all relevant knowledge, understanding, and activity that lead the enterprise to market-based decisions. But before we get to this framework, let's discuss the production and marketing concepts in greater detail.

In an era of growing populations and few choices, the production concept worked tolerably well. The Ford Model T mentioned previously—an innovative product in its time—was not born of focus groups, customer feedback, or any of the modern methods of determining the optimal mix of features, price, and performance. It was the creation of a small group of individuals who brought together the technical capabilities of the day and a new manufacturing process. The Model T was a commercial success because of what it represented: affordable automotive transportation for a large population that had never before had the opportunity to own an automobile. For a long period, the public bought as many Model Ts as Henry Ford could crank out of his wonderful new assembly line. It was a classic seller's market. And this is just the kind of market that the command-and-control organization was made to satisfy.

Countless other products have enjoyed success that would likewise support the notion of "Make the product, then go out and sell it." But, excepting new markets created through innovation, the production concept has become less and less supportable. Global trade has intensified competition in many key industries; customers have become more demanding and sophisticated; mass customization—mentioned earlier—is undermining product markets once characterized by standardized, mass-produced items. In a word, more and more of the world of commerce has become a buyer's market. And the production concept has given way to the marketing concept.

Steve Haeckel of the IBM Strategic Business Institute calls the production concept, the paradigm of the Industrial Age, "Make and Sell," aiming defined products at defined, segmented markets. The market-based concept is "Sense and Respond," in which strategy becomes an adaptive design intended to sense and respond to market changes before competitors do. "Sense and Respond" is required in an environment of discontinuous change, where forecasts, as well as plans, are unreliable. In this environment, a market-based enterprise requires a decision-making process that allows the enterprise to quickly gather its forces into an appropriate response; no longer can the enterprise simply invest in capital equipment to produce a defined product or service at what it believes to be the lowest possible cost.[1]

The marketing concept is a philosophy of management in which all phases of a company's activities are designed and executed to satisfy customer needs. Where the production concept ideal was make-to-sell, the marketing concept ideal is make-to-order. This chapter examines the evolution and practice of the marketing concept and its meaning for the market-based enterprises we hope to create. As we will see, it is not an isolated idea but one that connects with the structure of the organization, the flow of information, and business decision making.

THE RISE AND FALL OF THE MARKETING CONCEPT

Robert D. Buzzell, professor emeritus at Harvard, once traced the marketing concept to the late 1950s and the 1960s, a period of economic expansion that he views as a golden age for marketing. It was a period in which companies like General Electric, Pillsbury, and Procter & Gamble were guided by executives who actively integrated marketing into every phase of the business. As early as 1952, General Electric proclaimed an "advanced concept of marketing" that would "introduce the marketing man at the beginning rather than the end of the production cycle and would integrate marketing into each phase of the business."[2]

Peter Drucker, writing at about the same time, likewise identified the central role of marketing and innovation. To him, marketing encompassed the whole business and meant more than selling products and services or creating a marketing department. "Marketing," he wrote, "is so basic that . . . it is not a specialized activity at all. It is the whole business seen from the point of view of its final result, that is from the customer's point of view."[3] The same sentiment was articulated by Pillsbury president Robert Keith: "Soon it will be true that every activity of the corporation—from finance to sales to production—is aimed at satisfying the needs and desires of the consumer. When that stage of development is reached, the marketing revolution will be complete."[4]

At the end of this revolution, the customer—not the factory—would be at the center of the business universe, and marketing would have authority in production scheduling and inventory control as well as in the sales, distribution, and servicing of the product. It would also have a hand in product planning and innovation. Every activity would be oriented toward satisfying the customer or creating new customers through the development of innovative products.

The marketing concept held the high ground in management thinking (if not in practice) for almost two decades, and these were great years for American business. Personal incomes and markets expanded dramatically between the early 1950s and 1970. Consumer and industrial products sold briskly. Housing and all its attendant industries flourished as the middle class moved to the suburbs. The number of two-car families grew tremendously. Wall Street reflected the prosperity and optimism of the period in an outburst of speculative euphoria remembered today as the go-go years. Meanwhile, inside America's major industrial companies, marketing *as an organization* came into its own. And much of the "science" that marketers practice today—market segmentation, pricing, and market research techniques—was developed.

The extent to which the marketing concept contributed to the business prosperity of the late 1950s and 1960s has never been empirically determined. Did customer-focused marketing make a difference, or was it just along for the ride? When times are good, people are not inclined to spend lots of time trying to answer questions like this, and so we will never know. But these questions were asked in the unsettled 1970s and 1980s, which were lean times for many of America's largest established businesses. It is impossible to sort out the relationship between a managing philosophy such as the marketing concept and the poor performance that so many companies suffered during this difficult period. Empirical studies of the performance of companies that espoused the marketing concept (and actually practiced it), all other variables being controlled, are not available.

Frederick E. Webster, Jr., whose insightful writings trace the history of the marketing concept, underscores this problem: "There was virtually no convincing evidence that a commitment to the strictures of the marketing concept would actually improve profitability or other measures of organizational performance. The argument that profit was a reward for creating a satisfied customer seemed to be based on faith rather than hard data."[5] Webster also noted that while the basic wisdom of customer orientation was unarguable, the linkages between this high-minded philosophy and the resources and competencies of its adherent enterprises were weak. In other words, what customers asked for and what the enterprises could deliver—at a profit—were not necessarily the same. We will return to this important point later in this chapter.

THE RETURN OF THE MARKETING CONCEPT

Recognition of past failures and growing competition from abroad has (since the early 1980s) rekindled the interest of American enterprises in the marketing concept. As Webster observes, "After decades of thinking *that creating value for shareholders* was the ultimate objective, managers, consultants, and academic theorists have circled back to a *customer-value* concept of business strategy more consistent with the realities of the global marketplace and its stringent requirements for competitiveness."[6] The decline of the original marketing concept was really a function of the dearth of empirical evidence that customer satisfaction and corporate profits were directly linked. That evidence, he concludes, is beginning to emerge, and at the same time such popular innovations in management as total quality management and reengineering have very purposefully linked business processes and customer satisfaction.

It is difficult to say when the tide began to change—perhaps when corporate flirtation with the strategy of manipulating assets began to ebb and a deeper appreciation of customer satisfaction as a source of success began to flow once again. And it is a generalization to say that all or even most companies went through this transition.

Looking back from the perspective of the mid-1990s, we might identify the 1981 publication of *In Search of Excellence* by Thomas Peters and Robert Waterman, Jr., as an important benchmark in the process of change. Peters and Waterman, then management consultants at McKinsey & Company, took readers inside a number of American enterprises that had established themselves as "excellent" companies in terms of product or service quality. Among the characteristics common to these companies was the extent to which they would bend over backward to understand and please the customer. This corporate trait of "staying close to the customer—learning his preferences and catering to them" was listed by Peters and Waterman as one of the "eight basic principles" for staying on top. "The good news from excellent companies is the extent to which, and the intensity with which, the customers intrude into every nook and cranny of the business."[7] Clearly, these companies had never abandoned the marketing concept.

In Search of Excellence became a best-seller, inspired a PBS television series, and touched off much soul-searching and discussion in corporate offices large and small. In this sense, the book became something of a manifesto for the period of U.S. business reformation in which so many companies are now engaged. (It is also a sign of the times that some of the enterprises listed as "excellent" at that time would no longer be on the list.)

General Motors was among the many places where *In Search of Excellence* was being read and discussed in 1982. To its chagrin, GM had not been listed among America's excellent companies. In fact, the company had just completed an internal report on the causes for the development and production problems that had plagued its two most recent model series—the X and J cars. X cars, like the Chevrolet Citation released in 1979, had been GM's response to the energy crisis earlier in the decade and to the ongoing influx of small, fuel-efficient Japanese cars. These new GM cars were initially plagued by engine and assembly problems. The J cars, like the original Chevrolet Cavalier and Pontiac Sunbird released in 1981, had even more problems, which took two years to correct. In general, the internal report blamed pressures to stay within budget and on schedule for many of the problems afflicting production of these new models. Nowhere was any consideration of customer perception noted. The prevailing philosophy of the time as to what determined quality was "conformance to specifications" as defined by engineering.

The report on the X and J cars, coupled with a growing recognition that other companies were doing something very right, prompted management to form a cross-functional team of 150 managers and engineers to measure GM's means of ensuring quality against the practices of eleven U.S. industrial companies recognized for outstanding performance. This group included Boeing, Cincinnati Milacron, John Deere, Hewlett-Packard, IBM, 3M, and several other leading companies, most of them among the "excellent" companies profiled by Peters and Waterman.[8]

Over the course of a year, members of the GM team visited and analyzed the target companies and developed a report that, among other things, listed the practices that appeared to be tied to their success and market strength. Key among these was "customer satisfaction as job 1," a mechanism supported by feedback and problem-resolution systems.[9] Customer satisfaction was understood to be related to product quality and the many points at which company and customer meet.

Not coincidentally, the late 1970s and early 1980s witnessed a growing awareness of Japanese management techniques focusing on quality, continuous improvement, and customer satisfaction. Xerox was among the first major U.S. manufacturers to begin adopting these techniques—having been exposed to them through Fuji Xerox, its joint venture with Japan's giant film manufacturer. For Xerox, the relationship between quality and customer satisfaction was clear, and quality quickly found its way into company policy, which stated, "Quality means providing our external and internal customers with innovative products and services that fully satisfy their requirements."[10]

Typical of the Japanese techniques that gained adherents (sometimes zealots) in the United States was quality function deployment (QFD), a systematic process for planning products and services. QFD helps managers define the product requirements that satisfy customers and then develop the means to provide that satisfaction. It is a disciplined methodology that makes sure customer "wants" are understood, documented, and converted into appropriate product and service specifications. Part of the promise of QFD was its ability to integrate different functions of the organization, linking management, engineering, manufacturing, and marketing in the development of a breakthrough. This concept, including the direct involvement of customers, is explored in detail in later chapters. Hewlett-Packard is among the leading U.S. enterprises to have adopted this methodology.

Another management technique now widely adopted in North America is total quality management (TQM), a customer-focused philosophy and strategy that seeks continuous improvement in business processes through the application of analytical tools and teamwork. As in QFD, customers, not profits, are the focus. Quality is considered from the customer's viewpoint, and quality demands constant sensitivity to customer demands and perceptions and to market information. According to one author's description of TQM, "The voice of the customer is integrated into each process and system in the organization . . . [and] meeting and exceeding customer demands is the ultimate objective."[11]

Essentially, the many Japanese management techniques that found their way to North America and Europe in the 1980s shared two common understandings: first, that all business activities represent processes, and second, that these processes have only one purpose, *to satisfy customers*. The methodologies that underlie Japanese management techniques are at their core ways of fine-tuning and continually improving those processes to the point that they contain nothing that does not create value and satisfaction for the customer.

It takes little imagination to see that the basis for these new and widely adopted management approaches is the marketing concept, which, as defined earlier, is a philosophy of management in which all phases of a company's activities are designed and executed so as to satisfy customer needs. The marketing concept, along with the customer, has then moved back to center stage—perhaps even more overtly than people like Drucker proposed forty years ago. So powerful is its resurgence that Chrysler chairman Robert J. Eaton has told shareholders: "Focus only on the customer, and everything else falls into its proper perspective and proper priority almost automatically."[12] Learning how to act systematically on this conviction is what this book is designed to explain.

If business researchers of the 1970s failed to document a connection between superior business performance and the marketing concept, as Webster contends, the evidence is now becoming available. A number of recent studies have addressed the relationship between market orientation and various measures of business performance. All show a statistically significant relationship between a market orientation and most of the performance measures that managers pursue.

In research sponsored by the Marketing Science Institute (MSI), Ajay Kohli and Bernard Jaworski comment that "virtually all executives interviewed noted that a marketing orientation enhances the performance of an organization."[13] Positive consequences were reported for return on investment, profitability, costs, sales volumes, and market share. Nonmonetary benefits were also recorded, including customer satisfaction, repeat business, better customer retention, and enhancement of the enterprise's reputation. Perhaps as important was a sense among the interviewees that a marketing orientation provides strategic direction and an overarching goal for the organization.

What the Marketing Concept Can — and Cannot — Do

If the long-absent evidence of the marketing concept's value is now in hand, the concept is not without its critics. What theory isn't? In a now-famous article entitled "Managing Our Way to Economic Decline," Harvard professors Robert Hayes and the late William Abernathy cite a complaint that summarizes the case against the marketing concept:

> Inventors, scientists, engineers, and academics, in the normal pursuit of scientific knowledge, gave the world in recent times the laser, xerography, instant photography, and the transistor. In contrast, worshippers of the marketing concept have bestowed upon mankind such products as newfangled potato chips, feminine hygiene deodorant, and the pet rock.[14]

Hayes and Abernathy concede the common sense of conducting market analysis as part of the new product process but challenge the notion that consumer analyses and formal market surveys should dominate other considerations when allocating resources to product development.[15] Their case against unflinching allegiance to the marketing concept touches a raw nerve in the marketing profession, especially among market researchers. The two professors continue:

> Customers may know what their needs are, but they often define those needs in terms of existing products, processes, markets, and prices. Deferring to a market-driven strategy without paying attention to its limitations is, quite possibly, opting for customer satisfaction and lower risk in the short run at the expense of superior products in the future.[16]

It is a discomforting fact for marketing professionals that many if not most of the commonplace products that so enrich our lives were not plucked from customer wish lists by skillful market researchers. Christopher Sholes was a newspaper editor when he developed and sold the first typewriter patents to Remington in the 1870s. Sholes and Remington "knew" that people wanted to write faster and more legibly; no market research led them to the determination that "This is an idea that will revolutionize business"—but that's what it did. Not long thereafter, Thomas Edison brought forth the first practical incandescent lamp, from which was born one of the world's greatest enterprises: General Electric. Edison did not need market research to confirm that people want to "see in the dark." He recognized immediately the commercial potential of electric lighting. And the list goes on and on.

Experience shows that for the most part enterprises must provide leadership in the development of what may turn out to be breakthrough products. Customers themselves cannot always point the way. Depending on how they are asked to describe their needs, customers rarely venture beyond their current frames of reference. More likely than not, they'll describe incrementally improved versions of current products. In this sense, giving customers what they articulate as their needs, as distinguished from their unarticulated needs, puts the development of breakthrough products at greater risk.

The purpose of market research

The issue of whether or not market research can tell us about anything that does not already exist in the marketplace has been a source of open feuding for many years, and the warring parties have tended to see the issue in black and white terms. As in most heated disputes, the truth may lie in the gray areas. Having participated in these feuds for nearly thirty years, I have found some clarity in the writings of Henry "Buck" Weaver, GM's first director of market research. Weaver, who was hired by Alfred Sloan in the late 1920s, was an early pioneer in the field of market research and decision making. "Successful manufacturing," he writes, "rests upon a knowledge of natural laws on the one hand and a knowledge of human needs on the other hand."[17]

Weaver's practical grasp of this principle can be found in a 1932 edition of GM's market research newsletter, *The Proving Ground of Public Opinion*, in which Weaver and his colleagues address the issue of "Streamlining from the Consumer Viewpoint." His report points out that "it is not the purpose of Consumer Research to unearth new and original ideas on styling but to afford some indication as to the boundary lines of public acceptance." In an era dominated by box-shaped vehicles, Weaver reports more and more comments from the public on "the desirability of straight, rakish lines, low hung construction and a tendency toward the aero-dynamic design." The report speculates that "the Boundary Lines of Public Acceptance in this direction is in advance of the industry's offerings to date."[18]

Drawing on comments from car owners, the report speculates that the preference for streamlining might have come from the younger generation's interest in toy airplanes and models, pointing out that "There are few homes in America containing a child under 20 wherein the adults are not stumbling over streamline toy aeroplanes and 'Zeps.'"[19] GM researchers reference articles appearing in *Popular Science Monthly, Popular Mechanics*, and *Scientific American* and call attention to newsreels, futuristic motion pictures, and the Buck Rogers comic strip.

To drive home the magnitude of the issue, Weaver and his associates point out that with a population of 22 million males under the age of twenty (according to the 1930 U.S. Census), toy shops were selling well above 5 million toy airplanes each year. They also point out that toy cars had typically been four to five years behind current designs, whereas they were now (in 1933) more likely to have an ultramodern, streamlined design.

These many observations were tied to an understanding of the customer decision-making process indicating that the greatest influence of younger people in the car purchase decision was in the area of body lines. The report ties Weaver's philosophy of integrating knowledge of human wants and needs with the application of engineering and manufacturing skills by concluding, "Streamlining may bring about radical changes in chassis construction over the next few years."[20]

One of Weaver's techniques for plumbing the minds of potential car buyers was to ask them to submit suggestions for design changes by means of impromptu sketches. It is interesting to note that some respondents could not resist offering ideas that went beyond mere suggestions on appearance. The two 1932 sketches shown in Figure 2-1, for instance, depict ideas not yet in the market. The first was for a pneumatic bumper (eventually introduced by GM in 1973) and glass sunroofs (first introduced on a mass-production basis in the mid-1970s).

The case of the minivan

The development of the minivan, a new and now popular alternative to the standard motor vehicle, offers a useful example of how consumers can articulate needs that extend beyond the current framework of technology and product offerings. It also indicates how enterprises can hear this customer voice, yet fail to heed it—at least for a while.

Although most readers would take the position that the minivan concept was developed under the leadership of Lee Iacocca in the early 1980s,[21] automotive historians would point out that Buckminster Fuller had designed a three-wheeled, teardrop-shaped vehicle with analogous

Figure 2-1. *Respondent Concepts*

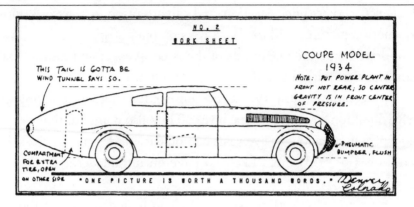

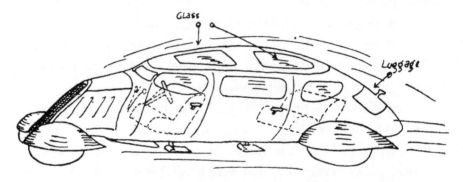

Source: General Motors Corp., "Streamlining from the Customer Viewpoint," *The Proving Ground of Public Opinion*, December 1, 1932. Reprinted by permission.

characteristics, the Dymaxion, as early as 1933. A prototype of a similar vehicle, the Stout Scarab, was featured in *Look Magazine* in 1939. But consider a sketch (Figure 2-2) from the GM market research archives. This rendering, submitted to GM in 1932, came from the mind of one of Weaver's respondents. The design's lack of elegance notwithstanding, it is clear that the respondent was articulating the details of a product not already in the market, one out of the normal frame of reference for auto drivers of the time. This respondent was saying: "I want better forward vision by placing the driver's position much further forward than in contemporary vehicles. I want the engine in the rear" (perhaps to avoid engine heat and odors in the passenger compartment). We could speculate that the "French doors" indicate a preference for improved entry and

Figure 2-2. *Minivan Precursor*

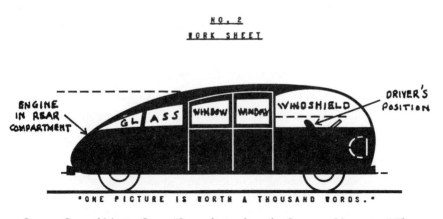

Source: General Motors Corp., "Streamlining from the Customer Viewpoint," *The Proving Ground of Public Opinion*, December 1, 1932. Reprinted by permission.

Figure 2-3. *Volkswagen Transporter*

egress. As silly as this vehicle appears, it is interesting to compare it with the Volkswagen Transporter (Figure 2-3), which entered the market during the mid-1950s, and flourished for the next two decades.

For the enterprise to hear the voice of the market is one thing; to respond to it with appropriate new products and services is another. In the case of the minivan, automakers may have been wise to ignore what was likely a weak signal from potential minivan buyers in the 1930s through the 1960s. The same cannot be said for auto executives of more recent decades.

David Halberstam tells part of this tale artfully in *The Reckoning*, a book in which he identifies the modern minivan as emerging in the late 1960s from the design shop of Ford Motor Company, then headed by Gene Bordinat.

> There were, thought Bordinat, a few times in a designer's life when he knew, *absolutely knew*, that he had a winner and this was one of them. [Don] DeLaRossa [the concept originator] had spoken of an all-purpose vehicle, neither station wagon nor van, which women as well as men could drive, a car for the suburban housewife during the week and for the family on weekends, a sawed-off hybrid of a van and a wagon, with lots of interior room.[22]

Meanwhile, Ford's market research on the concept, spearheaded by a company maverick named Norman Krandell, uncovered overwhelming evidence that the minivan would be a great success with the buying public, creating for Ford a hit vehicle with the potential to outshine even the Mustang, Ford's best seller since the Model A.

Krandell and other minivan advocates within Ford were repeatedly stymied by the powers-that-be in top management, particularly the finance people, who thought the new concept untested and risky. According to Halberstam, Henry Ford himself disliked the idea because it would require front-wheel drive, a technology that could not be cheaply adapted from another Ford vehicle. In the end, the big guns in top management scuttled the minivan, and its advocates found themselves in hot water. Within just a few years, however, a number of them followed Lee Iacocca to the Chrysler Corporation, a company in such dire straits that projects with big risks could be tolerated as long as big potential payoffs were part of the equation. The rest is history.

> [Chrysler] had the front-wheel drive and the platform from the K car, and the market research had been generously supplied by Ford. Norman Krandell's research turned out to be generally accurate. . . . In the fall of 1983 the Chrysler MiniVan, long planned at Ford and always side-tracked, came out and was an exceptional success.[23]

Ford management was not the only short-sighted party in this tale. GM had also been aware of the market potential of this new product concept. In fact, its consumer research essentially reflected Krandell's

Figure 2-4. *GM's MPC Compared with Chrysler's MiniVan*

General Motors MPC, 1978

Chrysler Corporation MiniVan, 1984

Source: General Motors Design Center Photo Archives. Reprinted by permission.

numbers, and GM had invested significant sums in prototype tooling tied to the 1979 X car front-wheel-drive program for a concept called the multiple purpose car (MPC) (see Figure 2-4). But GM misinterpreted the consumer research, which indicated potential buyers in virtually every existing segment of the market. Rather than recognizing an unmet need—the fact that many people were purchasing a wide variety of vehicles, none of which were fully satisfying—GM interpreted the research to mean that there was no market for the concept. Additionally, GM had a significant station-wagon product lineup that some feared would be cannibalized by a minivan. For these and other reasons the tooling gathered dust. Meanwhile, the struggling Chrysler Corporation captured a profitable new market that essentially put that company back on the map of U.S. automakers. GM was painfully reminded of its misinterpretation of the consumer research and its subsequent failure to go ahead with production by a couple of lines in the advertising script that introduced the Dodge Caravan in 1984: "Dodge Caravan, one vehicle that takes the place of an economy car, sporty car, station wagon and van. Dodge Caravan is a transportation revolution."

This tale of the minivan falls in the gray area of the marketing-concept debate. It shows that customers can occasionally think beyond their current frames of reference, beyond the known world of products and technology, to foretell innovations that would meet their requirements. At the same time, the tale makes it clear that enterprises and their researchers can proactively conceptualize new products, as did Ford and GM, and prove them out with good research methodologies. In neither case, however, will an innovative product see the light of day unless management is forthcoming with the right decisions and actions. The section that follows should make that clear.

The Marketing Concept and Current Practices

Whether we call it the marketing concept or a marketing orientation, the relationship between it and success in the tough market of the 1990s is becoming abundantly clear. And the idea of focusing the energies, intelligence, and resources of the enterprise on the creation and delivery of value to the customer is gaining—or regaining—broader acceptance. Recognizing the value of the marketing concept and acting effectively on its precepts, however, are two different things. In general, companies pursue one of two different approaches—company driven or marketing driven—to mesh themselves with their markets and to develop products and services that profitably meet customer needs. As we will see, neither approach is entirely satisfactory. Both are described here with respect to one of the key functions of the enterprise—the product development process.

The company-driven approach

The company-driven approach begins when one internal voice of the organization—usually not marketing—develops a product or service concept. The enterprise's official marketing organization is then asked whether the concept will sell (usually after other functional organizations have developed their positions). The marketing organization then directs research aimed at estimating the commercial viability of the concept. The resulting research is then presented to the other functions within the enterprise.

The product or program managers combine what they hear from marketing with what they hear from the other functions—engineering, finance, manufacturing, and so forth. Ultimately, a decision is made about the new concept based on the "official" market reaction represented by the marketing organization, and on technical and financial issues raised by others. For those concepts that are approved, the decision-making process leaves little room for improvements on the original idea.

Figure 2-5 illustrates the company-driven approach to product development using a new automobile as an example. In the first step, management develops a product concept. This concept is developed by engineers and designers working from management's original specifications and their own personal preferences and experiences. This design finds its way into some form of prototype, which becomes the basis for market research. That research becomes a "report card" for the concept and the basis on which decisions will be made. It will also be the basis for minor changes if the concept is approved for development.

As presented, this company-driven approach to product development is fundamentally flawed. First, it is sequential. Second, it does not encourage the identification of anyone with explicit responsibility for bringing together all aspects of the marketing concept (pricing, product development, promotion, distribution, etc.), with customer value as the inte-

Figure 2-5. *Company-Driven Product Development*

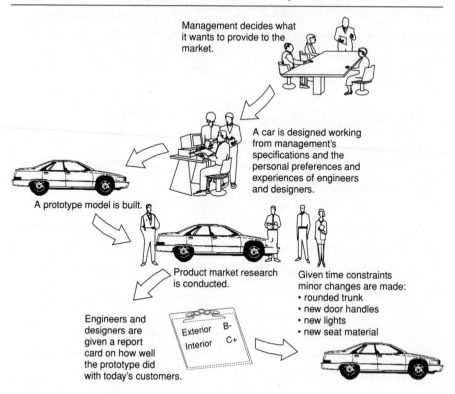

Management decides what it wants to provide to the market.

A car is designed working from management's specifications and the personal preferences and experiences of engineers and designers.

A prototype model is built.

Product market research is conducted.

Given time constraints minor changes are made:
• rounded trunk
• new door handles
• new lights
• new seat material

Engineers and designers are given a report card on how well the prototype did with today's customers.

Exterior B-
Interior C+

grating force. At best, the product concept is identified with the individual or groups that initiate it; no one else has much of a stake in it.

A third flaw of this approach has to do with the political nature of organizations. It is unlikely that a new concept generated in this manner would elicit forthright assessments of its strengths and weaknesses. It is "engineering's idea" or "so-and-so's idea." This tends to make the decision to advance the idea as much a contest as a collaborative effort. Fourth, there is no explicit provision in the company-driven approach for all interested parties to come together to discuss the many trade-offs required to design and manufacture new products. This is the "over-the-wall" issue so commonly understood and complained of in modern industry.

Consequently, if a market problem is found, the discovery is usually made late in the product development cycle. By then, it may be too late or too costly to make sensible changes. Organizational pressures impel the project forward, with an understanding that alterations can be made after the product launch. In the auto industry, in particular, there is plenty of evidence that Japanese producers in the 1970s and 1980s made relatively few design changes in the months prior to a new product launch; U.S. producers, on the other hand, made growing volumes of design changes in the months and weeks prior to launch, and these changes continued even as the first vehicles rolled down the assembly line. The results: added costs, quality problems, and dissatisfied customers.

Regis McKenna sums up the company-driven approach as outdated on several levels. "The old approach—getting an idea, conducting traditional market research, developing a product, testing the market, and finally going to market—is slow, unresponsive, and turf-ridden. . . . The alternative to this old approach is knowledge-based and experience-based marketing."[24]

The marketing-driven approach

The obvious weaknesses of the company-driven approach have led some enterprises to engage marketing at the beginning of the product development process. In this case, the marketing organization (or department) directs research to gather information from which market requirements will be determined. Based on its analysis of direct market measurements, the marketing organization looks for meaning through inference. On the basis of these inferences, it presents product requirements that the rest of the enterprise should develop to satisfy market requirements.

Product (program) managers, along with other functions, attempt to develop products that meet market requirements as articulated by the marketing organization. The marketing organization reviews these product concepts (sometimes taking them to the market for tests) and determines if they will satisfy their interpretation of the actual market requirements. Again, usually because of time pressure, only minor improvements are made to the original concept.

The marketing-driven approach to product development (Figure 2-6) attempts to put the customer at the beginning of the product development process. While this approach has lots of intuitive appeal, it also has at least three fundamental problems.

First, it too is sequential. The product requirements that flow from the

Figure 2-6. *Marketing-Driven Product Development*

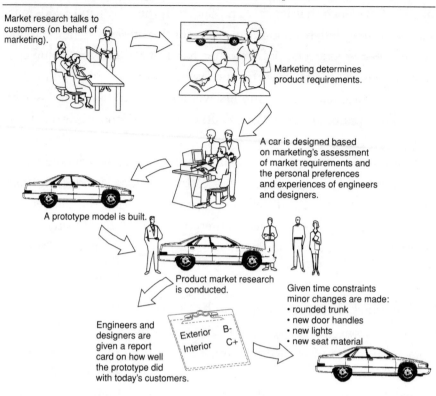

Market research talks to customers (on behalf of marketing).

Marketing determines product requirements.

A car is designed based on marketing's assessment of market requirements and the personal preferences and experiences of engineers and designers.

A prototype model is built.

Product market research is conducted.

Engineers and designers are given a report card on how well the prototype did with today's customers.

Exterior   B-
Interior   C+

Given time constraints minor changes are made:
• rounded trunk
• new door handles
• new lights
• new seat material

market may not be technically feasible, creative, innovative, or profitable. The process of presenting specifications followed by product conceptualization contributes to an adversarial relationship between the marketing organization and other functional departments.

Second, given the right sampling and questioning, the market is capable of stating its current needs and preferences for existing attributes. The market is also capable, to a lesser extent, of articulating its future needs. The market's ability to articulate its preferences for future technological innovations or advanced designs, however, is less reliable. After all, how could it ask to choose from concepts that do not exist, even in the imagination?[25]

Third, market information is available to everyone. You might say that there is an "efficient market" of market information. And if you assume that competing enterprises are equally competent in collecting and using market information, then enterprises would not differ significantly in their responses to market needs.

An external approach

Although the company- and marketing-driven approaches to product development appear diametrically opposed, they differ only in the orientation of the internal voice that starts the process. Indeed, although the marketing-driven approach has evolved as a response to the weaknesses of its predecessor, it nevertheless has its own limitations. The enterprise that wishes to operate within the marketing concept should reject the extreme positioning of both approaches. Instead, it should develop an alternative approach—one that integrates Drucker's original concept— embracing the idea that the business of an enterprise is to market and innovate.

If, as Drucker observed, marketing is to encompass the whole business, then the enterprise must find ways to connect integrated sets of decisions across functions and across all levels within the hierarchy of decision makers—always based on the common vision of satisfying customers. Benson Shapiro supports this observation in noting that "the term 'marketing oriented' represents a set of processes touching on all aspects of the company."[26] For Shapiro, the following characteristics are common to the market-based enterprise:

- information on all important buying influences permeates every corporate function; and
- strategic and tactical decisions are made interfunctionally and interdivisionally.[27]

All of this makes sense, of course. The value of having every part of a business highly tuned to its markets and eager to coordinate its efforts with other divisions is painfully obvious. Yet few enterprises follow this philosophy. Why? Why is it so difficult to find working examples of enterprises that are truly market oriented? One can only surmise that realization of the marketing concept is impeded by the lack of a truly actionable framework, which I call the market-based decision network.[28]

THE LINEAGE OF THE MARKET-BASED DECISION NETWORK

Gerald Zaltman and I extended the concept of the marketing-driven and the company-driven organization in the reconciliation of the voice

Figure 2-7. *Company Push/Market Pull*

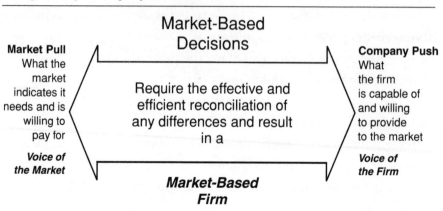

Source: Vincent P. Barabba and Gerald Zaltman, *Hearing the Voice of the Market* (Boston: Harvard Business School Press, 1990), 52. Reprinted by permission.

of the market with the voice of the firm in an earlier book.[29] As shown in Figure 2-7, we attempted to make the concept of "market pull" operational through what we called the "voice of the market," which we described as what the market wants or needs and is willing to pay for. We attempted to make the concept of "company push" operational through what we called the "voice of the firm," which we described as an all-encompassing statement of what all the firm's talent in engineering design, sales and marketing, and so forth are capable of and willing to provide to the market.

What we did not make fully explicit in our initial model is the fact that the firm's capability and willingness to contribute is seldom articulated by a single voice. What was missing is the cold reality that every enterprise operates under constraints. There are limits to what the enterprise can—or is willing to—deliver. There is only so much competence, only so much energy and money to go around, and there is bound to be disagreement on how these important assets should be allocated. Our original concept did not fully recognize this important reality. It did not explicitly recognize that there are different voices within the firm—often discordant voices.

Market-based decisions require that we understand both the many voices within the market and the many voices within the enterprise. A framework for decision making must be designed to allocate limited resources in a manner that satisfies the requirements of both the customer *and* the enterprise—creating a meeting of the minds.

The market-based decision-making network requires that the complexity, risk, and uncertainty of the environment be explicitly addressed as the enterprise attempts to reconcile what the customer wants and is willing to pay for with what the enterprise itself is willing and able to do. Getting these things right, harmonizing the many voices of the market and the enterprise, ultimately pays off in products and services of high "integrity."

The concept of product integrity derives from a cross-national study of manufacturing firms conducted by Kim B. Clark and Takahiro Fujimoto, who conclude that product integrity characterizes the more successful firms. Product integrity has both an internal and external dimension. Internal integrity refers to the consistency between a product's function and its structure: the parts fit smoothly, the components match and work well together, the layout maximizes available space. Organizationally, internal integrity is achieved mainly through cross-functional coordination with the company and its suppliers. Efforts to achieve internal integrity through this kind of coordination have become standard practice among product developers in recent years. External integrity refers to the consistency between a product's performance and customer expectations. External integrity is critical to product competitiveness, yet is for the most part an unexploited opportunity.

Besides uncovering the value of product integrity and its two dimensions, Clark and Fujimoto also identify an important unifying organizational philosophy, which underscores the value of the market-based decision-making network: "We found a handful of companies that consistently created products with integrity. *What set these companies apart was their seamless pattern of organization and management* [emphasis added]. The way people did their jobs, the way decisions were made . . . everything cohered and supported company strategy."[30]

EXTENDING THE MARKET-BASED DECISION MODEL

Having identified the company push/market pull decision-making model as being limited to a single simultaneous consideration of a single

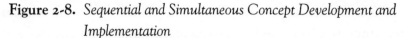

Figure 2-8. *Sequential and Simultaneous Concept Development and Implementation*

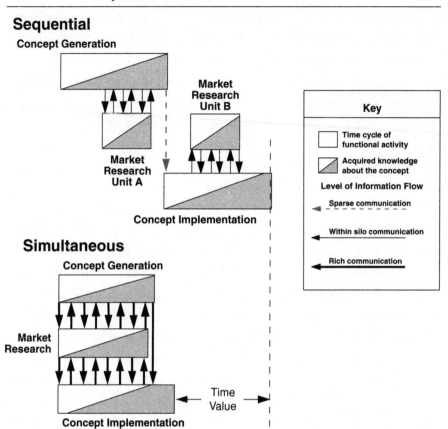

Source: Adapted from Steven C. Wheelwright and Kim B. Clark, *Revolutionizing Product Development* (New York: Free Press, 1992), 178.

voice of the enterprise with the voice of the market, let's now look at an approach that minimizes those limitations.

Figure 2-8 illustrates the benefit of having those who generate ideas and concepts address customer value simultaneously with those who must further develop and implement those ideas and concepts. There are three key variables shown in the key to the figure: (1) the overall unit of time, or decision cycle (determined by the time required for those groups involved at both ends of the process to interact and complete their activities); (2) the amount of knowledge available; and (3) the level and direction of information flow between the two groups.

In Figure 2-8, we see the difference between the traditional sequential and the more challenging simultaneous approaches to product and service development. In the sequential approach we observe the idea-generation group achieving a level of completion before market research is asked to check its validity and respond solely to the idea generators. Once checked, the developed idea is passed on to the concept implementers. In this example, the implementation group has no hand in the initial development of the concept. The problems that result from this type of over-the-wall generation and implementation of new business concepts are well known to any experienced manager and lead to the antithesis of Clark and Fujimoto's idea of "seamless" product integrity.

First, the concept may be developed in a vacuum—that is, it comes not from the marketplace of customer needs but from within the enterprise. While this is not always a fatal flaw, the odds do not favor new concepts that originate solely from within. Second, the concept generators ask their market research unit to "check" the validity of the concept after the fact—after an investment in the concept has already been made and after the generators' framework for thinking has already been formed. Feedback between concept generators and market researchers comes only in the late stage of concept generation. Then, it's over the wall to the implementers. In addition, the concept implementers are likely to use market research from a group assigned to their function. If differences emerge, a discussion of the value the methodologies used sometimes supersedes the significance of the differences themselves.

When compared with the sequential approach, the simultaneous approach entails obvious advantages. Here, all three parties interact and provide feedback from the start, which ensures that all parties to the new concept are fully engaged at the appropriate time. This is a sequence of activities that helps ensure the development of harmonious, high-integrity products and services that companies need and that customers want. Additionally considerable time value is gained with the simultaneous approach.

Although the benefits of this approach are obvious, it is not—as Clark and Fujimoto discovered—universally applied, primarily because

Figure 2-9. *Combining Market Pull/Company Push with Simultaneous Interaction*

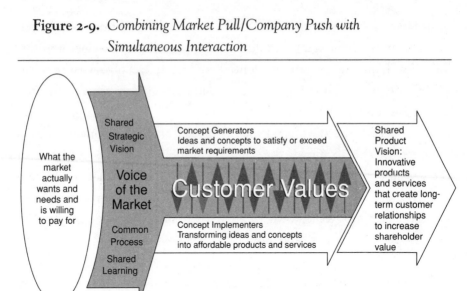

it is difficult both to create and to manage. Nevertheless, the two researchers identified three conditions associated with the adoption of this approach:

1. *A high need for upstream/downstream information flow.* The kind of information Clark and Fujimoto refer to is fragmented, incomplete, and informal—the type that does not lend itself to a formal presentation in taskforce or committee meetings.

2. *Ability of the downstream group to be flexible and able to live with ambiguity.* The early stages of the design process are by nature ambiguous. Because there are no finished drawings or final specifications at this stage, the downstream group needs a quick changeover mentality. It must also be less committed to initial implementation concepts.

3. *A short-cycle problem-solving capability.* Timeliness requires the capability to diagnose and solve problems quickly.

Figure 2-9 combines elements of both Figure 2-7 (traditional market pull/company push framework) and Figure 2-8 (simultaneous interaction) and positions the role of the voice of the market (the shaded area in the center of the figure) emanating from a shared understanding (vision) of customer requirements, enterprise objectives, common processes, and operating procedures. The principal benefit of this approach is that both the idea generators and concept implementers start their activities, at concept development, with a higher level of shared understanding and vision.

As a part of this shared understanding, the voice of the market (represented by customer values) is designed to provide both groups an approximation of how customers would react to the many trade-offs that must be made as an idea moves through concept development, refinement, and implementation.

The voices within the enterprise in this network of market-based decision making articulate what the enterprise is able and willing to provide. Ideally, these voices respond to market needs within the constraints just described. These internal voices interacting with customer values are, in fact, the missing element in much of the traditional thinking about the market concept and the notion of being market oriented. This is the actionable framework that has for so long been missing, making it possible to avoid the limitations of those earlier approaches and to develop products and services of high integrity.

THE MARKETING CONCEPT AND THE COMMAND-AND-CONTROL ENTERPRISE

If reconciling the two voices shown in the market-based decision network appears simple, know that it is anything but simple for the command-and-control enterprise. In most instances, these enterprises have shown themselves to be poor listeners—in the collective sense—and they rarely speak in a single, clear voice.

Consider the typical large corporation. The activities of the corporation are broken down into functions (engineering, finance, marketing, and so forth) and are performed by specialists organized for efficiency into specialized functional units. Chances are, these functional units do not communicate directly or clearly with one another. The real decision making, and the coordination of all efforts, is made at the level of top management.

How is the organization to speak to the market in a clear and unified voice? More likely it will be a babel that customers will hear. In most cases, the marketing organization, figuring that it "owns the customer," will do most of the talking. Cut off from direct contact with the customer, design, engineering, and manufacturing will rightfully question the views of the marketing organization and argue that their constraints and possible contributions are not fully considered. These discordant voices will give rise to products and services that fail the definition of product integrity.

And how does the functionally structured organization hear what the market voice says? Lack of coordination between functions typically results in one group hearing one thing and another group hearing something else. Too often, these different sounds are never brought together for dispassionate interpretation.

This is not to say that traditionally organized enterprises cannot succeed in the modern marketplace. The fact is that most of the business world continues to be dominated by these enterprises. Indeed, the organization of activities into specialized functions does create strengths that few enterprises can do without. Many such enterprises have found ways to minimize their organizational weaknesses while preserving and making the most of their strengths. As we'll see later in this book, this is accomplished through various forms of cross-functional coordination. In a 1992 MSI study, researchers Stanley Slater and John Narver point to cross-functional coordination as one of the three core strategic components of the market-based enterprise. This coordination, in their opinion, must be across the board. Salespeople, for instance, must see competitive intelligence as part of their job; they must acquire information about competitive products and pass it on to their own company's R&D personnel. As Slater and Narver say:

> Any individual in any function in a seller firm can potentially contribute
> to creating value for buyers. . . . To accomplish this, effective companies
> often manage projects through small multifunctional teams that can
> move more quickly than the traditional function-by-function, sequential
> approach. . . . The crux of the matter is that the responsibility for creating buyer value is beyond the scope of any one function.[31]

Kohli and Jaworski echo this opinion when they write that "becoming truly market oriented requires the effective coordination of multiple departments, people at various levels, organizational systems, and financial resources, and this takes time."[32]

For clear evidence of how a large, functionally organized company can create and deliver a new product that meets the test of the marketplace, we need look no further than Ford Motor Company's successful 1986 Taurus/Sable automobile program. Just how the company organized its personnel and resources around the Taurus project has been described often and with clarity. Suffice it to say here that Ford used the same people and the same facilities that until then had been turning out some of the worst vehicles to design and manufacture one of the best. They did not hire new managers or replace their veteran assembly workers to accomplish this feat. What they did was adhere to the marketing concept—at least within the bounds of the Taurus project.

The fact that the marketing concept could develop and prosper in a large, traditional company like Ford indicates that change in organizational structure is not an absolute requirement for the enterprise willing to be guided by a focus on the customer and a decision-making process tied to market knowledge. How we can make the marketing concept operational and put it to work in our own organizations is the subject of the next chapter.

NOTES

1. Stephan H. Haeckel, "Adaptive Enterprise Design," Whittemore Conference on Hypercompetition (Tuck School, Dartmouth College, 1994).

2. General Electric Company, Annual Report, 1952, 21.

3. Peter F. Drucker, *The Practice of Management* (New York: Harper & Row, 1954), 38–39.

4. Robert J. Keith, "The Marketing Revolution," *Journal of Marketing* 24, no. 1 (January 1960): 38.

5. Frederick E. Webster, Jr., *Market-Driven Management* (New York: John Wiley & Sons, 1994), 27–28.

6. Ibid., vii.

7. Thomas J. Peters and Robert H. Waterman, Jr., *In Search of Excellence* (New York: Harper & Row, 1982), 156.

8. For a complete case study of the GM benchmark study, see Gregory H. Watson, *Strategic Benchmarking* (New York: John Wiley & Sons, 1993), 129–148.

9. General Motors Corporation, Cross Industry Study, 1984.

10. Xerox quality policy as cited in V. Daniel Hunt, *Quality in America: How to Implement a Competitive Quality Program* (Homewood, Ill.: Business One Irwin, 1992), 139.

11. James Colleti, "Total Quality Management," in *Oliver Wight Instant Access Guide: World Class Manufacturing*, ed. Thomas F. Wallace and Steven J. Bennett (Essex Junction, Vt.: Oliver Wight Publications, 1995), 217.

12. Chrysler Corporation, Annual Report, 1993, 8.

13. Ajay K. Kohli and Bernard J. Jaworski, "Market Orientation: The Construct, Research Propositions, and Managerial Implications," *Journal of Marketing* 54, no. 2 (April 1990): 13.

14. Roger Bennett and Robert Cooper, "Beyond the Marketing Concept," *Business Horizons*, June 1979, 76. Quoted in Robert H. Hayes and William J. Abernathy, "Managing Our Way to Economic Decline," *Harvard Business Review*, July–August 1980, 71.

15. Ibid.

16. Ibid.

17. Henry G. Weaver, *The Philosophy of Customer Research* (Detroit, Mich.: General Motors Corp., Customer Research Staff, n.d.), 2.

18. General Motors Corp., "Streamlining from the Customer Viewpoint," *The Proving Ground of Public Opinion*, December 1, 1932, 1.

19. Ibid.

20. Ibid., 20.

21. Gary Hamel and C. K. Prahalad, "Seeing the Future First," *Fortune*, September 5, 1994, 70.

22. David Halberstam, *The Reckoning* (New York: William Morrow, 1986), 562.

23. Ibid., 566.

24. Regis McKenna, "Marketing Is Everything," *Harvard Business Review*, January–February 1991, 67.

25. This question is further developed and answered in Chapter 5.

26. Benson P. Shapiro, "What the Hell Is 'Market Oriented'?" *Harvard Business Review*, November–December 1988, 120.

27. Ibid., 120–121.

28. The market-based decision-making network is described more fully in Chapter 3.

29. Vincent P. Barabba and Gerald Zaltman, *Hearing the Voice of the Market* (Boston: Harvard Business School Press, 1990).

30. Kim B. Clark and Takahiro Fujimoto, "The Power of Product Integrity," *Harvard Business Review*, November–December 1990, 108.

31. Stanley F. Slater and John C. Narver, *Superior Customer Value and Business Performance: The Strong Evidence for a Market-Driven Culture*, Report No. 92-125 (Cambridge, Mass.: Marketing Science Institute, September 1992), 4–5.

32. Ajay K. Kohli and Bernard J. Jaworski, "A Grounded Theory of Marketing Orientation," working paper, June 1988, 27.

3

PUTTING THE MARKETING CONCEPT TO WORK

The customer determines what the business is.
Peter F. Drucker

The preceding chapter makes it clear that Peter Drucker's vision of the marketing concept has stood the test of time. Today, customer value must come before shareholder value if the maximum shareholder value is to be achieved in the long run. Marketing in the "Big M" sense—that is, marketing as an all-encompassing philosophy—as opposed to the "Small m" sense—as confined to the activities of a single department—is now understood to be the thread that makes the cloth of the successful enterprise. But this understanding has not resulted in widespread adoption of the marketing concept. Why not?

We learned in Chapter 2 that one of the things that stands in the way of the universal practice of the marketing concept is the absence of an *actionable* framework, or model. We'll shortly see that the lack of a common language, the internal complexity of the enterprise, and the external uncertainty of the marketplace are also impediments to the goal of becoming truly market oriented. The first half of this chapter examines these impediments in detail. The second half explains the operational framework of the market-based decision network and describes the tools managers can use to overcome its impediments and put it to work.

The use of the term *market-based decision network* has been selected for the following reasons:

- The *market* is where the exchange of goods and services takes place. It is where ideas meet their ultimate test: will they be accepted?

- To say market *based* as opposed to *driven* or *oriented* is to emphasize the fact that the relationship between customer, community, and enterprise can be improved by an open and continual dialogue in which each party learns from the other.

- *Decision* speaks of a commitment to action—to make a decision is to allocate resources based on an expected outcome.
- The choice of *network* over *center* emphasizes the need to consider the extended enterprise, comprising customer, community, and enterprise.

IMPEDIMENTS TO DEVELOPING A MARKET-BASED DECISION NETWORK

The following four impediments must be overcome if we are to achieve the promise of the market-based decision network. Later in the chapter we offer a set of tools for dealing with each of the impediments and their interactions.

Lack of a common (and operational) language

It is both remarkable and disconcerting that nearly half a century after people like Alfred Sloan and Peter Drucker articulated the philosophy of marketing as being something that "encompasses the whole business," both scholars and practitioners are still struggling to position marketing at the core of the enterprise. This failure may have its origin in the general confusion that surrounds the very idea of marketing. There are, in fact, at least three separate and distinct ways in which businesspeople think about marketing.

Some think of marketing as *an activity*. "This product launch will require a well-planned marketing effort" is a typical statement that reveals this form of thinking. To others, marketing is *an organization* that uses resources to produce a result. Advocates of this definition would say, "Marketing was able to provide the production schedulers with a sales forecast covering the next six months." More often than not, the perception of marketing as an organization assumes that marketing controls the conduit between the customer and the enterprise. Wilton Anderson articulates this popular view: "Marketing is and has always been in the business of controlling the interpersonal networks that form the living bridge between the organization and its environment to a degree that characterizes no other functional division of the firm."[1] Still others view marketing as *a form of knowledge*—the repository of understanding for such concepts as segmentation, competitive challenges, and so forth.

Lack of an actionable model

The lack of progress toward creating an actionable model for the market-based decision-making network can be attributed to a general failure to recognize the difference between the marketing concept and the market itself. Businesspeople use the word *market* regularly, but sometimes carelessly. So what do we mean by *the market*? Bill Lazer describes a market as "(1) people with (2) money and (3) the willingness to buy."[2] We should add to this definition the presence of enterprises with goods and services to sell. After all, if these two different parties—buyers and sellers—are not brought together, there is no market.

From the standpoint of the enterprise, the market is external and uncontrollable (although it can be influenced); it is where exchange takes place and where added-value relationships are developed. In this context, a market includes all types of customers and entities that can affect either the reality or the perception of a product or a service: consumers, distributors, suppliers, regulators, competitors, and so on.

The marketing concept, on the other hand, though promoting an external perspective, is actually an internal set of controllable resources and activities. Ideally, these activities integrate the internal functions of the enterprise for the purpose of planning and executing the development, pricing, promotion, and distribution of products and services. These integrated activities should lead to long-term relationships that deliver value to customers.[3] Given this definition, marketing is more than a functional unit—it is an entire approach to doing business. Although we call many organizations "marketing," we empower very few of them to make all the decisions involved in doing business.

Considering the confusion surrounding the terms *market* and *marketing*, it is not surprising that we have failed to develop a framework for putting the marketing concept to work. Arguments and agreements on the subject of marketing are handicapped by the absence of a common understanding. Fred Webster gets to the heart of this confusion: "It fascinates me that marketing, among all the so-called management 'functions,' is the only one that has never been able to define itself satisfactorily. Do you hear anybody asking 'What do you mean by finance?' We certainly hear that regularly about marketing."[4]

Internal complexity

The third major impediment to adoption of the marketing concept is internal complexity. Complexity comprises the many elements of an issue or problem and the manner in which these elements interact with each other. When these elements and their interactions are jumbled, confusion arises in analysis and decision making. Complexity mixes the many signals that decision makers receive into the equivalent of a scrambled television signal. It creates an environment in which command-and-control management—not the marketing concept—appears to be the best management option.

Although most human beings are provided with thinking tools like memory, intuition, imagination, and logic to address problems, our cognitive ability to deal with extremely complex interrelationships appears to be one of our more limited capabilities. Yet the complexity of the problems we face cannot be eliminated. In fact, the preponderance of evidence suggests that the environment in which we operate is likely to become even more complex.

To act on the marketing concept, an enterprise must recognize and come to grips with—rather than assume away—the problem of complexity. Complexity is part and parcel of operating a business, making decisions, and serving customers. To deal with complexity, we need decision processes that address our human limitations yet preserve the strength of our capacity of memory, intuition, imagination, logic, and even passion. Although complexity does have an external dimension, in this chapter we will focus on the complexity that naturally occurs within the enterprise.

External uncertainty

A market has its own rhymes and a mind of its own. It changes course in ways that even the best forecasters cannot anticipate. Every customer and every competitor creates an eddy in the pool of the market, and each of these in turn is carried along to some extent by the currents of the market itself. A number of forces account for market uncertainty. These are just a few:

- Customers create their own perceptions of competing products.
- Customers are continually changing what they need or desire and how much they are willing to pay.
- Societal and economic conditions have significant impact on market size and growth.
- Governmental assessments of voter concerns are reflected in industry regulations.
- There are no safe home markets for domestic businesses.
- Customer loyalty is replaced by value consciousness.

No enterprise—no matter how powerful or persuasive its arsenal of marketing tools—can control the market. Influence is possible, but not control. Bernard Berelson warned of the difficulty of influencing markets when we are uncertain when he said (some time ago), "Some kinds of *communication* on some kinds of *issues* brought to the attention of some kinds of *people* under some kinds of *conditions* have some kinds of *effects*."[5]

Not having a clear understanding of external markets undermines our ability to act as a truly market-based enterprise in that it encourages multiple realities for decision makers: marketing organizations see one reality, customer service managers see another, engineers and product developers may see something quite different. In the absence of a shared understanding of the external market, the loudest voice in the enterprise tends to have its way in critical decisions. In the absence of agreement, organizational power and not knowledge drives decision making. The resources of the enterprise are allocated in support of this one, loudest voice; and the richness of market understanding that normally exists in any organization is untapped.

The complexity/uncertainty matrix

For purposes of analysis, we can represent the internal complexity and external uncertainty barriers in a matrix, as in Figure 3-1. Internal complexity is shown on the horizontal axis. It is another way of describing the issue of particularism versus globalism, or the silo problem mentioned in the Introduction to this book. Internal complexity deals with both the number of different functions (or departments) involved in a decision

Figure 3-1. *The Complexity/Uncertainty Matrix*

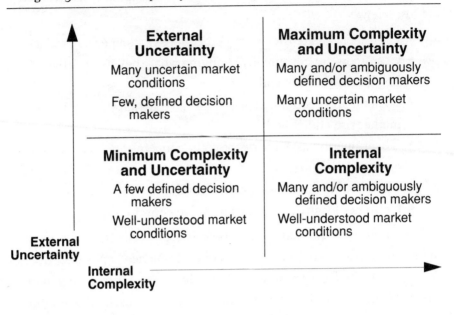

and the extent of agreement as to who will effect and who will be affected by the decision.

External uncertainty is shown on the vertical axis. The more market factors involved and the greater our uncertainty about them, the greater is the external uncertainty.

Obviously, the most complex and uncertain circumstances for the enterprise as a whole will be found in the upper-right quadrant, those with the least overall complexity and uncertainty in the lower left. The challenge for any organization attempting to make the marketing concept a reality is to find a way to deal with the difficult and "messy" situations found throughout the entire complexity/uncertainty matrix, with the exception of the lower-left quadrant, where life is simpler and more certain.

To address this challenge, the enterprise must develop a process that:

1. collects and understands customer values so that there is a shared vision between the customer and all elements of the enterprise; and
2. creates a unified internal vision that determines the most efficient way for the extended enterprise to satisfy those customer values.

Figure 3-2. *Impediments and Tools Related to the Marketing Concept*

Impediments	Tools
Lack of a common language	Enterprise business and process models
Lack of an actionable model	Market-based enterprise model based on influence diagram
Internal complexity	Strategy table
External complexity	Scenario table

OVERCOMING THE IMPEDIMENTS

With the impediments to making the marketing concept the driving force of the enterprise now recognized, we turn to the solutions. These take the form of tools—"thinking tools"—that make it easier to be systematic in identifying key issues and that provide a forum in which the many voices of the market and of the enterprise can make themselves heard and listened to. Figure 3-2 summarizes the impediments to the marketing concept and the tools offered here to overcome them. The overall goal is to build a highly integrated organization that delivers products and services within the "integrity" identified by Kim Clark and Takahiro Fujimoto (discussed in Chapter 2) as a major test of market competence.

Developing a common language with the enterprise business and process models

The first step is to create a common language and an understanding of how and why the enterprise operates. General Motors began doing this in early 1993, spurred by a key management objective to move toward common business processes and systems that would integrate GM's many and diverse business practices. With the assistance of the EDS Management Consulting organization, a group of GM business-process managers initiated a program to develop a common language to describe GM's business. As one key manager put it, "I don't care if we speak English, German, French, or Spanish, but we all need to use a consistent language to carry on a dialogue about our business." Given the sheer size of GM, an analogy to that of a country with many different dialects might be appropriate. In both cases, a single primary language is needed for effective self-governance.

Figure 3-3. *Enterprise Business Model with High-Level Functions*

Support Functions				Primary Functions			
Provide Administrative Services	Manage Financial Resources	Manage Human Resources	Develop Business Plan	Market and Sell	Design Product and Service	Produce and Deliver	Service

The anchor of this common language was the enterprise business model. Developed through interviews with key GM functional managers, the model tried to capture a description of the activities performed in each area of the business. Several hundred activity descriptions were classified into a structure representing the inventory of functions required to operate the business (Figure 3-3). At the highest level, the functions were named and labeled as either support (value-enabling) or primary (value-creating).

Figure 3-4 is a representation of the format to extend the model and begin categorizing each process within a supporting or primary function (proprietary substantive descriptions have been withheld). For example, "deliver the product," a value-creating process within the primary function of produce and deliver, is shown in the upper portion of Figure 3-4a as process G1, indicating it was a process within the primary function of "produce and deliver" (G). The initial categorization of the enterprise business model was then reviewed by GM's organizational units to ensure its accuracy as a recognized and accepted portrait of what and how GM conducted business.

The model became the taxonomy of terms GM would use to describe its business and to initiate dialogue at various levels. It was used broadly as a framework to describe GM's business to new members of the board of directors and narrowly as a financial budgeting model to understand GM's cost allocations. The model currently provides a mechanism for discussing GM's core competencies. It allows GM's management team to define those strengths they wish to leverage, the activities where performance is weak and needs strengthening, and the activities not key to GM's success that may be outsourced or eliminated.

The enterprise business model by itself is not revolutionary. Bob Hendry, then vice president of finance for North American Operations, commented somewhat disappointedly, "This model looks the same as one

Figure 3-4. *Enterprise Business Model*

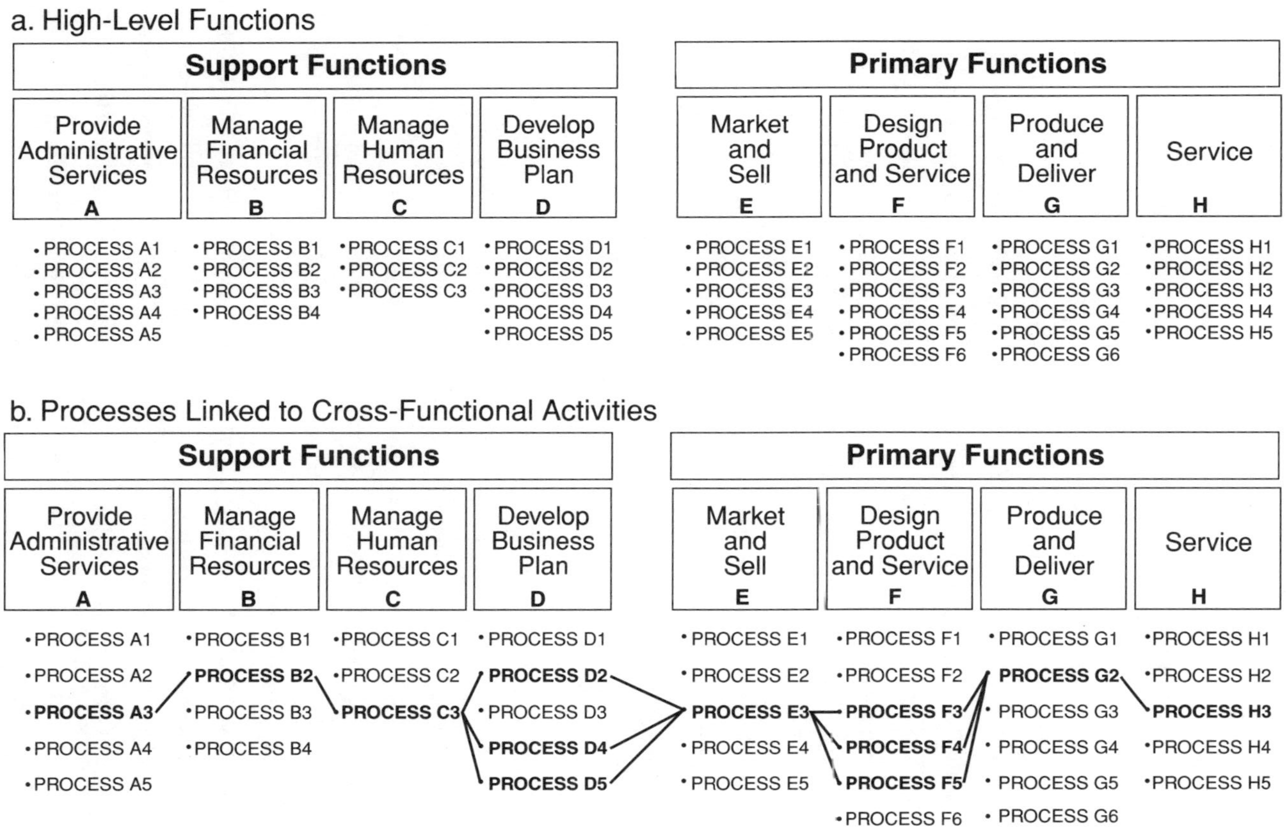

a. High-Level Functions

	Support Functions			Primary Functions			
Provide Administrative Services **A**	Manage Financial Resources **B**	Manage Human Resources **C**	Develop Business Plan **D**	Market and Sell **E**	Design Product and Service **F**	Produce and Deliver **G**	Service **H**
•PROCESS A1	•PROCESS B1	•PROCESS C1	•PROCESS D1	•PROCESS E1	•PROCESS F1	•PROCESS G1	•PROCESS H1
•PROCESS A2	•PROCESS B2	•PROCESS C2	•PROCESS D2	•PROCESS E2	•PROCESS F2	•PROCESS G2	•PROCESS H2
•PROCESS A3	•PROCESS B3	•PROCESS C3	•PROCESS D3	•PROCESS E3	•PROCESS F3	•PROCESS G3	•PROCESS H3
•PROCESS A4	•PROCESS B4		•PROCESS D4	•PROCESS E4	•PROCESS F4	•PROCESS G4	•PROCESS H4
•PROCESS A5			•PROCESS D5	•PROCESS E5	•PROCESS F5	•PROCESS G5	•PROCESS H5
					•PROCESS F6	•PROCESS G6	

b. Processes Linked to Cross-Functional Activities

	Support Functions			Primary Functions			
Provide Administrative Services **A**	Manage Financial Resources **B**	Manage Human Resources **C**	Develop Business Plan **D**	Market and Sell **E**	Design Product and Service **F**	Produce and Deliver **G**	Service **H**
•PROCESS A1	•PROCESS B1	•PROCESS C1	•PROCESS D1	•PROCESS E1	•PROCESS F1	•PROCESS G1	•PROCESS H1
•PROCESS A2	•**PROCESS B2**	•PROCESS C2	•**PROCESS D2**	•PROCESS E2	•PROCESS F2	•**PROCESS G2**	•PROCESS H2
•**PROCESS A3**	•PROCESS B3	•**PROCESS C3**	•PROCESS D3	•**PROCESS E3**	•**PROCESS F3**	•PROCESS G3	•**PROCESS H3**
•PROCESS A4	•PROCESS B4		•**PROCESS D4**	•PROCESS E4	•**PROCESS F4**	•PROCESS G4	•PROCESS H4
•PROCESS A5			•**PROCESS D5**	•PROCESS E5	•**PROCESS F5**	•PROCESS G5	•PROCESS H5
					•PROCESS F6	•PROCESS G6	

I would expect from any other large automotive company." This was very observant on his part. In fact, described at a high level, the activities performed by *any* company in a particular industry will be very similar. The unique differences between companies are in the execution of these activities—particularly managing the interactions.

Nevertheless, establishing a functional view of the business provided a good foundation for GM's common processes and systems efforts. It offered a reference point for GM's diverse practices, investments, and business processes and made visual the processes that needed to be common. What Bob Hendry was looking for was what Dr. W. Edwards Deming had referred to as a total system view of the business. Activities must be linked together as a total system if a business is to operate as an integrated whole. More often than not, these activities are executed by different functional areas. At GM, the activities that had been defined in the functional view of the business needed to be linked as a set of processes if the company was to complete the dialogue of how it wished to do business.

Linking activities together across functional areas was accomplished by leveraging work that had already been done on two cross-functional activities, product development and order fulfillment. The functional activities that made these two processes were "mapped" and "linked" across the enterprise business model to provide a view of how the processes were currently performed. The lower portion of Figure 3-4b illustrates the way the processes were initially "linked" for a major cross-functional activity.

Following the mapping of the two initial processes, the remaining core processes of the company were defined by a team of business-process managers representing multiple functions and organizations within GM. These process manager positions were developed to integrate common process and systems activities across the company. Teams composed of representatives from functional areas involved in each process defined and linked the appropriate activities together into an enterprise *process* model (Figure 3-5). Like the enterprise business model, the high-level processes of GM resemble the major processes found in almost any company in any industry. What is different, however, is the explicit manner in which the voice of the market, visualized through directional arrows such as those in the simultaneous concept development and implementation illustrations (Figure 2-8), is shown. This visual metaphor serves as

Figure 3-5. *Enterprise Process Model*

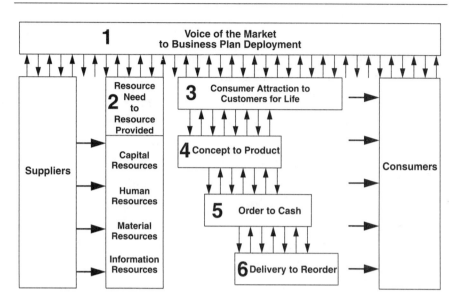

the tie that binds the day-to-day activities of the enterprise with the customer values expressed in the voice of the market.

These six processes (again, highly aggregated and somewhat disguised) represent the totality of business processes throughout the enterprise. Obviously, within each major process the model can reach different levels of detail. For example, the next level down in process 4, "concept to product," includes creatively thinking about the product, developing concepts, defining the product or service and its associated production or delivery process, validating both the product or service and the production or delivery process, and implementing the production or delivery capability. Similarly, the next level down in process 5, "order to cash," includes analyzing and forecasting demand, handling orders, scheduling the appropriate production and delivery capabilities, acquiring the necessary resources, producing and delivering the required products or services, and collecting money.

An important outcome of this process model is that people from different functions are—often for the first time—using a common language to describe "*what* GM does and *how* it goes about it." While the functional view of the business helped establish what competencies GM needed to compete in the automotive industry, the enterprise process model is the framework around which GM can define how it wishes to compete and what process capabilities it needs. This enterprise process model will also become the tool used for allocating resources for process improvement initiatives within GM. In this sense, it is analogous to the "war boards" used in military command centers during World War II. These boards created miniature representations of theaters of battle and troop movements, making it easier for commanders to visualize situations and make decisions. Just as changes were made to the generals' boards based on battles won and lost, GM's management team can now use a range of enterprise business and process models to make decisions on allocations of resources based on the competitive battles of the automotive industry.

Moreover, GM's growing acceptance of business models gives rise to the development of models for different levels of decision making. Models of varying levels of detail and scope are needed to facilitate the translation of high-level strategies, where business direction is formulated, to middle-level management, where the performance of processes is managed, to specific areas of the business, where processes are designed and performed. These multiple views will be integrated with the enterprise models to assist in communication across all levels.

Developing an actionable market-based enterprise model

The next step toward implementing a market-based decision network is to visualize an actionable market-based enterprise model.[6] An initial step in this visualizing is the creation of an influence diagram, which identifies the critical elements and relationships that exist within the enterprise and that create value for the customer. Figure 3-6 is a simplified example of an influence diagram.

Each element is indicated by a symbol:

- Rectangles for decisions or strategies composed of decisions. This is the part of the future we actually control.
- Ovals for risks or uncertainties. They are largely uncontrolled issues that stand between what we control and what we want.
- Octagons for ultimate values or results. Values represent those things in the future that are our ultimate desires.

Dan Owen made significant contributions to the section on pages 84 through 88.

Figure 3-6. *A Simplified Influence Diagram*

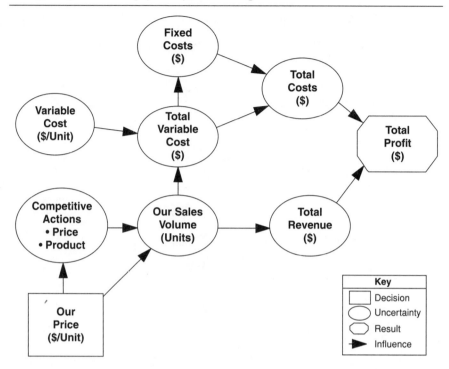

Arrows connect symbols to indicate the existence and direction of an "influence." An influence exists where there is a probabilistic dependency between two elements, so when knowledge about the influencing element changes, beliefs about the influenced element also change.[7]

Figure 3-6 is a relatively simple influence diagram for a decision about the price of a product. Notice that two types of relationships can be represented in an influence diagram: deterministic relationships, those for which one can write an equation such as the influence of "total revenue" on "total profit," and probabilistic relationships, those for which an equation cannot be written, such as the influence of a decision about price on competitive price changes or product changes. Known information on constants is not shown on the diagram. For example, although the tax rate is necessary to calculate total profit, it would not be shown unless some event of concern might result in a change in the tax rate.

The value of an influence diagram is that it provides discipline and clarity. It provides discipline by requiring that we make a distinction between what we can and cannot control through our own decisions. In

Figure 3-7. *A Market-Based Enterprise Model*

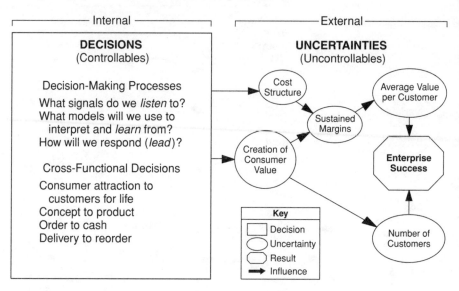

Figure 3-6, for example, the unit price is determined by the enterprise through decision making. Sales volume, particularly as it relates to retail sales without incentives, is not something over which the enterprise has absolute control. It provides clarity by facilitating communication among individuals. Different people inevitably have different views of the elements that appear in any influence diagram. They may differ, for instance, on the values that should be represented or the degree to which one element influences another. The diagram in this sense stimulates discussion and resolution of these differences. It helps to get everyone's view out in the open, where assumptions can be recognized and challenged and where the need for empirical information becomes more obvious.

Figure 3-7 is an influence diagram of the marketing concept, in effect a high-level market-based enterprise model. Here both the internal complexity and external uncertainties facing the enterprise are shown. This visualization fits our earlier definition of the marketing concept as an internal set of controllable resources and activities that integrate the internal functions of the market-based enterprise with shared understanding and vision of where and how the enterprise will achieve customer value.

The rectangle on the left of the figure represents the controllable, internal decisions to be made by the enterprise. The right side of the model contains the uncontrollable, external uncertainties facing the enterprise. This area contains the elusive concept of the creation of customer value, represented by the oval near the middle of the figure. As in Figure 3-6, an oval represents uncertainty. And uncertainty is appropriate here because no set of enterprise-controllable decisions can guarantee (for the reasons mentioned earlier) that the products or services of the enterprise will result in things that customers value over alternatives.

The octagon, on the far right, represents the outcome of the market-based enterprise model: enterprise success. If we were to accept the common measure of success as increased shareholder value based on long-term customer relations, then we could calculate enterprise success with a simple equation:

(average value per customer) × (number of customers) = enterprise success

This simple equation, of course, is directly affected by all the decisions made by the enterprise in the rectangle on the left side of the figure. In this simplified representation of the market-based enterprise model, the decisions fall into two categories: decision processes and cross-functional decisions.

Decision processes

- What signals do we *listen* to? Will we follow the company-driven, the market-driven, or the market-based decision model?
- What models will we use to interpret and *learn* from? Will we extrapolate from past experience? Will we develop prospective market models that help us determine what combination of attributes deliver the highest customer value?
- How will we act (*lead*)? Will we enhance existing products? Will we be a quick follower? Will we pioneer with *new* products and services?

Cross-functional decisions

- Consumer Attraction to Customer for Life. What management process will we use to integrate our understanding of customer requirements to resource allocations that will engender customer loyalty?
- Concept to Product. What processes will we use to translate cus-

tomer requirements to innovative product concepts that customers will value?

- Order to Cash. How can we anticipate market demand to make
  sure the product is there when the customer wants it?
- Delivery to Reorder. What will be our operating principles that
  ensure the customer's total product or service experience encourages him or her to make another purchase from us as well as to
  tell friends about the positive experience?

The decisions we choose will directly affect the cost structure of the business and, depending on the achieved level of customer value, the sustained margins over cost that can be charged in the market. In this way,
the influence diagram represents a simplified and actionable model of
Drucker's marketing concept.

Of course, the simplicity of this model masks the more complex environment in which the typical enterprise operates, in particular the many
uncertainties that every business faces and must consider. Figure 3-8
identifies some of these added uncertainties. Here we see that the ability
of our competitor to create sustained customer satisfaction has an influence on our customers and upon our own plans. Likewise, changing measures of market share, changing customer desires, changing market size,
and so forth all influence the equation by which we calculate enterprise
success. Even with the added complexity, Figure 3-8 masks other external
influences, such as the rate and type of technology development, societal
change caused by demographics, and the globalization of markets.

Crossing the complexity barrier with the strategy table

The strategy table makes it easier to deal with organizational complexity by laying out the set of decisions that have to be made in a complex
environment. Table 3-1 is such a table, kept simple here for purposes of
demonstration. You'll notice that the title of each column reflects a key
decision—be it how we listen, how we learn, how we lead, or whatever.
(At General Motors, we typically use five or more columns to represent
each of these decision-making areas.) In effect, these represent key decisions that must be integrated into a business plan—for a product, a product family, or an entire corporation. They represent areas within which
important business decisions must be made, determining resource alloca-

Figure 3-8. *Market-Based Enterprise Model with Added Uncertainties*

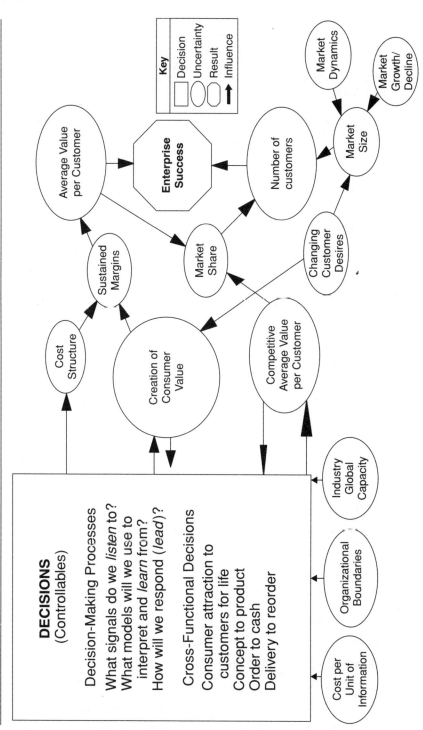

Table 3-1. *A Simple Strategy Table*

What Signals Do We Listen To?	What Models Will We Use to Interpret and Learn From?	How Will We Respond (Lead)?
Internal experienced and creative voices with successful long-term track records	Extrapolations from past performances and constant review of competitive activities	Continue to enhance existing products and services until a breakthrough product is invented (improve products and reduce costs)
External consumer voices as interpreted by the marketing organization	Extrapolation based on comparison of consumer reaction to past and current ideas and concepts	Effectively communicate those aspects of product (both tangible and intangible) that motivate consumers to purchase product
Appropriate internal experienced and creative voices directly involved in observing customers and consumers	Determination of which combination of attributes delivers the highest customer value	By knowing how much customers value our ability to satisfy their needs and wants, innovatively develop products and services at a price lower than that value

tions and strategic direction for the enterprise. Notice, too, that they correspond with the "controllable process decisions" shown earlier in Figure 3-7.

Listed under each column is a range of alternatives for decision making. For example, under the heading "What signals do we listen to?" are three alternatives:

1. Internal experienced and creative voices with successful long-term track records.
2. External consumer voices as interpreted by the marketing organization.
3. Appropriate internal experienced and creative voices directly involved in observing customers and consumers.

Similar alternatives are listed in the other two columns.

Because of space limitations, only the words that describe the various entries are depicted. Experience with strategy tables suggests, however, that the greatest clarity and likelihood of implementation are obtained when each strategy table entry has an additional paragraph that makes its meaning specific and includes a realistic assessment of the financial resources, personnel, and time requirements that are part of its implementation. For example, Table 3-2 shows how different strategies tie the strategic choice to specific actions the organization must take.

The rectangles in Table 3-2 show a strategy similar to the company-driven strategy discussed in Chapter 2. Notice that the table defines the strategy in terms of the specific decisions or resource allocations that are required to make it operational. In this company-driven strategy, the enterprise would:

- Listen to signals from internal experienced and creative personnel with successful long-term track records.
- Use models that extrapolate from previous experience and constantly review competitors' activities. The enterprise would also (to a lesser extent) use models that compare consumer reaction with past and current ideas and concepts.
- Continue to enhance existing products and services until a breakthrough period or service was invented. The enterprise would also (to a lesser extent) effectively communicate those attributes that motivate consumers to purchase the product.

Of course, the enterprise could have chosen other strategies that would have required quite different resource allocation decisions. For example, the ellipses in Table 3-2 show the marketing-driven strategy discussed in Chapter 2. Although this strategy starts out with a different approach to listening (beginning with the external voice of the customer as interpreted by the internal marketing organization), it allocates resources in a manner almost identical to the company-driven strategy—the differences being in emphasis.

The octagons highlight the market-based decision network strategy. In this strategy, the enterprise listens by having its most experienced and creative people observe consumers directly. The strategy calls for the identification of attributes that deliver the highest value to customers. The enterprise leads by knowing how much customers will pay for products or services that satisfy their wants and needs and then developing those innovative products and services at a cost below that value.

Each of the decisions requires a different allocation of resources. In the market-based decision network strategy, for example, the enterprise must

Table 3-2. *A Strategy Table That Links Strategy with Action*

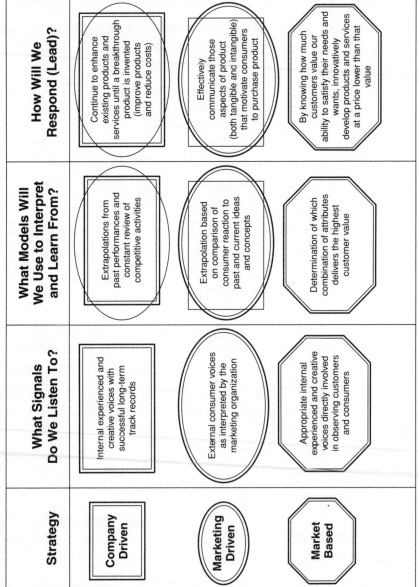

Strategy	What Signals Do We Listen To?	What Models Will We Use to Interpret and Learn From?	How Will We Respond (Lead)?
Company Driven	Internal experienced and creative voices with successful long-term track records	Extrapolations from past performances and constant review of competitive activities	Continue to enhance existing products and services until a breakthrough product is invented (improve products and reduce costs)
Marketing Driven	External consumer voices as interpreted by the marketing organization	Extrapolation based on comparison of consumer reaction to past and current ideas and concepts	Effectively communicate those aspects of product (both tangible and intangible) that motivate consumers to purchase product
Market Based	Appropriate internal experienced and creative voices directly involved in observing customers and consumers	Determination of which combination of attributes delivers the highest customer value	By knowing how much customers value our ability to satisfy their needs and wants, innovatively develop products and services at a price lower than that value

allocate sufficient time for the resources of engineering and design to ob-serve market activity, while in the marketing-driven strategy, it must allo-cate resources for market research specialists to collect information for marketing analysts to interpret. In this sense, the strategy table is a tool for visualizing alternative strategies and the resources required to imple-ment them.

The actions required of each function responsible for a particular col-umn in these three strategies are clear, specific, and different. This strat-egy table makes it easier for a group of managers representing different functions to understand the cost and the value of the different strategies. In fact, with further review, the managers could use the table to work toward an improved hybrid strategy. For example, the listening aspects of the marketing-driven and the market-based strategies might be merged so that the marketing department conducts market research and finds a way to more effectively involve engineers and designers.

It should be clear from this discussion how the strategy table can be used to overcome internal complexity. Obviously, the more the table re-flects the experience and judgment of the managers responsible for the choice of strategic direction, the more likely they are to come up with meaningful alternatives.

By displaying the strategy in table format, the strategy is explicitly linked to the resource allocations that define it. Also, no decision can be made without considering its impact on other choices. The two are presented side by side so that the decision makers can consider all the options within each column and connect them to an integrated strategy.

Managing uncertainty with the scenario table

While the strategy table serves as a mechanism for coming to grips with organizational (internal) complexity, the scenario table is a tool for dealing with the uncertainty that exists outside the enterprise—the "un-controllable" domain. The scenario table in Table 3-3 is similar in format to a strategy table, but its columns represent uncertainties, not decisions, and the entries within the columns are assessments of the potential range of events that can occur within that uncertainty. In other words, the pos-sible scenarios are developed horizontally, while the uncertainties are listed vertically. Like a strategy in a strategy table, a scenario is a set of

Table 3-3. *Scenario Table for Uncertain Events, Year 2000*

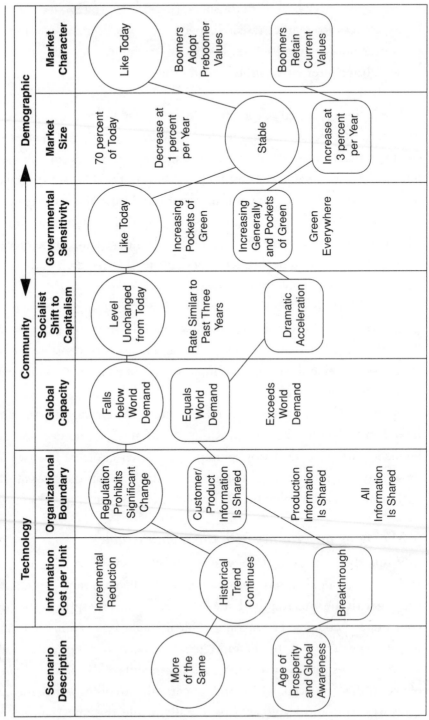

possible outcomes across the key uncontrollable factors that will affect the ultimate success or failure of any chosen strategy. Some of the uncertainties shown across the top of the table were identified in Figure 3-8.

Two scenarios, "more of the same" and "age of prosperity and global awareness," are illustrated here in terms of possible future events. The objective in defining alternative scenarios is not to portray every possible future event but to create a few likely, yet very different, scenarios that might occur in the future.

Finding the best strategy for an uncertain future

The strategy and scenario tables help address problems found in the upper-right quadrant of the complexity/uncertainty matrix (see Figure 3-1). But for all parties to appreciate the risks and rewards associated with each of the alternative strategies, we must understand the outcomes of each strategy over the range of possible future business environments. We can map these possible outcomes in a decision-tree format, as seen in Figure 3-9. While the figure shows a qualitative assessment of the outcomes, it is also possible to make a quantitative evaluation when the strategies are defined in terms of resource allocations and when the influence of the uncertainties that comprise the scenario table are quantified.

In this qualitative evaluation, the market-based strategy in a "more of the same" business environment does not develop outcomes that exceed the outcomes of the company-driven strategy. The rationale for this evaluation is that in an environment where "past is prologue," it matters little whether the enterprise listens to signals from internal experienced and creative personnel with successful track records or from experienced personnel directly involved in observing customers. The same is true across the other columns in Table 3-2.

If the environment qualifies as an "age of prosperity and global awareness," however, then the market-based strategy dominates the outcome of the company-driven strategy; it allows for substantial increases in the average value per customer and the number of customers, as opposed to reductions in average customer value and some increase in the number of customers. The rationale for this evaluation is that in an environment where information technology changes dramatically, enterprises are shar-

Figure 3-9. *Decision-Tree Format*

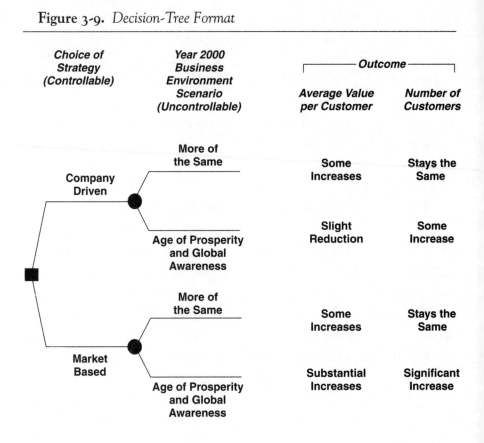

ing customer and product information, the market size is increasing, and baby boomers bring their values with them as they move into maturity, the value of the enterprise's past experiences is diminished greatly. With this amount of change, the enterprise must find new ways of finding out what customers want, need, and value and then design products and services at a cost below the value that customers place on them.

When the full process is used and strategies are evaluated quantitatively, the results often lead to the development of a composite, or hybrid, strategy that has a greater value than any of the initially identified alternatives. A hybrid strategy offers at least two advantages for the enterprise: (1) while individual functions may take ownership or lean toward one strategy or another, the whole team can take ownership of the hybrid; (2) the development of hybrid strategies forces learning to take place and shifts people's attention from defending positions to searching for value.

The key point is that the true value of the process is in the personal discussion held by key stakeholders as they evaluate the potential out-come of different decisions under different circumstances.

SUMMARY

Taken together, the tools described in this chapter provide a frame-work for putting the philosophy of the marketing concept to work in the modern enterprise—including the enterprise organized by business functions. Following is a summary of their purposes.

The *enterprise business model* represents what an enterprise does in the conduct of its business and provides a taxonomy of terms that describes the business and initiates dialogue at various levels. The model also pro-vides a mechanism for discussing the core competencies of the enterprise, making it easier for management to identify those strengths they wish to leverage, the activities in which performance needs to be strengthened, and nonessential activities.

The *enterprise process model* describes major cross-functional processes regardless of their functional origin. While the functional view of the business helped establish what competencies are needed to compete, the process model defines how the enterprise will compete and what process capabilities it needs.

The *market-based enterprise model* (visualized in an influence diagram format) identifies all the critical elements and relationships within the enterprise that create value for customers. It visualizes the internal, controllable issues with which the enterprise must be concerned (deci-sions) as well as the external, uncontrollable variables that exist outside its boundaries.

The *strategy table* is a tool for mastering the complexity that exists in every organization and for critiquing alternative strategies within the framework of the marketing concept. The voices of each relevant func-tion of the enterprise are brought to bear in discussing and developing strategies that represent "what the enterprise is capable of delivering." In this collaborative activity, no one voice becomes the owner of the strat-egy, the contribution of each function to the strategy becomes known, and the possibility of creating high-integrity products and services is enhanced. This tool makes it possible for functionally organized enterprises to act in cross-functional ways.

The *scenario table* deals with the problem of external uncertainty. It helps decision makers understand the range of uncontrollable alternatives and serves as a facilitating device to encourage imaginative forays into the future.

The *decision tree* depicts the qualitative impact (quantitative, when necessary) of a broad range of uncertain futures on alternative decisions facing management, leading to creative discussion concerning the robustness of current decisions over future uncertainties.

NOTES

1. Wilton T. Anderson, "Is the Purpose of the Organization 'to Create Satisfied Customers'? No!" *Marketing and Research Today* 19, no. 3 (August 1991): 138.

2. William Lazer, *Handbook of Demographics for Marketing and Advertising: New Trends in the American Marketplace*, 2d ed. (New York: Lexington Books, 1994), 6.

3. C. Whan Park and Gerald Zaltman, *Marketing Management* (Chicago: Dryden Press, 1987), 8.

4. Frederick E. Webster, *It's 1990—Do You Know Where Your Marketing Is?* Report No. 89-123 (Cambridge, Mass.: Marketing Science Institute, December 1989), 5.

5. Bernard Berelson, "Communications and Public Opinion," in *Communications in Modern Society*, ed. Wilbur Schramm (Urbana, Ill.: Univ. of Illinois Press, 1948), 172.

6. An actionable market-based enterprise model grew out of a conference on the future of marketing sponsored by Quest and Associates at the Chaminaude Conference Center in Santa Cruz, California, in 1992.

7. Daniel Owen, "The Use of Influence Diagrams in Structuring Complex Decision Problems," in *Applied Decision Analysis*, ed. Derek W. Bunn (New York: McGraw-Hill, 1984), 213.

4

The Market-Based Enterprise

*Indeed it has been said that we are now living in a second
industrial revolution; but instead of steam, the new
revolution is being propelled by information. And, as in the
first revolution, relative success will be determined by the
ability to handle the propelling force. . . . There can be
little doubt that the need today is for conceptual skills, that
is, the ability to process information and make judgments.*
Robin M. Hogarth

The foundation of a market-based enterprise is neither its physical assets nor the shape of its organizational chart. Its foundation is an open information system that allows a free flow of knowledge between individual employees across functions. At its core, it is a network of market-based decisions that take place in an environment that encourages and rewards the sharing of knowledge. This "core competence" is what gives the enterprise its competitive edge in product development, pricing, and so forth.

At this point we must ask: What does a truly market-based enterprise look like? What is its form and what are its behaviors? And what are some examples of enterprises that use market-based decision making to satisfy customers on a consistent basis?

The Vertical Organization

To answer the first question, we need to discuss the structure of the enterprise. This book began with a description of the command-and-control organization, which is characterized by separation of activities into distinct functions, or vertical silos. In the classic command-and-control organization, decisions and activities are controlled hierarchi-

cally both within the individual silos and collectively through top management's control of all functions.

From the customer viewpoint, this enterprise too often ends up being
a creature with many faces and uncoordinated voices. Customers know
it through its outward representations: through the design, the features,
and the performance of its products and services; through its promotional
messages; through the dealers who sell and service its products. For the
silo enterprise, these representations are typically unharmonious—like a
living room in which the furniture, carpeting, and draperies clash. The
outward results of such conflicts may be minor irritants to the customer—
such as the U.S. Postal Service's priority mail envelope, which is made
of a high-finish paperboard to which the Postal Service's own postage
stamps do not stick well. Or they can be major aggravations, like the
nonsmoking woman's car with a factory-installed cigarette lighter and
ashtray but no place to put a purse.

What is lacking in these examples is the Clark and Fujimoto definition
of "product integrity" (see Chapter 2). Without this integrity, the aes-
thetics of design and materials are neither pleasing nor harmonious with
the product's quality and functionality. If the customer can spot this lack
of integrity from the outside, chances are that the enterprise lacks integrity on the inside—in its structure, in the way information is passed
around, and in the way decisions are made.

More often than not, lack of integrity stems from the fact that one
group of people determines what customers want; another group designs
the product; other groups do the engineering, manufacturing, and promotion; and still other groups have individual responsibility for selling,
for servicing, and for determining the terms of trade. Unfortunately, too
few of these people talk to each other in a systematic way in the classic
silo enterprise. And the fault for this lack of communication has less to
do with individual employees than with the structure of the organization
and the way work processes link people together.

The late W. Edwards Deming was among the first to teach manufacturers that the problem of quality had much less to do with people than with
processes—the way work was structured. Inferior product quality, in his
view, was not so much the fault of uncaring workers as it was the fault of
processes designed without adequate care. Manufacturers should spend

less time managing people, he told them, and more time managing and honing their processes. This important idea virtually revolutionized the world of manufacturing, which quickly discovered that the same workers who had turned out second-rate goods for years could produce top-quality goods once their work processes were changed and managed as if quality mattered.

Deming's injunction to manage the process and not the people is as important to the production of services as it is to manufactured goods, and the current movement of business "reengineering" is a direct descendent of this fundamental idea. The story of the ill-fated Ford Edsel is a useful example of the lack of coordination and shared learning that gets silo companies into trouble.

Over the years, conventional wisdom has clung to the notion that Ford's disaster with its Edsel, which appeared in September 1957, somehow showed that market research is of limited value in the development of new products. In 1989, *Investor's Daily* perpetuated this notion in telling readers that "the infamous Edsel was the most heavily researched vehicle of its day, yet it turned out to be perhaps the auto industry's biggest bomb."[1]

There is no disputing the magnitude of the Edsel fiasco. Some $250 million was spent on its development, a huge sum for its day and the largest amount ever spent on the development of a commercial product up to that time. The return on this investment was also monumental— but inversely so. Estimates of the company's losses on the new vehicle over a two-year period run to some $350 million, or nearly $2 billion in current dollars. Ford Motor Company had forecasted sales of 200,000 units in the new automobile's first year, with healthy continuing sales in the years to follow. In reality, only a few more than 100,000 vehicles found buyers during the first *two* years.[2]

I can still vividly recall a presentation made by Fairfax Cone, of Foote, Cone and Belding, to the Sacramento, California, Advertising Club in 1957. Cone explained how his agency had access to research on every aspect of the Edsel's entry into the market, down to developing a long list of names for the car, and how I would soon see one of the world's most successful new-product entries. Of course, not everyone had the opportunity to hear Fairfax Cone personally discuss the launch his agency had helped prepare. Nearly everyone, however, had an opportunity to hear about the Edsel through one of the most extensive launches conducted up to that time. Indeed, we all expected something quite spectacular.

Market research was indeed conducted on behalf of the new automobile, but its scope was limited to developing an appropriate name, to determining the psychographics of potential buyers, and to crafting a promotional campaign. The Columbia University Bureau of Applied Social Research was hired to interview eight hundred recent car buyers in Peoria, Illinois, and San Bernardino, California. Most of the questions had to do with determining the image, the social status, and the masculine and feminine characteristics associated with various Ford and competing vehicles. One way the researchers attempted to gauge the sophistication of respondents was to assess their ability to mix cocktails. Questions relating to the cost, the performance characteristics, and safety features of these vehicles appear to have been left unasked.

This superficial probing of the market is a far cry from what most in the auto industry—or any industry for that matter—would have considered appropriate for a major new product. And even this limited research was corrupted in the way it was used. As John Brooks wrote in a *New Yorker* series on the Edsel:

> Science was curtly discarded at the last minute and the Edsel was named
> for the father of the Company's president, like a nineteenth-century
> brand of cough drops or saddle soap. As for the design, it was arrived at
> without even a pretense of consulting the polls, and by the method that
> has been standard for years in the designing of automobiles— that of
> simply pooling the hunches of sundry company committees.[3]

Indeed, the advanced (or bizarre, depending on your viewpoint) styling of the Edsel was developed in isolation from the market and drew little from the research.

In today's parlance, we would say that the Edsel was a "company push." Instead of listening to its customers and potential customers, its automotive engineers and dealers, Ford management made the mistake we all make from time to time: It tried to push a product into the market. Instead of spending millions on listening and learning about the market, it spent millions on a campaign to launch the product it had developed in isolation. In this sense, the Edsel story is a classic of what so often goes wrong in a silo-based enterprise: Organization and ego got in the way of sound decision making.

To conclude that this type of failure is a natural result of the functional form of organization, or to imply that failures are preordained, would be incorrect. It is more correct to conclude that the likelihood, or the pre-conditions for such failures, are at hand. We should remember that the same functionally organized company that gave the world the Edsel also gave it the hugely successful Mustang. Years later Ford would again rise to the occasion in its development of the popular Taurus model—this time drawing on each company function to form a long-term, empowered team to get the job done end to end.

THE HORIZONTAL ORGANIZATION

Many companies are trying to eliminate the problems of the vertical structure by redrawing the organizational chart. Organization pundits have prescribed many new architectures for the posthierarchical enterprise, chief among them the virtual corporation, the modular organization, and the horizontal organization. Each is seen as having important advantages for competitive success in the Information Age. It is the horizontal organization that has the greatest relevance to this discussion.

Before we discuss the horizontal organization, consider the familiar organizational chart for the vertical corporation in Figure 4-1, which shows just three of the typical functional silos. The common complaint about this structure has to do with the gray areas between the silos. These are the areas where coordination must take place. Unlike the vertical, hierarchical organization structured around functions or departments, the horizontal organization—seen in Figure 4-2—is rebuilt around a handful of "core processes," such as product development, sales and fulfillment, customer support, and administration.[4] According to its advocates, the horizontal organization has a number of important benefits: the elimination of non-value-added activities; reduced supervision responsibilities; less money and energy spent on maintenance of the vertical, multidepartmental edifice; elimination of the "disconnects" that occur when work

Figure 4-1. *The Vertical Organization*

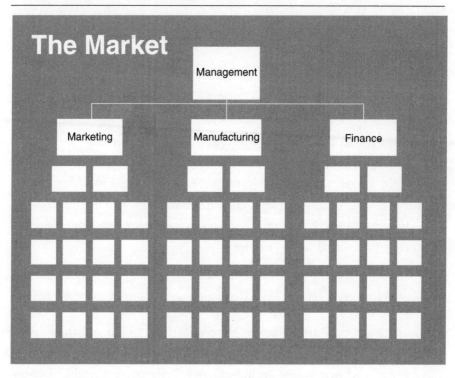

moves from one functional area to another; and closer contact between customers and decision makers in the enterprise. Unfortunately, there is still plenty of gray space in this organizational chart, meaning that the horizontal enterprise may be subject to the same coordination problems that afflict its vertical counterpart.

The horizontal organization is the kind of structure that the apostles of business reengineering have been working so mightily to create. Reengineering is a direct descendent of the many Japanese programs that were developed to improve work processes. According to Fred Adair of Mercer Management Consulting,

> Reengineering is a natural outgrowth of the quality movement that began in the 1970s. That movement encouraged companies to think about customers and to focus on how work was accomplished. What reengineering added was, first, an understanding that customers and processes were the most important aspects of the quality movement, and second, a recognition that quantum leap improvements in the way business was done

Figure 4-2. *The Horizontal Organization*

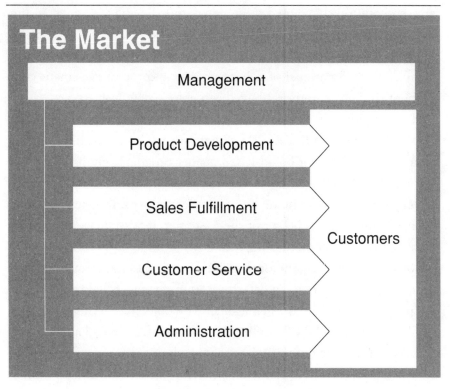

[were] both possible and necessary. It's the magnitude of these improvements, and their necessity, that has made reengineering so popular.[5]

Working back from the customer, determining which activities directly serve that customer, and then organizing those activities into coherent and efficient processes constitute an organizational method for aligning resources in a very direct way to serve the customer. When properly designed, each process contains all the decision-making capabilities needed to create customer satisfaction, and all the human elements see the customer as the object of their labors.

This new structure has the potential to improve the focus of work on value-adding activities, to eliminate costly bureaucracy, to improve communication between the enterprise and the marketplace, and to enhance communication and decision making within the business. The fact remains, however, that our experience with these new forms is extremely limited. Enterprises that have adopted them wholly tend to be new and small businesses; in fact, organizing around activities instead of formal structures has always been a natural way to begin a new business. When large corporations have used these new forms they have done so in limited ways—an accounts payable department here, a production facility there. Across-the-board reengineering is not only rare but exceedingly difficult, requiring a level of culture change and top management commitment that few enterprises have been able to demonstrate.

Most providers of reengineering consulting services report implementation failure rates in the 50–70 percent range. This is roughly twice the failure rate reported for broad-based quality programs, giving rise to the warning, "If you thought TQM was hard to implement, wait until you try reengineering." Given the high costs associated with this new approach to organizing work on behalf of the customer, most managers will want to think twice about attempting it in any but limited situations.

The current enthusiasm for these new organizational forms is uncomfortably reminiscent of the great expectations managers held out for similar "panaceas" of the past: management by objectives, synergy through conglomeration, and the "excellence" movement. Each had much to recommend, and many enterprises benefited when these philosophies were thoughtfully applied, but none has proven to be a definitive solution to the endless challenge of creating products and services that satisfy customers.

Speaking of the attractions of horizontal organization in a *Business Week* interview, management scholar Henry Mintzberg observes that "the danger is that an idea like this can generate too much enthusiasm. It's not for everyone."[6] Unfortunately, the consultants who develop these ideas and beat the drum for them around the country are as guilty of overselling as senior managers are hungry for universal solutions. The two create a dangerous mixture of hype and hope.

Promoters of the current obsession with creating flatter, nonhierarchical organizations fail to recognize that these concepts are not something new; they have a history of their own. According to Robert Eccles and Nitin Nohria, management scholars in the 1920s were writing about practices involving "cross-functioning," the replacement of "vertical authority" with "horizontal authority," and so on. The vertical, hierarchical organization, today's most popular villain, is, say Eccles and Noria, "an old dog that has been kicked for a long time."[7] They make it clear that what many management consultants package today as leading-edge organizational practices were actually facts of corporate life seven decades before. Indeed, the brave new workplace of nonbureaucratic, "networked" organizations is anything but new.

The persistence of the functional organization—even in the long presence of alternative forms—suggests that it is not totally wrongheaded and may be with us for some time to come. As of this writing, however, many scholars and business pundits have written off the traditional, functionally organized model of enterprise that has carried most of the burden of large-scale commerce since the days of Henri Fayol. As Frederick E. Webster, Jr., describes it, "the benefits they provided in terms of specialization and control have been offset by their inefficiency and lack of flexibility."[8] Still, traditional functions have been instrumental in developing and harboring real depths of practical know-how that horizontally construed organizations have yet to match. The real challenge for top managers is to find mechanisms for capitalizing on the deep know-how of the functions and putting them in the direct service of the customer.

THE HYBRID ORGANIZATION

All protestations about the new age of horizontal enterprises notwithstanding, it is not likely that the concentrated effort and expertise characteristic of the functions of large corporations will soon be abandoned. Small firms might do so with good effect; quickly growing new enterprises that have yet to adopt a strong functional organization orientation—that have no tradition or investment in it—might also benefit from the new style of organization now capturing managerial interest. Others ought to be wary.

In the final analysis, the most serious problem of the functionally structured organization is the problem of coordination within and across functions. It is in the gray space between functions on the organizational chart that this coordination must take place. Consider the idea of turning the functional organizational chart on its side, so that finance, marketing, engineering, and so forth are horizontal. Now re-label them as product development and manufacturing, sales and order fulfillment, and so on.

The gray space is still there. Instead of silos we have processes, but they are still disconnected. So how much has really changed?

Henry Mintzberg, in his essay "The Innovative Organization," favors a hybrid approach. He would group people with specialized skills in functional units but deploy them in project teams to attack specific tasks. With this arrangement, information and decisions flow informally; coordination becomes the responsibility of these skilled people and not those normally endowed with hierarchical authority. The downside of this arrangement, according to Mintzberg, is the high price paid for frequent communication and coordination.[9] Stanley Slater and John Narver point to studies of high-tech firms that rely on formal organizational structures as a base, with temporary teams drawing from appropriate functional areas to attack new product projects, strategic assessments, and other tasks requiring cross-functionality.[10] Also, no less an authority than Thomas Davenport, credited by many as being the father of process reengineering, recognizes the continuing importance of strong functions: "I can see shrinking functions, but I can't see getting rid of functional expertise completely. Process management is an important dimension of structure, but it should simply be added to the multidimensional matrices most organizations already have."[11]

By the 1980s, American automakers were learning how to do what Davenport had described. As Clark and Fujimoto discovered in their auto industry study, "even the most resolutely functional development organizations had established formal mechanisms such as coordination committees, engineering liaisons, project managers, matrix structures, and cross-functional teams to improve product development."[12] And while I hate to lavish praise on a direct competitor, the Ford Taurus case speaks eloquently to the potential of cross-functional teams drawn together to spearhead an important project. The project leader of "Team Taurus" was a Ford "lifer" named Lew Veraldi. Veraldi had learned a number of important lessons about the problems of silo thinking during a stint in Europe. There, Ford divisions did not communicate, either within or across national borders, and that lack of communication and cooperation resulted in visible quality problems, notably in the company's Capri model.

Veraldi was successful in bringing management and engineering together in solving the European Capri quality problems and in subsequently developing the Fiesta model. When he got the top job on the Taurus project, he was determined to be even more eclectic, bringing in people from marketing, manufacturing, customer service, public relations, and assembly as well as people from outside the company—namely, the dealers and independent auto mechanics who would one day have to service the new vehicle. Veraldi's attempts to recruit the best and brightest from various departments for his own long-term project were not universally appreciated, however. As one case study of the project relates:

> Ford, at the time, had its share of fiefdoms and powerful departmental barons. Some department heads, who did not like having their best people pulled away from them for Veraldi's project, at first resisted by putting forth their second- and third-level players. However, top management, which solidly supported Veraldi and his team concept, let it be known that they knew who the top people were in each division, and they wanted them on the Taurus team. The department heads had little choice but to acquiesce.[13]

While the Taurus story points to the great potential of using cross-functional teams on long-term projects, this passage points out some of the behavioral challenges involved as well as the need for support at the highest levels.

A VISION OF THE MARKET-BASED ENTERPRISE

The previous discussion should make it clear that there is no one way to structure an organization in fulfilling the philosophy of the marketing concept. The new, horizontal structure may be fine for some, particularly smaller enterprises, but there are many examples of enterprises that have retained a strong functional orientation while meeting the definition of being truly market based in the way they do business. Indeed, the response to the challenge of becoming market based is in the process, not in the structure. One of the reasons that command and control no longer works as it once did is that its process is rooted in its hierarchical structure. The process of the market-based enterprise is not limited to one organizational structure.

So if we cannot describe the market-based enterprise by its structure, how can we describe it? Here it is useful to create a vision of what we might agree are the characteristics of a truly market-based enterprise. Visioning can be a powerful and creative tool. A vision is an idealized image of what we hope to create; it offers an ideal pattern against which we can begin building a common vision among relevant team members. An ideal vision of the market-based enterprise is pictured in Figure 4-3; it could be described as follows:

- An unambiguous sense of direction, relative to developing customer-satisfying products and services, permeates the entire organization. No one needs to be told the mission of the enterprise.
- Strategic and operational plans reinforce each other, and there are no downstream disconnects between activities.
- Decision makers understand how their roles contribute to the total enterprise, and their accountability is clear—all the arrows are aligned.
- Planning and execution recognize the full complexity and uncertainty of the market. There are no simplistic ideas about how customers or competitors will respond to the actions of the enterprise.
- There is empowerment throughout the enterprise. Direction is clear, resources necessary to meet the objectives are allocated with the decision to proceed, accountability is well-defined, guidelines for implementation are clear, and there is no micromanagement from above.
- Conflict and differences of opinion are not suppressed. When they surface they are channeled into a process that seeks win-win solutions.
- Market knowledge results in a steady stream of innovative and customer-satisfying products and services that leverage the capabilities and resources of the enterprise.

This ideal company has formed itself in such a way that the customer sees and recognizes one face and hears a familiar and consistent voice. Every point of customer contact—from printed material to products to after-sale service—must present the customer with a clear and harmonious impression of the company, its products, and its services. And this unified outward image is a reflection of the company's internal consis-

Figure 4-3. *Market-Based Enterprise Process Model*

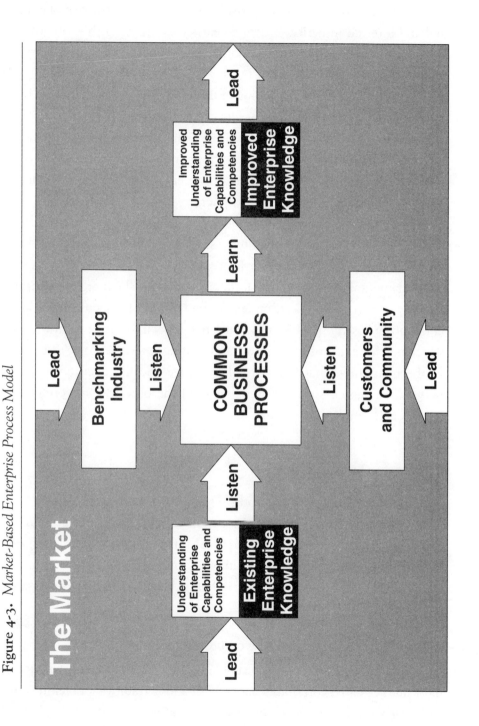

tency. In this sense, the market-based enterprise meets the test of external and internal integrity, as defined earlier. Underlying this integrity is a high level of cross-functional coordination between the many parts of the enterprise and its suppliers.

As pointed out in the beginning of this chapter, the foundation of this market-based enterprise is neither its physical assets nor the shape of its organizational chart. Its foundation is an open system of information and a free flow of knowledge shared across functions by individual employees who use common business processes. The network of market-based decisions that take place in this atmosphere of shared knowledge (for example, going from existing enterprise knowledge to improved enterprise knowledge) is what gives the enterprise its competitive edge in product development, pricing, and so forth.

Fundamental to this seamless form of enterprise—be it organized horizontally or vertically—is an understanding of industries, customers, and community based on decision-making networks informed by knowledge developed from listening, learning, and leading (processes to be discussed in the next three chapters). This knowledge and the decision-making networks it supports are the ties that bind the otherwise disconnected pieces of the enterprise.

Two Case Studies

Market-based decision networks. Free flow of knowledge. These are pretty ethereal concepts. You cannot exactly hold them in your hand or see them on a piece of paper. That's why the following two cases are offered. Both describe enterprises in which market-based decision making is operational and for which it has paid off in customer-pleasing products.

Procter & Gamble and the disposable diaper

Cincinnati-based Procter & Gamble is often cited as one of America's most market-based corporations, one with a long tradition of seeking out and articulating customers' unmet needs. P&G's disposable baby diaper is one product of that tradition, and it provides us with a picture of a market-based enterprise in action.

Legend has it that the principle of buoyancy was discovered because Archimedes took a bath. Procter & Gamble's lore has it that the first truly successful disposable paper diaper came about because Vic Mills had a grandchild. In 1956, Vic Mills was privileged to spend some time caring for the newest member of his clan. We can be sure that Mills was charmed by the baby, but there is no charm in a bucket of dirty diapers—even for a doting grandfather. Mills, as chance would have it, was also director of P&G's exploratory development, and his diaper duty inspired him to assign some of his most talented people to the job of developing a practical method for producing a disposable diaper.

The idea of the disposable diaper was not new. In fact, a number of different brands had been on the market for years. Market research quickly indicated why these pioneering brands had failed to capture more than 1 percent of the U.S. market: first, they were expensive; second, parents viewed them as ineffective and suitable only when travel or other circumstances made regular cloth diapers impractical. Research also suggested the potential market for disposables was huge. America was in the grip of the postwar baby boom, and simply multiplying the number of infants by the average number of daily diaper changes produced a staggering number of potential sales. And American babies were just the tip of the iceberg.

Over the next year and a half, P&G product developers labored to develop a product that would do the job and appeal to parents. Their initial prototype—an absorbent, pleated pad inserted into a plastic pant—almost scuttled the entire project. In the summer of 1958, the P&G staff conducted field tests of this product in torrid Dallas heat. The tests produced nothing but negative reviews from parents and heat rashes for baby Texans. Back to the drawing board.

By March 1959, P&G had redesigned its disposable diaper in a form similar to the current product and produced 37,000 in its development labs for test marketing in Rochester, New York. There, two thirds of the subjects (that is, parents) rated the product as superior to cloth diapers. Eureka!

As anyone who works around product development knows, product innovations must often be accompanied by process innovations that address the quality and cost aspects of the new product. In this case, development of the cost-effective process for manufacturing the disposable diaper was a greater challenge than development of the product itself. One engineer described it as "the most complex operation the company had ever faced." Production methods and equipment had to be created from the ground up. By December 1961, however, the project had progressed to the point that P&G could go to a market test with a product produced in a verified manufacturing process.

"But will it play in Peoria?" is a catchphrase in every American marketer's lexicon. And Peoria, Illinois—a most middle-American town—was chosen as the test market for the product that would be called Pampers. Peoria mothers liked Pampers, but not at 10 cents per diaper. The price would have to come down. But by how much? Further market testing in six geographic areas indicated that pricing at 6 cents per diaper would support retail sales in the volumes needed to make a go of the new product line. Some P&G manufacturing engineers found ways of reducing production costs and building the capacity that would make it possible for the company to offer Pampers at that price on a nationwide scale.

Today, Pampers is still a powerful component of the P&G product line and indicative of what can be accomplished when a company is truly market based. One person's observation of a true market need was verified through direct market research. Research also determined the level of price sensitivity in the market. New product development was directed and improved by responses from potential users, whose viewpoints were brought into the development process in its early stages. Different functions—primarily production engineering, design, and marketing—worked together on the continual testing of product and pricing changes. In the end, the company created a win-win proposition: a product that ameliorated one of every parent's most unpleasant chores, and a significant new source of revenues and profits for P&G.[14]

Regaining customer focus at Hewlett-Packard

In early 1992, managers at Hewlett-Packard's Santa Clara Division (SCD) recognized that they had a serious problem.* SCD designed and

---

*Material for this case study was generously provided by Stu Winby and Jenny Brandemuehl of Hewlett-Packard Company and an HP internal document, "Santa Clara Division: Becoming a Customer-Focused Division Through Fast-Cycle Work Redesign," by Mark Allen, Jenny Brandemuehl, Peter Gaam, and Deone Zell, October 8, 1993.

manufactured electronic test and measurement instruments. Its techno-logical prowess and excellent products had made it an acknowledged leader in its field, but deep cuts in defense spending, changing manufacturing processes, and new competition from rival technologies were making it a leader in a declining industry. The division's revenues had declined by 47 percent between 1984 and 1992, and employment had fallen by almost equal measure. SCD's returns on new product investments were very low by HP standards.

Obviously, something had to change if Santa Clara was to remain a contributing member of HP's confederation of operating divisions. Marty Neil, who joined SCD as general manager in November 1991, recognized both the need for change and the issue that stood between the organization and a brighter future. Through individual discussions with a number of employees, he came to realize that a problematic relationship between the division's functional staff and cross-functional teams was hindering effective business decision making. Functions were being optimized at the expense of the business decisions that would put SCD on the path to growth. Specifically,

- The division was slow to recognize change in the business environment.
- Product development cycles lasted too long.
- The decision makers were the functional staffers, who were removed from the business and lacked sufficient information, rather than the people closest to the business.

On the basis of Neil's analysis, a cross-functional team of twelve middle managers was set up in spring 1992 to redesign the "front end," where the SCD came nose to nose with its customers and where decisions about market choice, product strategy, and new product development were ideally made. SCD would shift its focus to customer needs, become nimbler, and empower the employees closest to the business to make decisions.

Following ten weeks of analysis and design, SCD management adopted the reorganization proposal. The division would be restructured as front-end businesses (organized around key customer segments) and back-end processes (order fulfillment and product development). The businesses would focus entirely on external customers, while the processes would be reengineered to better serve internal customers, emphasizing speed and flexibility. R&D and marketing would no longer exist as functional silos; instead, they would now support the businesses and processes. Perhaps the most dramatic change involved the division's design engineers. In a break with company tradition, these engineers would be moved out of R&D to the front-end businesses, putting them in closer contact with customers and effectively ending the "next bench" syndrome that had long characterized Hewlett-Packard and other technology companies. Future innovations would be designed to impress customers, not fellow engineers.

Over the two to three years following its reorganization, the Santa Clara Division changed from an inward-focused business unit to one with a clear focus on customers and their requirements, significantly altering the way people worked and marking a cultural shift in the values underpinning their work. By 1995, a number of indicators confirmed the success of the initiative. SCD revenues had rebounded by almost 23 percent from 1992 levels and were forecast to take another leap forward by the end of 1995. Profits rose apace. Of HP's twelve Electronics Instruments Group divisions, SCD rated second in 1995 business performance metrics. And the number of products and new markets increased dramatically.

The SCD experience reaffirmed the tradition developed by company founders Bill Hewlett and David Packard, who resisted centralizing their company's organization as it grew over the decades. Hewlett and Packard regularly broke large divisions into smaller ones, giving them their own sales and R&D resources, in an effort to keep technical development and business decision making closer to the pulse of their markets. The effectiveness of that tradition is confirmed today in the excellence and utility of HP products and in the business results that make HP one of the world's most admired corporations.

If we think about what P&G and Hewlett-Packard do that makes them so successful, we can conclude the following:

1. They *listen* to and learn from both internal and external voices.
2. They *lead* by making decisions at the forefront of their industries.

3. They *learn* still more by observing the impact of their decisions on the marketplace and on their own organizational competencies.

This interconnected set of activities—listening, learning, and leading—is dynamic, enriches the enterprise when performed well, and defines the enterprise as one that is truly market based. Subsequent chapters spell out in detail what is meant by *listen, learn,* and *lead.*

NOTES

1. Paul A. Eisenstein, "Car Makers Fine-Tune Market Research Use," *Investor's Daily*, May 31, 1989.

2. John Brooks, "The Edsel: 1—The E-Car Has Faith in You, Son," *New Yorker*, November 26, 1960, 57.

3. Ibid.

4. John A. Byrne, "The Horizontal Organization," *Business Week*, December 20, 1993, 76–81. See also Chapter 3, pages 79–84, for a discussion of how the enterprise business and process models are used to develop the "core processes."

5. Fred Adair, interview with Richard Luecke, Boston, June 23, 1994.

6. Byrne, "The Horizontal Organization," 78.

7. Robert G. Eccles and Nitin Nohria, *Beyond the Hype: Rediscovering the Essence of Management* (Boston: Harvard Business School Press, 1992), 121.

8. Frederick E. Webster, Jr., *It's 1990—Do You Know Where Your Marketing Is?* Report No. 89-123 (Cambridge, Mass.: Marketing Science Institute, December 1989), 4.

9. Henry Mintzberg, "The Innovative Organization," in *The Strategy Process: Concepts, Contexts, Cases*, ed. Henry Mintzberg and James B. Quinn (Englewood Cliffs, N.J.: Prentice-Hall, 1991), 731–746.

10. Stanley F. Slater and John C. Narver, *Market Oriented Isn't Enough: Build a Learning Organization*, Report No. 94-103 (Cambridge, Mass.: Marketing Science Institute, March 1994), 17.

11. Thomas Davenport, "Special Report: Reengineering," *Enterprise*, January 1994, 22.

12. Kim B. Clark and Takahiro Fujimoto, "The Power of Product Integrity," *Harvard Business Review*, November–December 1990, 112.

13. Gregory H. Watson, *Strategic Benchmarking* (New York: John Wiley & Sons, 1993), 117. The idea of *teams* and more fluid organizational forms is all the rage these days. But they seem to have enjoyed an earlier vogue. In his 1973 edition of *Management*, Peter Drucker comments: "Teams have become very fashionable and are indeed in danger of being damaged

by becoming popular. Countless books are being written on task forces, project teams, free-form organizations, small groups, and so on." See Peter F. Drucker, *Management: Tasks, Responsibilities, Practices* (New York: Harper & Row, 1973), 564.

In 1981, Russ Ackoff offered an alternative to the current cross-functional-teaming phenomenon when he introduced the notion of the "circular organization," a form of democratic hierarchy. This organization's characteristics included the absence of an ultimate authority, making it possible, through manager and employee boards at many levels, for each employee to participate in some way in the decisions that affect him or her directly. Like cross-functional teams, these boards are meant to bear much of the burden of coordination between functions. See Russell L. Ackoff, *Creating the Corporate Future* (New York: John Wiley & Sons, 1981), 163–168.

14. For a full discussion of the Pampers story, see Oscar Schisgall, *Eyes on Tomorrow* (Chicago, Ill.: J. G. Ferguson Publishing Co., 1981), 216–220.

5

LISTEN

*Few executives yet know how to ask: What information do I
need to do my job? When do I need it? And from whom
should I be getting it?*
Peter F. Drucker

Effective listening is one of the three activities common to all market-based enterprises. The ability to listen, listen well, and listen to the right voices is a precondition to creating market knowledge in the enterprise. For the business enterprise, listening has a definite purpose with respect to building a foundation of knowledge on which market-based decisions can be made. For our purposes here, listening is a metaphor for all perceptual sensing of the outer world. As individuals, we are separated from the rest of the world by the outer surfaces of our bodies. Touch, smell, sight, taste, and hearing provide us with sensations that the brain interprets to form an understanding of that outer world. The ancient Greeks were the first to formally speculate about this process of sensing and the particular reality it creates in our minds. Organizations likewise rely on sensing to create their own notion of reality.

Military organizations have long understood the critical importance of "listening" to their environments, both at strategic and tactical levels. They probe the unseen world beyond their own lines to evaluate the terrain, to determine enemy plans and dispositions, and to detect preparations for incoming attacks. Thus, their use of aerial and ground reconnaissance, forward observers, intelligence gathering, "listening posts" situated outside defensive perimeters, and spies. What legendary war strategist Sun Tzu understood 2,500 years ago remains true in the age of surveillance satellites and sophisticated covert intelligence networks: "What is called 'foreknowledge' cannot be elicited from spirits, nor from gods, nor by analogy with past events, nor from calculations. It must be obtained from men who know the enemy situation."[1] These mechanisms

Figure 5-1. *Lawson's Process of Command and Control*

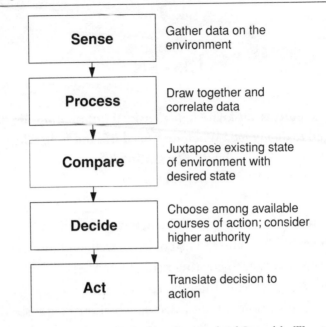

Sense	Gather data on the environment
Process	Draw together and correlate data
Compare	Juxtapose existing state of environment with desired state
Decide	Choose among available courses of action; consider higher authority
Act	Translate decision to action

Source: Adapted from Thomas P. Coakley, *Command and Control for War and Peace* (Washington, D.C.: National Defense University Press), 1991, 31–32.

for listening extend the sensing capabilities of the organization beyond what otherwise would be distinct and rigid boundaries. With effective listening, the distinct boundaries between the inner and outer world blur.

In military theory, what we here call *listening* is generally called *sensing*, and it is the first in a series of activities that ultimately lead to action on the part of a commander. These activities are often represented in a model of command and control proposed by Joel S. Lawson, as shown in Figure 5-1. In the Lawson model, sensing provides the commander with data about the environment. Data about terrain, weather, troop strength and deployment (friendly and enemy), supplies, and so forth are collected. These raw data are processed and combined with other available data, and a comparison is made between the state of the environment as it is and as the commander would wish it to be. Based on this comparison a decision is made; the commander—perhaps in consultation with a higher authority—chooses a course of action that will lead to the desired state. Finally, that decision is translated into action.

Stephan Haeckel, director of strategic studies at IBM's Advanced Busi-

Figure 5-2. *The Haeckel-Nolan Business Learning Loop*

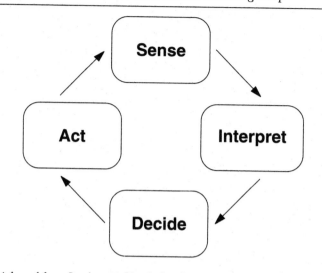

Source: Adapted from Stephan H. Haeckel and Richard L. Nolan, "Managing by Wire," *Harvard Business Review*, September–October 1993, 128.

ness Institute, and Richard Nolan of the Harvard Business School have likewise identified this important continuum of activities in their "business learning loop," the steps of which are to *sense, interpret, decide,* and *act.* Their model (Figure 5-2) draws on the Lawson tradition but represents it as a "loop," emphasizing the important fact that in acting we alter the original environment and thus create the need to begin the sensing activity again.

Our own model of listen, learn, and lead likewise recognizes the importance of a feedback loop. Because we define a decision (decide) to include the allocation of resources (act), however, we have subsumed "decide" and "act" into one activity: leading. In either model, the quality of the listening—or sensing—is a key determinant of the appropriateness of the ultimate response. Insufficient or inaccurate listening corrupts all else that follows: "Garbage in, garbage out," as the saying goes.

How We Listen

Market research has been the traditional sensing mechanism for the enterprise. If we were to accept the notion that the marketing organization "owns the customer," it would naturally follow that marketing take responsibility for listening to the outside world—gauging and evaluating customer needs, forecasting demand for current and future products, and identifying competitive threats. And in this functionally organized world, it would also naturally follow that a specialized group *within* marketing—namely, market research—take charge of the technical side of this work.

Over the past half century, market research has developed into a specialized field requiring extensive training and practice. Its mission, generally, has been to:

- assess market information needs;
- measure the marketplace;
- store, retrieve, and display the data;
- describe and analyze market information; and
- evaluate the research and assess its usefulness.[2]

Each of these activities contributes to the listening that every enterprise must undertake. The problem with market research as generally practiced, however, has little to do with the validity of *what* it does. The problem lies in *how* it does what it does. The real problem is the fact that too many organizations rely on the market research and, worse yet, the market research organization for all their listening. "You're the market research department," many executives say, "so tell us what's going on in the market. That's your job." To functionally organized companies, this statement makes perfect sense. Every important activity, after all, is owned by some individuals or some department. And market research is one of those departments. As we'll see shortly, listening is a job that must involve just about everyone.

Simply having the means of listening (market research tools) and people who know how to use them does not guarantee that good listening and meaningful action will take place. Kim Clark and Takahiro Fujimoto found that automobile companies with powerful capabilities for gathering market data rarely develop distinctive product concept when the market data constrains the imagination and passion of product designers.[3]

People-proofing versus people-involving market research

The problem described by Clark and Fujimoto may have its origins in the discipline of market research as traditionally practiced. Traditional market research aims to "people proof" the information that passes from the market to the enterprise. People proofing is a deliberate effort to minimize human bias in experimental design, sampling procedures, the construction and administration of questionnaires, and the many other things that data gathering involves. Unfortunately, although appropriate for ensuring reliability and validity, people proofing also screens out the benefits of imagination, creativity, and personal insight—the very qualities that contribute to the development of breakthrough products and services. "Imagination," as Gerald Zaltman says, "is the mechanism that links needs and products." So when our methods of listening deliberately prevent the mingling of imagination with what customers tell us, it is little wonder that so few breakthroughs occur.

People-proofed data gathering is an important but small part of what we mean by listening. The listening that is more likely to generate new ideas is "people involving." People-involved listening is thus most important "upstream," in the initial stages of conceptual development, when people's imaginations must not be constrained. Downstream, when product design must be finalized and numbers produced, people proofing becomes more appropriate.

Focused versus open listening

Listening can be described in two modes: *focused* and *open*. We could try to listen to everything, but this would be beyond our resources. It is much more efficient to focus our efforts. This means that we must know what we are listening for and that we ask ourselves the following questions:

1. What do we already know about the issue at hand?
2. What don't we know? This indicates the degree of uncertainty associated with pending decisions.
3. What level of certainty must we have to move toward a decision?
4. What new information must we have, and at what level of precision, to bring us toward that level of certainty?

With these questions answered, we can design a plan to obtain the information we need using traditional or unconventional methodologies. Focused listening is an efficient means of satisfying most of the information needs of most enterprises. Properly executed, it is capable of answering questions about the needs and wants of customers, the dimensions of specific markets, and anticipated demand.

The criticism of focused listening is that it encourages tunnel vision. Because focused listening is consciously directed and reflects the reigning assumptions of the enterprise, it is unlikely to uncover anything new. Focused listening only picks up signals from the areas toward which it is directed, leaving others silent and unexplored.

Fortunately, the efficient use of focused listening frees up some time and resources for probing those silent areas using what we call open listening. Open listening is serendipitous, a broad search for the unexpected, a means of exploring a broad spectrum in search of insights, surprises, opportunities, and threats. It helps to avoid tunnel vision, addressing what Zaltman describes as the "need for wide cognitive peripheral vision." It is insurance against the mistake of thinking about a problem based solely on what we currently precisely know, which leads us sometimes to ask the wrong questions, which in turn leads sometimes to solving—precisely—the wrong problem.

An example of open listening is the consumer idealized design (CID) developed by Russ Ackoff. In this methodology, actual or potential consumers are asked to create their idealized design of the product or service under consideration. This exercise is particularly helpful when consumers cannot articulate their expectations. The idealized designs created by consumers help producers—and the subjects themselves—to define those expectations.

In an article on CID, Susan Ciccantelli and Jason Magidson describe its application in several settings, including a men's clothing store.[4] In this case, a retail chain offering high-quality men's clothing at discount prices had failed, despite many changes, to attract the affluent customers it wanted. All that it got were low-income bargain hunters. After repeated failures, the retail chain hired researchers who employed CID techniques.

The researchers selected fifteen representatives of the targeted customer population and asked them to design their "ideal" of a men's clothing store. The ideal store, it turned out, was quite different from the real retail chain stores with respect to the arrangement of items, interactions with salespeople, pricing, and so forth. For example, the target customers "arranged different articles of similar types of clothing by size, rather than by type." In their scheme, all available styles of suit jackets, sport jackets, vests, shirts, and outerwear for the upper body were grouped together by size. The reason was that they didn't like hunting all over the store to retrieve different articles. Implementation of some of the customer-designed features resulted in success in attracting the upscale clientele originally sought.

Gerald Zaltman has also pioneered a new approach to open listening. Called the Zaltman metaphor elicitation technique, or ZMET®, it probes the attitudes of individuals relative to particular subjects deeply and systematically through the use of metaphors and visual images. While many, including myself and Zaltman, have sought to "hear the voice of the consumer," Zaltman wants to go further and "see, touch, smell and feel the voice." Unlike traditional methods of market research, which look for the response of many subjects in a fairly narrow channel of probing, Zaltman uses just a handful of interviewees, seeking their innermost thoughts on a given subject. The interviewees take photographs or clip magazine pictures of images that evoke their inner thoughts and feelings. (My personal experience with this technique is described in the Introduction to this book.) It is Zaltman's contention that a better understanding of the voice of the customer requires the use of research tools that engage customers' nonverbal and especially their visual channels of thought and communication.[5]

BARRIERS TO EFFECTIVE LISTENING

As intuitively obvious as the importance of effective listening may seem, organizations create barriers to it. Key among these self-imposed barriers is the intervention of the "information handlers" and the myth that market research cannot tell us anything about products or concepts not already on the market.

The intervention of information handlers

"Information handlers" are those who collect, package, and interpret information and construct data bases. Typically, these individuals are attached to specific functional areas and operate on behalf of their respective functions. They transmit information within the function's hierarchy, offer advice, and act as "keepers" of the function's accumulated data, information, and knowledge. These information handlers may be market research managers, sales analysts for an operating group, or those individuals who by virtue of long tenure have a unique grasp of the information on which others depend.

Information handlers, no matter what their titles, have one thing in common: their position and status in the organization are closely bound up with the control of information—the outcome of the listening we are discussing. Information and its methods of acquisition form the coin of their realm, and they guard it carefully. This is neither unnatural nor entirely bad. Market researchers in particular are naturally uncomfortable with the idea of people who lack training in research methodologies—engineers and others—talking with focus groups and existing customers, then drawing inferences for the target market that cannot be supported by the statistical requirements of professional research. Their discomfort leads to people proofing.

Here I am reminded of the story about President Harry Truman and his abrupt firing of Gen. Douglas MacArthur, then commander of UN forces in Korea and a popular national hero. "How did you reach this monumental decision to fire MacArthur?" one reporter asked. "I asked the voting public what I should do," Truman responded, describing how he had gone into a Washington tavern and asked three men at the bar how he should handle MacArthur. "They said, 'Fire him,' and I did." While this story may or may not be true, information handlers' fear of top managers, engineers, sales managers, and others estimating the sentiment of the market based on this type of unscientific polling is real, and it explains their determination to control information and the means by which it is acquired.

Information handlers are justifiably concerned that "insights" into markets or customer sentiments be genuinely determined. They are aware of how information gained from listening can influence decisions involving large sums of money and other resources. As a result, information handlers prefer to be the singular channel for listening, the intermediary between the outer environment and the many individuals in the enterprise who have an interest in probing that environment.

This use of information handlers was developed during the Industrial Age, which viewed the enterprise as a machine of interrelated parts. Its negative aspects are more apparent today, particularly as we attempt to move to greater cross-functional activities. Since most information handlers are bound to particular functions of the enterprise, they inadvertently maintain barriers to cross-functional information sharing. Their tradition has been to collect, order, and analyze information for the particular uses of their parent functions, not to make it available or meaningful to outsiders. And just being part of a function skews listening toward those things the function is keen to hear.

Functional information handlers also serve as absorbers of the uncertainty surrounding their organization's information base. They do this by drawing inferences from a body of evidence and then communicating the inferences instead of the evidence itself.[6] For example, designers and salespeople at GM might come to me and say, "Vince, you've seen all of the customer studies, what do you think of our new product concept?" There is a great deal of uncertainty in all of our new model studies, but in asking this question they would want me to hold the bag of all the uncertainty and give them a straightforward answer, such as: "Generally, the product concept is all right," or "Customers won't accept it for these two reasons." Neither of these responses transmits the complete richness of customer feelings or the ambiguities that naturally exist in most product markets. The questioners know intuitively that these answers are underpinned by uncertainty, but the range of that uncertainty—from low to high—cannot be communicated in the answer they seek. As we will see later in a discussion of the dialogue decision process, the enterprise needs a mechanism to communicate the range of informational uncertainty to all decision makers.

It is this absorption of uncertainty that has led some individuals and organizations to hold implicit power over portions of their function's decision making. The information handler is in a position to tip the scales in favor of one product or project over another. The symbolic ways in which we recognize this power are several. For example, we tell individuals with ideas, especially junior people, "You'd better check the information that supports your idea with Charlie if you are to gain its acceptance," or "We are going to accept Bill's insight on this issue because he knows more about that subject than we do." It also occurs when staff functionaries make forecasts or price estimates in such a way that the specific relationships of underlying assumptions are implicitly and not explicitly tied to outcomes.

Although "control" over information has always been a legitimate concern, as long as the information handlers and those affected were both operating at the direction of functional management and stayed within the accepted decision-making domain of that function, the system was sufficient. Because these systems seemed to be working, vertically optimized information systems flourished, leaving little incentive to consider horizontal communication or integration. Many decisions made within individual functions, however, had a negative impact on the efficiency and effectiveness of other functions and of the enterprise as a whole. In today's more comprehensively competitive environment, this is something few enterprises can afford.

What is needed is a process that makes possible cross-functional decisions, optimized at the enterprise level, without disrupting or giving up the benefits of strong functional management and information systems. If we are to achieve these benefits, we need to design decision-making processes that encourage trust, information sharing, knowledge creation, and institutional learning.

The myth about what can and cannot be heard

The second barrier to listening is best told by the following example. In 1990, in a *Wall Street Journal* article titled "Marketing 101 for a Fast-Changing Decade," Peter Drucker made the observation that "one can use market research only on what is already in the market." In other words, an insightful person with a deep understanding of business practices was saying that one of the key forms of organizational listening is stone deaf with respect to future product markets. As support for this statement, Drucker cited the failure of American companies to perceive the demand for the now-ubiquitous fax machine, the technology for which had been pioneered in the United States. "The Americans did not put the fax machines on the market, because market research convinced them that there was no demand for such a gadget. But we have known for decades that one cannot conduct market research on something not in the market."[7]

Drucker was correct in saying that Americans failed to bring the fax machine to the marketplace, but he was incorrect in stating that market research can tell us nothing about product areas for which no product currently exists. And his use of the fax case is doubly wrong.

As early as 1974, Xerox Corporation conducted research to determine, through customer response, the extent and frequency of urgent messages delivered outside the firm, the amount of time within which these urgent messages needed to be delivered, the form of these messages (number of pages, graphics, etc.), the bearer of their cost (a central staff or end users), and so forth. Xerox market research estimated sales of facsimile devices based on the prevalence of *customer need* rather than strictly on intent to acquire a hypothetical product. Its mid-1970s research indicated the initial market potential for facsimile-device sales in business and commercial applications alone of approximately 1 million units.

So, if Xerox had the technology to produce a fax machine, and if it had evidence of market demand, how did it allow this new product opportunity to slip through its fingers to Asian competitors? The answer is that Xerox believed it had a better product concept—namely, a system that would integrate the digital and imaging technologies then within its circle of competencies. In this product concept, computers would communicate with each other, with the receiving computer putting the message on paper by means of Xerox imaging technology.

Unfortunately for Xerox, it chose the wrong path to this latent market, just as Sony had wrongly chosen its beta video format technology instead of the VHS alternative that became the market standard, and just as Edwin Land (Polaroid) chose the silver-haloid-based Polavision over the magnetic-based camcorder. But Xerox's fault did not lie in the inability of its market research to recognize the latent demand, as Drucker and so many contend.

The lesson from the fax case is clear: the challenge of utilizing market research to uncover previously nonexistent markets is in the *use* of the information, not in its collection.[8] Sleuthing out these undisclosed markets requires creativity. As Gerald Zaltman says, "When needs are not well-articulated or understood by the market itself, you need to develop a deep understanding of customer thinking and behavior."[9]

LISTENING TO THE RIGHT PEOPLE

"Listening to customers is a lousy idea," according to Tom Peters. "Listening to the 'right' customers is a matchless idea."[10] There is much more to becoming a market-based enterprise than simply listening to customers. Some customers can tell us more than others. And some are more worth pleasing.

In the simpler world of the past, it was easier to listen to the people who purchased and used a given product or service. The shoemaker of the last century dealt face-to-face with the people who purchased and wore his shoes. He took their foot measurements himself and asked them directly for their preference on style and details. He made the shoes himself and watched as they tried them on for the first time. If they had a problem with the fit or with some errant stitching, these customers would return to the shop and tell him about it directly.

Today many intermediaries and competitive alternatives stand between many large enterprises and their final customers. General Motors, for example, does not sell cars directly to individuals but to its network of dealers. Most fast-food companies do not deal directly with the people who eat their products; their franchisees are the point of contact with the consuming public. Likewise, the publishers of most popular books seldom have direct contact with people who read their books. Their customers are almost entirely intermediaries—book wholesalers, bookstores, book clubs.

Each of these producers—GM, the fast-food company, and the book publisher—must either find ways of hearing from the final consumers of its products or accept the intermediaries as customers and take cues from them. Unfortunately, listening strictly to intermediaries can be like hearing a news story after it's been told and retold. The retelling may make the story more interesting, but it doesn't add much to its authenticity— indeed, it may actually distort the original message, as was pointed out in the three misquotes used in the Introduction to this book.

Producers have ways of dealing with this lack of direct contact with final consumers. GM and other automakers listen to both dealers and final consumers by using sophisticated research methodologies. Fast-food companies like McDonald's themselves own and operate a number of franchises for a number of purposes, one being direct access to customers. A number of book publishers, except those that focus on mass-market titles, maintain direct selling channels to both enhance revenues and get customer feedback. If you found a response card in your copy of this book, you encountered the publisher's attempt to hear about your occupation, reading interests, and opinion of the book. One would think that the intermediaries in these examples—the auto dealer, the fast-food franchise owner, and the corner bookstore—would have their own ways of listening to existing customers, whom they encounter during virtually every hour of operation. And many do.

Most listening is directed toward current customers, but several other types of customers should be considered: innovators, opinion leaders, market mavens, and lead users. *Innovators* are generally referred to as the first 2 or 3 percent of the population to actually adopt a new product concept. *Opinion leaders* are those who informally influence the thoughts or behaviors of others, typically with regard to just a few or related products. For example, we all know someone who is an opinion leader on stereo sound systems. We trust this person's expertise in this product area, but we would only coincidentally ask his or her advice on the purchase of a hair drier. *Market mavens* have valued knowledge about where to shop and how to buy. Typically, they are knowledgeable about buying clubs, consumer buying reports, discounters, sources of information, and buying strategies. Unlike opinion leaders, market mavens have knowledge that is not product specific. As a result, their networks of influence cross many boundaries. According to work done by Gerald Zaltman, there is little correlation between market mavens and opinion leaders; there is some overlap, but not much, so they do tend to be different people.

Lead users are the pioneering adopters of newly developed products. Many lead users buy off-the-shelf products and either adapt them to uses the manufacturer had never imagined or enhance, upgrade, or make other alterations that significantly improve product performance. In the first instance, listening to these users can open the manufacturers' eyes to new applications and markets; in the second, it can lead to valuable improvements in the next generation of products. Eric Von Hippel, a professor at MIT's Sloan School of Management, and Ronald Rice and Everett Rogers have documented the value of being in close contact with lead users.[11]

An interesting example of listening to the "right people" is found in research GM conducted for its electric vehicle (EV) program. Early in the product concept development stage, Ken Baker, the program manager, went so far as to have GM's engineers and market planners ride to work in the vehicles with the research respondents in Los Angeles. Their goal was to "get a feel" for the Los Angeles commute prior to initial concept development and to find out what commuters would like changed—if it could be changed.

Following that initial test, from 1991 through 1994, GM then conducted in-depth research to more specifically understand the potential size of the EV market and to obtain both technical information and attitudinal/behavioral information for use in the product development phase. Traditional market research techniques were supplemented by one of the first implementations of a new method called the Information Accelerator®, developed by Glen Urban and several colleagues at MIT. This new method puts respondents in a virtual buying environment that allows them to simulate the purchase decision, including accessing information that would be available to them in a future time period. The Information Accelerator® uses an interactive multimedia computer simulation to place interviewees in a future time in which they can be asked a set of structured questions relating to buying decisions and product specifications. In effect, it creates a frame of reference for interview subjects.

In these studies, the accelerator had subjects participate in interactive discussion with individuals knowledgeable about EVs through electronically stored videotaped interviews. The subjects were also given news reports from the future about environmental issues and about the development of an infrastructure supporting the use of electric vehicles. Hypothetical television ads featuring the electric vehicle were likewise part of the simulation. Against this background of a simulated future, respondents were asked how they would make their buying decisions, what sources they would use to seek out information, and other details.

The studies were augmented by the innovative application of conjoint measurement techniques supplied by Dick Smallwood of Applied Decision Analysis in Menlo Park, California. These studies identified a priority list of customer values that provided considerable insight into how consumers might react to the introduction of a vehicle completely unfamiliar to them.

In 1994 a fleet of GM's prototype electric vehicle, the Impact, was produced for nationwide testing with potential consumers in twelve U.S. cities. During the course of the study, EVs were made available to hundreds of people for their personal use for a two- to four-week test. Special units installed by local utilities, which also had an interest in the program, recharged the EVs' batteries.

Public announcement of the study in each of the twelve cities resulted in a flood of calls to an 800 number. In Los Angeles alone, thousands of calls came in within just a few days. More than six thousand of these L.A. callers were sent a questionnaire designed to identify those few individuals who ranked high on GM's measures of innovators, opinion leaders, and market mavens. These were the people GM wanted to listen to—the "right people," in Tom Peters' view.

Staying with the example of Los Angeles, more than one hundred respondents fit the bill as the "right people." And were they an amazing group! Among them were a racing car driver, an auto enthusiast whose collection of seven cars included a '53 Chevrolet and a '54 Pontiac, the president of a battery-recycling company, an experienced instructor of auto mechanics, and a member of a team that had won a GM-sponsored structural design competition.

These and dozens more like them represented a gold mine of informed feedback on the Impact, raising user-related issues that few people in Detroit could have anticipated. And almost universally, they were enthusiastic about helping to design and develop a new vehicle concept that would meet their high standards. The chief engineer for the project was on hand during our debriefing of the individuals. He was able to answer the participants' questions about the EV, and in doing so he gained a more intimate understanding of their likes and dislikes—what they had experienced and what they were looking for. Some market researchers would view this interaction with the subjects as a source of bias; their instinct is to people proof any study. But at an early stage in new product development, when the enterprise is listening to learn and not to forecast, a people-involving approach yields a richer set of insights.

One important discovery of this exercise in planned listening was this: innovators, opinion leaders, and market mavens talk a lot to other people. We quickly learned that they were spreading the word about the electric vehicle to their friends and associates—usually people who represented the broader market for the vehicle—and that these other people were willing to share their insights and concerns at a level different from that of the original test group. Since the first impression of a new concept is important to market success, GM valued the concerns of this second group during the early stages of development. Some of this feedback was captured through an auxiliary program.

DEALING WITH MANY VOICES

In the Preface to this book, we discussed the idea of the extended enterprise and its becoming the norm in the near future. We discussed the stakeholders in this enterprise as being those individuals or entities that can affect or be affected by the decisions of the enterprise, and we collapsed them into three groups:

- The customer, which includes both consumers and individuals in the distribution system that accept products from the enterprise.
- The community, which is made up of consumers in a societal context, the government interests that attempt to represent them, the special interest groups that carry strong views on specific issues, and the competition for customer and community attention and resources.
- The enterprise, which in addition to itself includes everything on the opposite side of the customer and the community: suppliers, investors, and so forth.

We also stated that, as a system, these stakeholders in the extended enterprise must deal simultaneously with each others' interests, seeking synergy from their relationship. If the total value of that relationship is greater than the sum of stakeholders' individual contributions, the relationship will flourish; if its value is equal to or less than the sum of the individual contributions, the relationship will and should fail. We concluded by stating that the interdependence of the extended enterprise is likely to flourish when customers, the community, and the enterprise come to a meeting of the minds. In this context, it is perhaps appropriate to update our interpretation of GM president Charles Wilson's famous quote: *What is good for the customer and community is good for General Motors and vice versa.*

Because even the careful listener receives very few clear signals, this task of creating a meeting of the minds is difficult. Within the groups described above, some dissonance is to be expected. As we listen more broadly, the dissonance almost always increases, if only for the fact that we start to hear voices representing very different groups. For example, customers, the community, and the enterprise itself have different voices, and they are often in conflict. A laundry detergent producer might find that customers want the "whiter than white" wash delivered by phosphate-based detergents, while the community—which includes customers, government regulators, and employees—want "cleaner than clean" public waters, which are compromised by the introduction of phosphates. Meanwhile, the enterprise—the shareholders and the employees—want to produce a customer-satisfying *and* profitable product that is compatible with its sense of environmental responsibility. Figure 5-3 represents these different voices of the market: the customers, the community, and the enterprise. Needless to say, there are plenty of opportunities for agreement and conflict between these different constituents of the market. Listening makes it possible to capture the breadth and depth of both. It falls to decision makers to understand the conflicts and agreements in reaching market-based decisions.[12]

The positioning of the values represented in this figure is not necessarily fixed. For example, vehicle safety used to be solely a community value, reflected in government regulations on safety belts and other features. It is now an enterprise and customer value as well, to the point that safety features are a regular selling feature for most vehicles. The same could be said, to a lesser extent, for environmental issues, which began as community values and have begun to take on meaning for both the enterprise and the customer.

Figure 5-3 serves as a visual reminder that customers do not live in a

Figure 5-3. *Different Voices, Different Values*

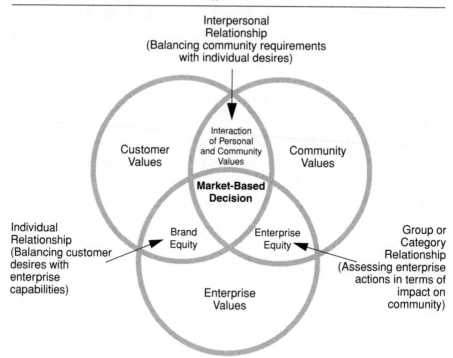

vacuum. Customers live in communities. Thus, we must simultaneously consider the desires both of the individual customer and of the community made up of those individuals; people's values in a personal buying situation do not necessarily map to their values in a community situation. Consider, for example, the case of some Wal-Mart customers.

Wal-Mart is a tremendous success in the retail business. In 1994, one-fifth of the U.S. population shopped at a Wal-Mart every week, and two of every ten dollars spent at department stores went into a Wal-Mart cash register. Projected sales for 1995 were $100 billion. This is an enterprise that clearly hears and responds to the voice of the customer. And customers like Wal-Mart because of the great variety of products it carries, the value of those products, and the services it provides. Most communities like Wal-Mart as well. It creates jobs, attracts customers from other communities, and pays taxes.

But not all communities, like not all customers, have the same view. Small retailers who can't compete with the buying power of a giant like Wal-Mart claim that Wal-Mart sets its prices low to drive them out of business. When these small enterprises close down, the community's downtown business district shrinks, its tax base errodes, its services decline, and its middle class flees. "Wal-Mart is accused of turning the downtown of small town after small town into ghost town after ghost town,"[13] according to one observer.

Another observer articulated the interaction of personal and community values in these words: "We don't care if we save a few cents on underwear. We're looking at the real cost to our overall community. We don't want to see Main Street boarded up. We don't want to see property values negatively affected. And we don't want to put some of our friends and neighbors out of business just so we can have another Wal-Mart, because we've already got one probably 10 or 20 miles away."[14] A man whose store closed after Wal-Mart came to his small Louisiana town admitted that he shops at Wal-Mart. "We have to—not that we like to."[15] Wal-Mart counts him as a customer, but he doesn't particularly like the enterprise. In some parts of the country, an active and occasionally successful grass-roots movement is under way that uses zoning regulations to keep Wal-Mart stores out of the community.

Careful listening to the different constituencies of the enterprise provides, at a minimum, the opportunity to reach decisions that address what customers say they want, what the enterprise is capable of providing at a profit, and what the community values. These market-based decisions lead to the development of products and services that customers, as both purchasers and citizens, feel satisfied in buying. These are products and services that

- offer performance features that the target market wants and can afford to buy;
- can be provided by the enterprise at a profit; and
- are within the boundaries of community constraints.

This model for harmonizing different values in a set of market-based decisions will be reviewed in subsequent chapters.

MAKING SURE THE RIGHT PEOPLE LISTEN

If it is important that the right people are listened to, it is equally important that the right people in the enterprise do the listening. We've already described the problem of information handlers controlling the listening process through formal market research and other means. These specialists must participate, but they cannot be relied on exclusively. We cannot depend on intermediaries but must see to it that the engineers, the designers, and everyone else privy to decision making does some direct and active listening.

We saw in the case of the electric vehicle how the presence of the chief engineer enhanced the richness of the listening experience. The importance of direct listening by people other than information handlers is further illustrated in another test case. In 1988, GM engineer Harvey Bell attended customer focus groups with the market researchers conducting a study aimed at understanding customer requirements for the next Pontiac Firebird and Chevrolet Camaro. During the discussion, Bell heard strong opinions voiced around the need to be "in control" during the braking process. This emphasis on control differed from conventional wisdom, which held that "stopping distance"—how long it takes to drop from from 60 to 0 mph—was the customer's primary concern. As Bell listened to the customers talk about these sporty cars, he understood that the ability to control the vehicle while braking was critical to overall customer satisfaction and confidence. The traditional parameter of stopping distance was a necessary, but insufficient, measure of customer concern.

Using his knowledge of braking systems, Bell was able to translate the targeted customer's need to feel calm and assured while braking into appropriate design requirements. In addition, his team created new measures for braking performance that incorporated this customer concern into subsequent GM brake testing and evaluation. The value of his efforts was publicly recognized when the newly designed braking systems were introduced. An article in the *Pennsylvania Times Leader* closed the loop on listen, learn, and lead: "The brakes, which provide terrific road feel and stop the Z28 like an egg hitting the sidewalk, were helpful in New York's rush hour. But I appreciated them the most when a deer decided to say hello while I was on the interstate heading toward Virginia."[16] The writer closed his story by saying, "See what happens when a car company listens to the people who buy their products?"

The lesson of this story—and there are many like it—is that the people who are privy to decision making and the people who are responsible for innovation and design need to be directly involved in active listening.

Listening to Learn and to Lead

Earlier in this chapter we described two models of sensing that ultimately lead to action: the military model of sense-process-compare-decide-act and the Haeckel-Nolan business model of sense-interpret-decide-act. In both cases, the sensing (our "listening") has a definite purpose: to open a window onto the outer world. But the sensations gathered through this window must be imbued with meaning before they have value to the organization. By themselves, sensations are mute; to have value they must be either processed and compared (as in the military model) or interpreted (as in the business model). In our own model, we listen for the purpose of learning and leading.

Some forms of listening are more suited to learning than to action. Open, people-involved listening is motivated by the need to learn in a general way. Ackoff's consumer idealized design, Zaltman's metaphor elicitation technique, and the methodology used by GM in the electric vehicle project are examples of listening designed more to enrich our understanding than to help us make decisions. Other forms of listening are intended to facilitate an immediate decision. For example, in the case of auto vehicle development, we typically reach a point at which we have a high level of confidence about most of the vehicle's design characteristics and market strengths and weaknesses. To clear up the few remaining areas of uncertainty—for example, accessory packages, the optimal market segment, etc.—we would design highly focused research. This research has the immediate purpose of facilitating a decision. This is *listening to lead*. The Frito-Lay case that follows shortly represents another example.

Using Information and Information Technology

We like to think of ourselves as living in the Information Age, but information, and the knowledge generated from it, has always played a critical role in the success or failure of an enterprise. Only the means for gathering, storing, retrieving, and distributing have changed. In the sixteenth century, the great merchant house of the Fuggers developed and operated a network of businesses in banking, mining, textiles, and trading that spanned the globe—from China and Peru to Britain and Europe. Jacob Fugger linked this empire with information. Offices in London, Paris, and Antwerp and agents elsewhere were connected by caravelles, horses, and runners to Augsburg, where their reports were analyzed and interpreted, and instructions then sent back. Though their means of communication was primitive by modern standards, the Fuggers nevertheless armed themselves and their agents with an information system that was far superior to that of other enterprises of the day, and this gave them tremendous advantages in their undertakings. In the nineteenth century, the Reuters company relied on carrier pigeons to speed the information that investors and speculators needed to gain an edge in market trading. Both Reuters and the Fuggers made excellent use of what was available to them.

More recently, Frito-Lay provides an excellent example of listening—or sensing—in which human contact with customers is combined with an integrated information system to provide the kind of cross-functional decision making that both Reuters and Fuggers used to competitive advantage. Frito-Lay uses three information systems—the pipeline system, the category management Apollo system, and the executive information system—each of which plays a critical role in supporting cross-functional behavior and decision making.

The pipeline system is an integrated, order-to-cash information system that focuses on customer transactions. Frito-Lay salespeople (store delivery route salespeople) upload store orders via hand-held computers as they physically replenish shelves; these computers are then uploaded at the distribution center. The orders act as "triggers" for the entire Frito-Lay supply chain, which responds in the "demand pull" (or *kanban*) approach pioneered by Japanese manufacturers. In this approach, customer demand pulls new production on a just-in-time basis through the system, from distribution centers back through production centers and their outside suppliers. All products must reach the last inventory location in no more than four or seven days for high-volume and limited-sourced products, respectively. This rule is reinforced by Frito-Lay salespeople, who can refuse all products that reach them after the expected freshness date. The pipeline system allocates customer and salesperson orders to plants and logistics centers based on service, cost, and constraint limits. Manufacturing schedules production, transportation schedules delivery routes, warehousing creates pickup lists, and route salespeople set up deliveries to stores—all using the customer order information.

The discipline of short product shelf lives (thirty-six to fifty-one days) with the Frito-Lay system reinforces the customer focus. By design, manufacturing, warehousing, and transportation have just four days to ship the order. The transportation function has three days to deliver the product to the salesperson. Thus, no more than seven days can elapse between the time the order is taken and the time the salesman receives freshly produced product. Anything received after these allocated time limits can be rejected by the recipient. These rejected orders are charged as an expense item against the offending party (manufacturing, warehousing, etc.), and the rejected goods are shipped to a local soup kitchen or other charitable institution. And because Frito-Lay departments have no planned expense line for "stales" or mistakes, everyone has an intense interest in performance.

The category management Apollo system uses store point-of-sales data for all brands within a category. The system recommends "store sets" of products that should maximize throughput and profitability for the store owner by linear foot of shelf space. (It helps that Frito-Lay has six or seven of the ten top-selling products in the "salty snack food" category.) This strategic positioning capability—based entirely on careful listening and analysis by Frito-Lay—forges a value-adding partnership between the company and the customer.

The executive information system combines the raw data obtained from its frontline sales- and delivery people with information obtained through other sources to create a broader picture for higher-level decision makers. Figure 5-4 represents this system. With it, Frito-Lay is able to combine detailed point-of-sales data with the other signals it gets from customers, competitors, and its own storehouse of market understanding to form a broader-based knowledge of its markets and its industry. This knowledge then becomes the basis for market-based decisions. For ex-

Figure 5-4. *Frito-Lay's Executive Information System*

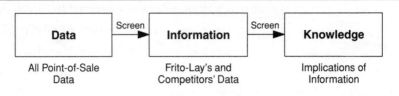

ample, if corn chips sales decline significantly in southern Texas on May 6, the system would "know" better than to sound an alarm. It would "know" that Cinco De Mayo, the celebration of Mexico's independence, is on May 5. If the year-to-year, Julian calendar day-to-day comparisons signal a sustained downturn, however, then competitive positioning would be a candidate for root-cause analysis.

University of California at Berkeley professor Rashi Glazer describes this process—of collecting data (listening) and transforming it into information, which when analyzed and interpreted becomes knowledge— as the information value chain. "For organizations that manage from this perspective," he tells us, "the goal is to capture the value of the information at each point along the chain."[17] This is very much what Frito-Lay is doing, and it is very close to the market-based decision network that will unfold over the next two chapters.

In the right hands, information technology makes it possible for enterprises—even large, functionally organized ones—to "sense and respond" to markets and customers in ways unimagined just ten years ago, as the Frito-Lay case makes clear. This capability has as much to do with *orientation* as with the technology itself. Hierarchical organizations are prone to be inward looking in their orientation to information, and this fits in with their whole approach to doing business. For them, information is used for internal sensing and control. Information acts as a signaling device, indicating where performance is out of line with predetermined standards. What goes on in the outer world of customers, suppliers, and competitors is less adequately addressed.

While information systems for internal control remain important, they do not actively create business success. They may help managers to steer their companies along a chosen road, but they do nothing to help them decide which fork in the road to take. The real story about information technology is being written by companies whose systems are outwardly oriented. Starbucks Coffee, one of America's fastest-growing companies, invested heavily in a computer network that makes it possible to track and respond to the changing tastes of coffee drinkers on a daily basis. Regular guests of Ritz-Carlton hotels don't have to tell the registration clerk if they want a no-smoking room or a nonallergenic pillow or if they are entitled to a corporate discount. The clerk already knows these things because Ritz-Carlton's guest-history database records such information with every stay. Companies like L. L. Bean, American Express, and Fingerhut (a catalog firm) have likewise made themselves masters of the art of knowing their customers—their interests and their preferences—through the use of information systems that have an *outward* orientation.

FROM THE ARCHIVES: HENRY "BUCK" WEAVER'S PHILOSOPHY OF CONSUMER RESEARCH

It's always humbling when we discover that principles we've struggled to determine through our own study and experience were well understood by our predecessors. Such is the case with listening to the customer, a craft understood and articulated more than sixty years ago by GM's chief of consumer research, Henry "Buck" Weaver. In the following excerpt from Weaver's work,[18] it's clear that he and his staff recognized the importance of listening to and understanding the customer and the extent to which the modern, functionally structured organization impairs its own ability to communicate with and serve the customer. Weaver and his people went beyond understanding to creating the mechanisms for overcoming these impairments.

> Under the conditions of the one man shop, with the head of the business serving as designer, manufacturer, purchasing agent, salesman, and service expert, an intimate understanding of customer tastes and desires was automatically assured. . . . [The shop owner] enjoyed a distinct natural advantage in being able to *observe first hand* the relations between his various duties and the major objective of his business, in fact the major objec-

tives of all business, namely, *serving the customer in the way that the customer wants to be served.* . . .

By the very nature of things, the bigger an institution grows, the wider becomes the gap between the customer and those responsible for directing the destiny of the institution. With producer and consumer so widely separated it becomes increasingly difficult to keep the business sensitively attuned to the requirements of the customer. . . .

. . . Mass production and mass distribution have tended to obscure the fundamental necessity of reckoning with the detailed tastes of the individual buyer, and yet the principle is just as true today as it was back when our forefathers first began laying the foundations upon which rest our great industrial structures of today. . . .

There is a need for some kind of liaison which would serve as a substitute for the close personal contact which existed automatically back in the days of the small shop. Consumer research fills this need by providing an auxiliary and more direct line of communication between producer and consumer.

Customer research is not merely a matter of sending out questionnaires—calling on car owners—compiling a lot of dull statistics. These are *only incidents.* It's really a matter of recognizing the retail buyer as the hub about which all our activities revolve.

From this broad viewpoint customer research cannot be looked upon as an isolated departmental activity. To be truly effective, it must be in the nature of a *spirit or attitude of mind* permeating every phase of a business. Or putting it another way, we might say that customer research is simply a tool for developing a greater degree of *human understanding*.

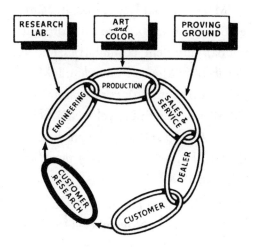

NOTES

1. Sun Tzu, *The Art of War*, trans. Samuel B. Griffith (London: Oxford University Press, 1963), 145.

2. For a complete discussion of these market research activities, see Vincent P. Barabba, "Market-Based Decisions," in *Marketing Managers Handbook*, ed. Sidney Levy (Chicago: Dartnell Corporation, 1994), 328, and Vincent P. Barabba, "Problem Formulation and Research Design," in *McGraw-Hill Handbook of Market Research*, ed. Michael J. Houston (New York: McGraw-Hill, forthcoming). For a graphic summary, see Vincent P. Barabba, "The Market Research Encyclopedia," *Harvard Business Review*, January–February 1990, 105–116. Also reproduced in Vincent P. Barabba and Gerald Zaltman, *Hearing the Voice of the Market* (Boston: Harvard Business School Press, 1990), 100–111.

3. Kim B. Clark and Takahiro Fujimoto, "The Power of Product Integrity," *Harvard Business Review*, November–December 1990, 113.

4. Susan Ciccantelli and Jason Magidson, "From Experience: Consumer Idealized Design: Involving Consumers in the Product Development Process," *Journal of Product Innovation Management*, no. 10 (1993): 341–347.

5. Gerald Zaltman and Robin A. Higie, *Seeing the Voice of the Customer: The Zaltman Metaphor Elicitation Technique*, Report No. 93-114 (Cambridge, Mass.: Marketing Science Institute, September 1993), 7.

6. Nigel Piercy, *Marketing Organisation: An Analysis of Information Processing, Power and Politics* (London: George Allen & Unwin, 1985), 13.

7. Peter F. Drucker, "Marketing 101 for a Fast-Changing Decade," *Wall Street Journal*, November 20, 1990.

8. This was not the first time that Xerox let a good idea get away. See Douglas K. Smith and Robert C. Alexander, *Fumbling the Future: How Xerox Invented, Then Ignored, the First Personal Computer* (New York: William Morrow and Company, 1988).

9. Gerald Zaltman, interview with Richard Luecke, Boston, July 6, 1994.

10. Tom Peters, "For Better Products, Listen Right, Well," *San Jose Mercury News*, May 25, 1992, 2D.

11. Eric von Hippel, *Sources of Innovation* (New York: Oxford University

Press, 1988); Ronald E. Rice and Everett M. Rogers, "Re-Invention in the Innovation Process," *Knowledge* 1 (1980): 499–514. Again—nothing is new. In 1941, GM's Henry "Buck" Weaver discussed how difficult it is for the consumer to "project himself very far beyond that which he sees and feels in his day to day experiences":

> In recognition of this fact, we have, over a period of years, as an incident to our general surveys, built up a panel of "special correspondents" or what we call "Motor Enthusiasts" restricted to the names of people who make motoring a hobby—who take more than a passing interest in problems of engineering design—and who *do* have the ability to project their thinking somewhat beyond what they actually see in the cars of today. . . .
>
> Along this same general line of thought, I'd like to say that Customer Research, if it is to provide dependable guidance for future planning, must aim to get two types of reactions.
>
> 1. *Offhand Reactions*—what is the existing state of the public mind as regards a given proposition?
> 2. *Deliberative Reactions*—what are the reactions to the same proposition after the pros and cons are brought to the attention of the respondent?
>
> The former aims to take a cross section of public opinion just as it exists—without reference to the soundness or unsoundness thereof. The latter type concerns itself not with *existing attitudes* but with what the attitudes will most likely be *after* the motoring public—through experience or otherwise—has come into possession of the full and complete facts. While there can be no question but that spontaneous reactions are highly significant as bearing on the short haul, deliberative or well thought out reactions are likely to be more significant as bearing on the long haul or ultimate trend of public thinking.

Henry G. Weaver, "Proving Grounds of Public Opinion," *Journal of Consulting Psychology* (July–August 1941): 149–153.

12. Abraham Maslow elaborates on the internal and external conditions that affect these interactions in *Eupsychian Management: A Journal* (Homewood, Ill.: Richard D. Irwin and The Dorsey Press, 1965). This is a book worth reading, for his insights still hold.

13. "Up Against the Wal-Mart," *60 Minutes*, April 30, 1995, transcript.

14. Ibid.

15. Ibid.

16. Scott Wasser, "Simply Z Best," *Pennsylvania Times Leader*, April 26, 1993.

17. Rashi Glazer, "Measuring the Value of Information: The Information-Intensive Organization," *IBM Systems Journal* 32, no. 1 (1993): 100.

18. Henry G. Weaver, *The Philosophy of Customer Research* (Detroit, Mich.: General Motors Corp., Customer Research Staff, n.d.), 6–9, back cover. Sketches reprinted by permission of General Motors Corp.

6

LEARN

Knowledge resides in the user and not in the collection.
It's how the user reacts to the collection of information
that matters.
C. West Churchman

Many organizations struggle with the paradox of being data rich and knowledge poor. They may "listen" to what is going on in their environment yet fail to make sense of what they hear in a way that will enhance their knowledge of customers, competitors, or their own capabilities so as to make decisions that will improve the value of their enterprise.

Information technology can be part of the problem and part of the solution. While it is now possible to collect and store quantities of data and information undreamed of a generation ago, data and information in and of themselves have little value. Tom Davenport in *CIO* magazine addresses this issue head-on:

> I think we've had a very narrow view of what it takes to create an information environment. We'd like to have an environment where people share information across the business processes, or use information to make decisions. And the way we've attacked those problems is we've thrown technology at them. We assume that once we get that database in place, we'll have that information environment we want. Once we get Lotus Notes, we'll be doing information sharing. And [yet] there are so many other areas that are involved in creating an information environment.[1]

Unless information is converted into what will shortly be described as the intelligence, knowledge, understanding, and wisdom needed for

Wendy Coles, Alice Hayes, and Dan Owen made significant contributions to this chapter.

decision making—as Frito-Lay and a number of other leading companies are now doing—the enterprise will be no better off. It may actually be less well off, buried under a mountain of data and information that makes decision making that much more difficult. Learning is the solution to this problem; it is the act of processing data and information in a way that creates insight or wisdom that leads to efficient and effective decision making—that is, to the actual allocation of resources to both do the right things and do them right.

CEO Jack Smith of GM took a step in the direction of advancing the development of organizational knowledge. In June 1994, he announced the formation of the Strategic Decision Center to support management in the integration of market and business knowledge, the management of information systems, and the development of a global direction on core business and strategic intent. He directed the center to create a knowledge-sharing network that would support GM's efforts to:

1. better align strategic and operational business plans;
2. improve management's understanding of complexity, uncertainty, and opportunity in the market;
3. determine the required resources for knowledge development and clarify roles and responsibilities;
4. effectively capture ideas for innovative products and services;
5. develop organizational learning as a system.

The Hierarchy of Knowing

There is a hierarchy that extends from the smallest components (data) of "knowing" to the most sublime (wisdom). Russell Ackoff's description of the stages of this hierarchy is a memorable introduction to this hierarchy:

An ounce of information is worth a pound of data;
an ounce of knowledge is worth a pound of information;
an ounce of understanding is worth a pound of knowledge; and
an ounce of wisdom is worth a pound of understanding.[2]

- *Data* are codified observations of symbols that represent objects, events, and/or their properties. Only when data are put into context do they become a kind of information. Because context is critical to the transformation of data to information, not only the data but the context of the data must be stored so that it is visible and available to the decision makers who determine the data's role in the creation of information

- Once the data have been sifted through and organized so as to be relevant to the context of the decision at hand, the data can be called *information*.
- *Intelligence* is where the collection and use of information come together. The transformation of information to intelligence requires the drawing of inferences as to how the information relates to the specific issue or decision. It is critical that the inferences are apparent (visible), understood, and shared by those who will eventually use the intelligence.
- *Knowledge* is gained from the certitude that comes from experience, a logical argument, or a preponderance of evidence. Knowledge is knowing what works and how it works.
- *Understanding* is the ability to explain or answer the question, "Why?" Understanding is subjective; it cannot be taught. Understanding comes from observing what is (and is not) taking place and taking advantage of experience—both good and bad.
- *Wisdom* requires the ability to synthesize all that is developed from data, information, intelligence, knowledge, and understanding and to apply it in judging what is right to do.[3]

The Learning Process

Experience helps form the filter or lens through which we process information in the creation of knowledge (see Figure 6-1). Experience gives us a basis for evaluating information and knitting it into an ordered pattern that establishes meaning. This is a *learning process*. In business, the learning process involves taking information about customers (as individuals or as groups), competitors, communities, and the enterprise itself as raw material and then passing it through the lens of experience, which connects it with other bits and pieces of processed information to form a meaningful picture of market reality, or market knowledge. The word *meaningful* is important here. This picture of market reality is more than

Figure 6-1. *The Learning Process: From Information to Knowledge*

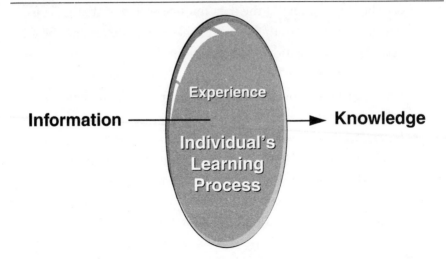

a collection of random information; it is a picture that conveys under-standing. Customer opinions, a chance remark overheard at a trade show, recollections of past successes or failures, and sales information are each bits of information gained from listening or previous learning. By them-selves they mean little. But when we process them in the context of other experiences and understandings—that is, of our human judgment—they are transformed into knowledge. This knowledge, in turn, becomes the raw material for market-based decisions.

As important as the individual learning process is in creating knowl-edge from information, it is not without its problems. Perhaps nothing is more detrimental to learning—for the individual or the enterprise—than a distorted lens of experience or context. The distorted lens pro-duces an erroneous understanding of reality that ultimately leads to bad decisions. Perhaps the most powerful and dangerous case of the distorted lens is the predisposed mind—one that is prepared to see what it expects to see and that filters out what does not fit comfortably with its under-standing of how things should be. This is reminiscent of the old saying, "When you're a hammer, everything looks like a nail." Consider the fol-lowing case of the predisposed mind, as told to me by a colleague.

Sandra and Karen were on a business trip to Boston. Both were dog owners—but theirs were not just any dogs; theirs were Labrador retriev-ers. And they knew that just a short drive and ferry boat ride away, on

Martha's Vineyard, was The Black Dog, a place they both wanted to visit. But how could they wiggle in a visit with days full of meetings?

Sandra and Karen headed off to their first meeting on Monday morning, accepting the fact that a trip to the Vineyard might not be in the cards. But what did they see on the drive into the city but a sign that read, "Labrador Training Center, 2 Miles to the Right!"

"Wow!" Karen remarked. "If only we could take time from classes to see the training center."

On Monday and Tuesday they saw the same sign again as they drove in for their meetings. But no time for detours. Finally, on Wednesday morning, Karen said, "We're running a little ahead of schedule, so we can take a few minutes, turn off the road, and see the Labrador Training Center." And they did.

As the two women approached the facility, they were impressed by the lush, well-manicured grounds. "What a nice place for walking dogs, huh?" The landscape showed off a rich variety of rhododendrons, hibiscus, and ivy, complemented by tall trees. The facility itself was a three-story, dormitory-like building. "This must be where the owners stay when they bring their dogs for training," Sandra concluded. "Let's go inside and check it out."

Despite the many cars in the parking lot, the two women encountered no one as they entered the front door. Photographs of construction projects adorned the walls of the lobby. "These pictures must have been taken when they built the place," Sandra remarked.

They meandered past a cafeteria, a pool room, and a gymnasium. "They must keep the dogs out back," Karen surmised. "I just wish there were someone here so I could pick up a brochure—my dog would love this place."

As they walked down a corridor they passed an office, where a man dressed in green coveralls sat doing paperwork. "Can I help you?"

"Well, we're a couple of black dog lovers who were just looking around the place."

"Dogs?" the man responded in puzzlement. "This is the Labor Training Center. You must be lost."

Labrador? Labor? How did two capable people manage to misinterpret the situation? One may have read the sign wrong. But to read it wrong three days in a row, to have a second person also misread the sign, and then to walk through a building making all the wrong interpretations? Sandra and Karen had viewed reality with predisposed minds. They interpreted everything through lenses that disposed them to find a training center for dogs. What Sandra and Karen did is what decision makers in business do every day.

Gerald Zaltman and I once referred to the problem of the predisposed mind as the "Law of the Lens":

> Knowledge creation, dissemination, and application are themselves not separable processes. Their integration is further complicated by the assumptions, truth tests, expectations, and rules about decision making that make up a viewing lens through which managers and researchers, or information users and information providers, view the marketplace differently.[4]

Because each of us brings experience and context to our learning, each of us has the potential to hold an image of a different "reality." This fact represents both a danger and an opportunity for an organization: a danger in that conflicted notions of reality result in conflicted decisions; an opportunity in that the sharing of different understandings of reality may create a robust sense of reality and better decisions. What is required is a process that permits the enterprise to accommodate and share different notions of reality. The "thinking tools" described in earlier chapters, along with the decision-making process explained in the next chapter, in effect represent that process. Together, they are the result of shared, or organizational, learning.

Just how we learn things, as individuals and in groups, has been the subject of much study over the years. What is presented here represents a small window on that large subject, and one based on my experience. For decades, scholars have pointed to "mental maps," language and story telling, systems thinking, and dialogue as means through which learning takes place—in effect, as learning tools.

Peter Senge, who along with Chris Argyris and others has opened our thinking to the importance of learning and the ways in which it occurs, also talks about mental models. In *The Fifth Discipline*, he describes these models as "deeply ingrained assumptions, generalizations, or even pictures or images that influence how we understand the world and how we take action."[5] Mental models, or *mental maps*, are essential to the learning process, but, as the story of the two women and the "Labrador" Training Center makes clear, they can easily lead us—as individuals and in groups—down the wrong path.

Language and story telling are also important learning tools. In his book *Reality: Isn't What It Used to Be*, Walter Anderson describes language as the "tool with which a culture creates its reality."[6] He illustrates how language is a means by which people categorize their thinking and put it in a context to share with others. Words by themselves have a dictionary meaning, but they convey a great deal more if we understand them in the framework of sentences and what the speaker's body language conveys. Story telling provides a broader dimension of learning through language, a venue for creating an even deeper context through words. Business processes that invite us to communicate and make decisions together provide an opportunity to knowingly use words in context and help us to avoid misinterpretations.

C. West Churchman, Russell Ackoff, and other scholars have given us another powerful learning tool: systems thinking. *Systems thinking* has been described as "seeing the 'structures' that underlie complex situations . . . seeing whole . . . a framework for seeing interrelationships rather than things . . . for seeing patterns of change rather than static 'snapshots'."[7] The power of a systemic perspective has long been recognized in the "hard" sciences and broadly applied.

For business organizations, there is another powerful, if not more complex, system operating: the human system. There is value in understanding the dynamics of a group effort. Thinking of a team as a system of interdependent beliefs, and not a collection of replaceable parts, for example, helps us understand interrelationships between team members and the impact of each on the whole. What we learn about the dynamics of team interaction helps us to leverage the strengths of all its parts.

Dialogue is the last and perhaps the most important of our learning tools. Its power comes from the fact that it subsumes all of the learning tools already discussed. The word *dialogue* is often used to mean a conversation between people. David Bohm describes it as a stream of meaning flowing among and through us and between us. This will make possible a flow of meaning in the whole group, out of which will emerge some new understanding. It's something new, which may not have been in the starting point at all. It's something creative. And this shared meaning is the 'glue' or 'cement' that holds people and societies together. . . .

. . . The object of dialogue is not to analyze things, or to win an argument, or to exchange opinions. Rather, it is . . . to listen to everybody's opinions, to suspend them, and to see what all that means. If we can see what all of our opinions mean, then we are sharing a common content, even if we don't agree entirely. It may turn out that the opinions are not really very important—they are all assumptions. And if we can see them all, we may then move more creatively in a different direction. We can just simply share the appreciation of the meanings; and out of this whole thing truth emerges unannounced—not that we have chosen it.[8]

Dialogue as Bohm describes it presents the opportunity for both individual and collective learning. That possibility is held open even as people listen to others with no intention of relinquishing or changing their own perspectives. Nor does dialogue require a commitment to a decision on completion. It merely implies a faith that understandings are made richer by suspending one's own assumptions and beliefs long enough to consider those of others. (As will be fully discussed in the next chapter, however, the systematic review of realistic alternatives employed in GM's dialogue decision process does in fact lead to a well-understood commitment of resources, one that achieves the best value for the customer, the community, and the enterprise.)

ORGANIZATIONAL LEARNING AND KNOWLEDGE

The need for individuals to learn on a continual basis is universally accepted today. Both rapid technological change and the accelerating rate at which knowledge increases require that individuals continue to learn at a fast pace. From an organizational standpoint, an enterprise is better off as its individual members increase their storehouses of knowledge. To the extent that someone in finance becomes more knowledgeable, the enterprise will be more skillful in obtaining capital and hedging its commitments against interest- and currency-rate changes. To the extent that individual product designers are more knowledgeable about new developments in materials and technology, the new products that emerge from the product development pipeline will better represent the leading edge.

Individual learning is necessary for an organization to succeed in a dynamic and complex environment, but is it sufficient? For sustained, successful functioning as an organization, employees must not only learn individually, but their learning must contribute to the shared knowledge of the internal and external environments in which members of the enterprise, as individuals and as a group, think and work.

Shared knowledge makes it possible for individuals to act in concert with integrated actions flowing from a common understanding of "how the world works." Since the purpose of an organization is to create value through the collective action of its individual members, it follows that a powerful base of shared knowledge will enhance the organization's ability to create value over time.

There is irony in the fact that the increasing availability of information compounds the problem of organizational learning. The organization must be increasingly judicious in deciding what it learns, what information is relevant to its business. To create value, we must not only learn, we must learn the right things. Success at systematically advancing organizational knowledge depends on how well the enterprise uses what it currently knows and how judiciously it selects from the increasing volume of information in the environment.

Organizational knowledge can be defined as the agreed-on, shared portion (the intersection) of what individuals, working on a specific problem, know that is relevant to their collective action. It is established through a dialogue in which each individual brings forward his or her knowledge to the group, which then jointly arrives at shared, relevant organizational knowledge. Dialogue is of value not only for its result—shared knowledge—but for its potential to arrive at a synthesis of what individuals know rather than a simple aggregation. The resulting "organizational" knowledge, then, is far richer than any individual's knowledge and more deeply understood and internalized by all concerned.

Figure 6-2 illustrates the concept of organizational knowledge. The in-

Figure 6-2. *Organizational Knowledge*

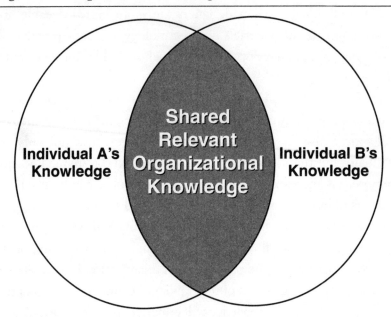

tersection of individual knowledge sets A and B is that portion of knowledge held in common and relevant for collective action. In addition to their shared knowledge, A and B have individual knowledge (the non-shaded area), but this is not considered "organizational" in that it either has not been agreed on by A and B, or is not relevant to their joint activity. Thus, organizational knowledge is not the sum of all the knowledge among individuals but what is relevant and shared. Knowledge that is not shared by those who must act together cannot contribute to their effective collective action.

Some knowledge, often referred to as tacit knowledge, is not easily shared. Ikujiro Nonaka describes tacit knowledge as subjective understandings about the way things work, informed intuitions, and so forth. The challenge to the organization is to develop processes that bring the individual's tacit knowledge to the surface so that it can be leveraged by the organization. As Nonaka says, knowledge-creating companies are adept at converting tacit knowledge into explicit knowledge and at perpetuating the dynamic interaction of tacit and explicit knowledge to create a spiral effect of ever-advancing knowledge.[9]

If individuals engage in an activity without a process that encourages

Figure 6-3. *Learning in the Silo*

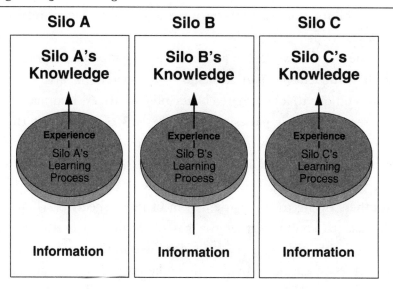

shared understanding, the learning that occurs will likely be predominantly individual learning. Nor will the knowledge gained by any single individual likely be as rich as it would be if individuals had the benefit of one another's knowledge. And absent a shared knowledge base, the level of coordination in the actions of an organization will increase only by happenstance.

In considering the problem of transforming individual learning and knowledge creation to organizational knowledge, we should consider an intermediate problem—that of the functional silos. In Chapter 1, we saw how functionally organized enterprises encourage the development of specialized knowledge within their separate functions.

There are relatively few problems with learning and sharing knowledge within functions. Communication within silos—while not completely trouble-free—is not the problem that it is across the organization. This is because the inhabitants of each silo are more likely to have a common set of responsibilities and to speak a common technical language. They generally share common business processes as well. The accumulation of specialized knowledge within functions is fundamental to the strength of the traditional organization; ideally, the entire organization would operate in the same way. Unfortunately, the sharing of specialized knowledge outside the silo walls is not encouraged. Figure 6-3 illustrates the learning process for the functional unit. As with individual learning, information passes through the lens of experience and context to form knowledge.

Anyone who has worked in a functionally organized enterprise understands how the lens of a particular silo—be it marketing, finance, or any other—is unique to it and shared by its inhabitants. As information falls into a separate silo it passes through the lens of experience through which that silo sees the world. What is viewed as meaningful to that silo is processed and retained as new knowledge; that which lacks meaning for the silo is discarded. The silo learns some things and possibly fails to learn others owing to the particularism of its perspective. There is no mechanism to connect either the basic information or the resulting knowledge with understanding held elsewhere in the organization. This learning process cannot provide the market knowledge we are looking for. Finance people, for example, tend to process information about a proposed new product (or other issue) in terms of capital costs, the timing and uncertainty of receipts and expenditures, and so forth. Marketing people view the same proposed new product proposal through a lens that focuses on sales features and benefits, possible channels of distribution, and promotional requirements. In short, the two different lenses produce quite different views of the world.

In this sense, the problem of relating silo knowledge to organizational knowledge is the same as relating individual knowledge to that of the organization. The situation is analogous to that of Pearl Harbor, as described in the Introduction. There, pieces of information fell into separate pockets from which they could never be pieced together into an alert that Japanese forces were preparing to attack.

Organizational knowledge need not be shared and accepted by all individuals within the organization. It must, however, be shared and accepted by those individuals who must act together and by those who must approve their actions. For example, in the design of a new product, a group of individuals from the engineering, design, manufacturing, and marketing functions must share knowledge to ensure an integrated design, but that shared knowledge need not be extended to every individual within their respective functions. By the same token, some aspects of shared knowledge can be accepted by deference. The marketing person, for instance, need not understand in complete detail the engineering of the product design but can defer to the expertise of the engineer, confident that they share a common understanding of the design's intent.

In general, it is in the interest of the organization to increase the intersection of individual knowledge, thereby increasing the breadth and depth of shared knowledge. The value of this shared knowledge to the organization, however, depends on its quality, its relevance, and the degree to which each individual understands the knowledge, not just on the amount of knowledge. There are conditions under which a small intersection may be appropriate. For example, an R&D scientist may be studying some new and theoretical approaches to road and engine noise on future vehicles. As a result, the scientist must share the market researcher's understanding of customer attitudes toward noise. The scientist's understanding of noise and how it is created and reduced is naturally greater than the market researcher's. But they do share a small intersecting interest in customer attitudes and, with respect to noise, that intersection might not extend further.

Of course, however important we believe learning and shared knowledge to be, few successful managers would say that they are in the business of learning, per se. As such, we should not be surprised that most business processes—demand forecasting, product development, inventory planning, and others—were not designed with the idea of stimulating learning or advancing knowledge. But, for better or worse, business processes are learning processes, the crossroads of organizational learning. As such, business processes should be explicitly designed to encourage learning and to develop the knowledge that comes from that learning. In the market-based decision-making process to be introduced in Chapter 7, individuals on cross-functional teams learn to create the shared knowledge they need to work effectively. The process does not presume that organizational knowledge is a natural outgrowth of individual knowledge. Individual knowledge may have little organizational value unless the organization takes steps to ensure that it does. Just what the organization can do will be made clear as we move through this chapter.

Knowledge States and Business Processes

We have discussed how organizational learning and knowledge generation occur through the execution of a set of business activities by a group of individuals. As such, the business process can be represented as the transition between consecutive organizational knowledge states.

We can define a knowledge state for a business process as the complete set of information necessary to the future execution of the process; each information element of the knowledge state is a variable. While the content of a knowledge state is particular to the process, it is generally of two types: information about relationships and information about issues (the variables). The concept of organizational knowledge, defined as that which is shared among individuals (knowledge, mental models, etc.), extends this concept of knowledge states and describes an organizational knowledge state. For example, in the development and design of a new vehicle, individuals from sales and service, product engineering, manufacturing engineering, and the design studios will need shared knowledge before completing a vehicle of high-product integrity. The sharing of knowledge is a requirement that allows them to come together with a clear definition of the informational requirements of the design process. This process of sharing knowledge should enable each of them to bring their individual knowledge states, containing information based on their experience, to best use. The set of information these individuals agree to share is the organizational knowledge state for that business process.

As learning proceeds, new information becomes available. The newly developed knowledge state, then, is some combination of the current knowledge state and the new information, as determined by the learning through the execution of the common business process. Consequently, common business processes are a natural vehicle for dynamic organizational knowledge.

There are three important observations about the relationship between knowledge states and business processes.

1. Knowledge states are the complete and sufficient set of information required to execute the prospective business process to which they are being applied. Consequently, when the process

Figure 6-4. *One Learning Cycle*

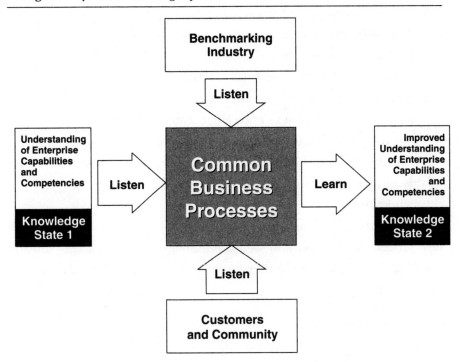

is completed, a newly developed knowledge state, appropriate
to the next application of the process, supersedes the previous
one.

2. The business process itself may be dynamic; consequently,
changes in the process require modifications in the knowledge
state.

3. This model represents learning as a discrete activity that takes
place in a particular time period, followed by another discrete activity. Learning is represented as a sequential dynamic process.

Figure 6-4 illustrates the relationship of a business process and knowledge states for one learning cycle. Prior to engaging in a business process,
a group of individuals might define their organizational knowledge
state—that is, take an inventory of what they agree they know about
various topics relevant to the business process in question (knowledge
state 1). As they do this, they will encounter new information, some of
which may be prescribed by the activities that compose the business process, some unintended. When the process is complete, the group of indi-

viduals can reflect on what they have come to understand and document a new, hopefully improved, knowledge state (knowledge state 2).

In deciding what new information to include in the next knowledge state—that is, what is judged relevant to the next application of the process—the group will augment topics in the current knowledge state and add new and relevant information. It may also eliminate knowledge deemed irrelevant. The next knowledge state, then, may represent revisions to the current knowledge state, the addition of new elements of information, and the elimination of certain elements of information. As a consequence, the dimensionality of the knowledge state may change through learning.

The quality of the learning and the knowledge that results from a business process depends on how well the individuals use what they already know and how judiciously they select from the range of all available new information.

Current knowledge

Imagine a business process that admits no new information per se during decision making and that operates only on current knowledge. To avoid stagnation, the working group would have to design the process in such a way that its understanding of the relationships between current information elements are successively improved. As bizarre as this approach may seem, it offers three valuable benefits:

1. The group may identify previously unknown relationships within elements of the current knowledge state, some that individual group members could not have perceived on their own. Today the more sophisticated application of data base management makes this idea more feasible.
2. Introspection may lead the group to admit information to the knowledge state that was previously known to some members of the group but not accepted into the organizational knowledge state by others. In these cases, individuals perceive things the group has not yet come to understand.
3. Informational deficiencies in the organizational knowledge state can be identified. These deficiencies can be rectified by the active collection of specific new information in the next decision.

In this type of review, the participants improve on their current knowledge by reinterpreting or striving for a deeper understanding of what is already known. Profound learning occurs when dialogue around current knowledge triggers its reinterpretation, leading to a new agreement on what it is that we know.

The value of new information

Now imagine a learning process that calls for as much new information as possible. If the business process does not call for any review of what is currently known, the tendency will be to add all new information to the existing knowledge state. Information added indiscriminately will compound to the point where the size and complexity of the knowledge state will reduce its effectiveness in advancing the knowledge of the business process.

Unless the learning process is discriminating, the knowledge state will increase in size to the point where relevant information is obscured. Thus, the ancient adage: "Water, water, everywhere, but nary a drop to drink." When new information is added without regard for its value to subsequent activities, the knowledge state is, at worst, swamped with information and starved for knowledge. A well-designed business process identifies deficiencies in the current knowledge state and provides for the collection of specific new information. Any other new information that becomes available is carefully scrutinized for its relevance to future applications of the learning process.

Processes that combine explicit dialogue (for the purpose of understanding and agreeing on what is known) and judicious selection of new information (adding what is necessary to know) give an organization the capacity to sustain dynamic organizational knowledge.

A record of knowledge states

With the dynamic relationship between organizational knowledge and business processes understood, how can we ensure the advance of organizational knowledge with successive applications of business processes? Western science has reached its current heights because each generation of scientists has, in effect, stood on the shoulders of Newton and thousands of other scientists, living and dead. Science codifies its current state

Figure 6-5. *Consecutive Knowledge States*

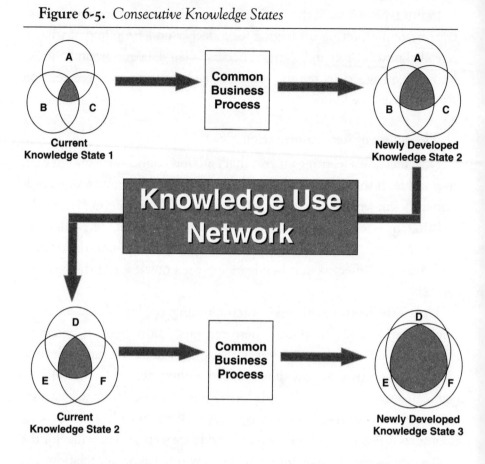

of knowledge and passes it forward. Each era of scientific development becomes the baseline from which further advances in knowledge are made. We can do the same with organizational knowledge by recording each development in the knowledge state. This ensures that successive groups of individuals who engage in a business process begin from the organization's best current knowledge of that process. As in science, the rate of learning and advance of knowledge depends on the willingness of each successive group to carefully consider the knowledge passed to them from the previous team.

Figure 6-5 illustrates the flow of knowledge states. Individuals A, B, and C begin by defining the knowledge they share that is relevant to the set of activities in which they are engaged (current knowledge state 1). After going through a common business process, their newly developed shared knowledge has increased, as indicated by the enlarged intersection (newly developed knowledge state 2). The formal record of this advancement in organizational knowledge can be made available to the next set of individuals (D, E, and F) prior to their engagement in this common business process. The knowledge state is made available through the knowledge use network, described in Chapter 8 as "a functioning network for the development and transfer of knowledge both between the outside world and the enterprise and within the enterprise itself." Knowledge state 2, with which D, E, and F begin the set of activities, then, will be some combination of the current knowledge state (i.e., of A, B, and C) and that portion of individual knowledge that D, E, and F agree to share. As Figure 6-5 indicates, on completion of the common business processes, individuals D, E, and F have significantly increased the newly developed knowledge (state 3). Their increased organizational knowledge state would then be recorded and made available to the next group of individuals to engage in that business process.

While the act of recording the knowledge state does not guarantee that the knowledge will be used by the next participants, it does provide the opportunity. Failure to systematically record knowledge gained dooms the organization to a cycle of learning the same things while the more efficient enterprises have moved on.

Implications for information management

Traditionally, generating knowledge meant managing information. Information managers were charged with organizing and analyzing data and delivering to the organization the knowledge resident in its information. This approach to knowledge creation followed a sequence: build from the data, compile information, and see what we know. From the perspective of process-based learning, knowledge creation is decision based: build from what we know, identify what we need to know, and seek that information. By recording what we know of the knowledge state, we put in place a mechanism for managing information based on our knowledge. If the knowledge state is kept current, it can be used to guide the changes introduced to information systems.

Knowledge states, then, provide management with a tool for use in the continual alignment of information systems with information needs. Individuals executing common business processes will demand to be apprised of the current organizational knowledge state and will create the pull for new information. The result is that the organization has a complete, efficient, and dynamic information system to support business processes. The systematic use of business processes with companion knowledge states makes possible the controlled growth of information through the judicious selection of relevant information by those who will use it.

LEARNING BY DESIGN: GM's DIALOGUE DECISION PROCESS

An organization that designs and manages its processes with the intent of using what the organization currently knows and of learning what it needs to know will reap enhanced dynamic knowledge as a natural by-product of its decision-making process. Given the current pace of change in many markets and industries, it is time to start thinking proactively about designing business processes in ways that account for the importance of learning and knowledge as outcomes. These processes must, of course, deliver the goods, but if they can be designed to maximize the generation and sharing of knowledge within the enterprise, so much the better. As Alice Hayes and Daniel Owen theorize, "It is our contention that if we explicitly design learning into business processes and systematically record and share the knowledge gained, an organization will realize efficient, rapid and sustainable increases in relevant knowledge."[10]

Enlightened management can see the advantage of using the business processes to encourage systematic learning and to generate knowledge. It knows that improvements to a process come from the direct experience of the individuals who execute the process. Management should guide the evolution of the process in response to—not apart from—the knowledge gained by those who experience it. The intent is to offer the next participants the best process with the most current set of information. Actively managing process evolution will also increase the appropriateness and quality of knowledge.

Managing processes as evolving systems is important not only to ensure adaptability to change but also to ensure appropriate commonality across successive executions of the process so that knowledge does not merely change but advances. Common processes are important and can result in a widely held common knowledge state. Common processes also increase the quality of the knowledge state, because with each execution, individuals start from a more advanced level of understanding.

GM has redefined many existing business processes. It has also developed new ones, one of which is a decision-making process called the dialogue decision process (DDP). Eight years and more than one hundred major applications of the DDP have given us the opportunity to observe and document both the increase in the shared knowledge among participants and the systematic increase in organizational knowledge in successive applications of the same process using different participants.

Our comparison of the DDP with advocacy-driven business processes at GM and at other enterprises suggests two things: (1) that the rate of organizational learning is greater when the business process is well-defined, and (2) that some business processes are inherently better for organizational learning than others. Observations indicate that the DDP has both of these things in its favor.

GM has also been developing and recording knowledge states. Our initial experience included the development of four organizational knowledge states for groups ranging in size from two to twelve individuals. These knowledge states have been captured in dialoguing sessions of several hours in duration. The sessions were led by an experienced facilitator whose primary responsibility was to get the groups to define with precision and clarity the information elements of the knowledge states. The following actions appear to make the facilitated session more productive:

- Prior to the session, develop a "straw man" organizational knowledge state by interviewing some participants. The object is both to identify the informational requirements of the process and to obtain an initial assessment of the knowledge state. Participants seem able to add, delete, and modify more easily than they create.
- During the session, provide participants with an explanation of a *knowledge state*. Emphasize that the objective is to arrive at shared insights of prospective value to the process, not to record individual experiences.

- Define as well the process to which the knowledge state pertains. This keeps the discussion focused and ensures the relevancy of the knowledge state.
- Enlist computer support for on-line, real-time changes to the informational elements to be made during the session. This helps the group reach clarity and consensus.

Most participants, but not all, react favorably to this process. Many say that they learn a great deal through the dialogue. What becomes apparent is the potential of the knowledge state to serve as a guide, indicating where new knowledge is most needed. In making explicit what we know, we also make clear what we don't know or can't agree on. With the knowledge state, then, we can manage knowledge advancement, and in so doing direct our learning to what is most essential to our ability to create value as an organization.

An Ensemble of Learning and Knowledge

Peter Senge's popular and influential book *The Fifth Discipline* describes five disciplines for organizational learning: personal mastery, mental models, vision sharing, team learning, and systems thinking. These, according to the author, are the disciplines that must be practiced to create an organization that is as rich in skills and intellectual capital as the competitive marketplace requires. But these disciplines in themselves are insufficient. As Senge observes, "It is vital that the five disciplines develop as an ensemble."[11] Like the many instrumental voices of an orchestra, the five disciplines must unite in a harmonious and mutually supporting way if effective and continuing learning is to take place. The next chapter describes a practical and proven method for doing just that.

NOTES

1. From a *CIO* magazine interview with Tom Davenport, December 15, 1994/January 1, 1995, 47–51.

2. Russell Ackoff, "The Content of Learning," unpublished manuscript.

3. The hierarchy of elements that go from data to wisdom is more fully discussed in Vincent P. Barabba and Gerald Zaltman, *Hearing the Voice of the Market* (Boston: Harvard Business School Press, 1990), 40–46. Both an information pyramid and Haeckel's hierarchy are presented.

4. Barabba and Zaltman, *Hearing the Voice of the Market*, 41.

5. Peter M. Senge, *The Fifth Discipline: The Art and Practice of the Learning Organization* (New York: Doubleday, 1990), 8. See also Chris Argyris, "Teaching Smart People How to Learn," *Harvard Business Review*, May–June 1991, 99–109, and Chris Argyris, "Good Communication That Blocks Learning," *Harvard Business Review*, July–August 1994, 77–85.

6. Walter T. Anderson, *Reality Isn't What It Used to Be: Theatrical Politics, Ready-to-Wear Religion, Global Myths, Primitive Chic, and Other Wonders of the Post Modern World* (San Francisco: Harper, 1990), 58.

7. Senge, *The Fifth Discipline*, 68.

8. David Bohm, *On Dialogue* (Cambridge, Mass.: Pegasus Communications, 1990), 1–14.

9. Ikujiro Nonaka, "The Knowledge-Creating Company," *Harvard Business Review*, November–December 1991, 96.

10. Alice Hayes and Daniel Owen, "Organizational Learning: A Process-Based Approach," GM Internal Memorandum, November 4, 1993, 3. Chapter 6 relies on conversations with Hayes and Owen.

11. Senge, *The Fifth Discipline*, 12.

7

LEAD

The nature of consensus is not understood. It is complete
agreement, not in principle, but in practice. It is this
distinction that is not widely grasped.
Russell L. Ackoff

The development of products and services that satisfy customers and create profits are the point of all the listening, learning, and knowledge creation discussed up to this point. The final activity is *leading*. Listening
and learning are indispensable activities, but they create no change for
the enterprise or its customers. By themselves they are sterile. They do,
however, create the organizational knowledge that is the basis for action,
or market-based decisions; and these decisions ultimately determine the
character of the products and services by which the enterprise is known
to the market. As a preface to our discussion, consider this true story from
the annals of modern warfare. The story dramatizes the human behaviors
that so prevent our organizations from making the kinds of decisions that
challenging circumstances demand.

In June 1942, two U.S. carrier task forces steamed out of Pearl Harbor
for an engagement that proved to be the decisive action of the war in the
Pacific. They were guided by intelligence reports indicating that the next
target of the Imperial Japanese Navy would be tiny Midway Island,
America's last remaining outpost in the eastern Pacific. Everyone understood the significance of the battle that lay ahead. Its outcome would be
determined, in no small measure, on how various operating units would
interpret and respond to gathered information.

Thanks to the code-breaking abilities of its Combat Intelligence Unit
(CIU), U.S. forces were privy to many enemy plans during the war. But
the intelligence gathered through code breaking was generally incom-

---

Dan Owen and Michael Kusnic made significant contributions to this chapter.

plete, telling the likely target, but not the date. Or, if the date were known, the size of the enemy force was unknown. When the CIU intercepted a coded message on May 20, 1942, it learned only that a large invasion force was headed toward "AF." But what was AF? Suspecting AF to be Midway Island, U.S. Fleet Commander Chester Nimitz secretly instructed the Midway garrison to send out a radio message that its water distillation plant had broken down. Sure enough, the CIU soon intercepted another Japanese message indicating that AF was running low on drinking water. But the strength and attack plans of the Japanese force remained a mystery.

The U.S. Navy during World War II, like most other large organizations, had its "silos," and these didn't always work closely together. In particular, the Combat Intelligence Unit and naval operations officers did not see eye to eye during the early period of the war. Captain E. T. Layton was the fleet intelligence officer reporting the findings of the CIU to Nimitz. As such, he had responsibility for briefing operations officers on CIU reports and assessments of enemy activities, which were not always accepted. Many operations officers viewed Layton as an alarmist and would automatically discount his assessments. If Layton said, "There are six enemy ships," operations would discount that figure to four. And if there proved to be only four, this would be taken as proof of Layton's tendency to overstate enemy strength and would reinforce their tendency to reduce his estimates.

As it turns out, Layton learned from experience how operations officers would reduce the CIU estimates, and so would inflate them, tricking operations into the right answer. Layton would be satisfied that operations had taken the bait for the right estimate, and operations would pat itself on the back for discounting Layton's "wild" estimate.

Actually, Layton could be uncanny in his predictions. At the Battle of Midway, he estimated the time and place of the first discovery of Japanese vessels to within five minutes and five miles.[1]

To any manager, the Layton story should have a familiar ring. Layton and the operations officers he briefed on a daily basis were members of a closed system, yet each maintained a unique view of events based on their various training and responsibilities. Each had his understanding of reality; each interpreted information through the lens of his own experience. Each party to the game of estimating true enemy strength was sincere in what he was doing, yet each felt obliged to be less than candid with the others in the effort to reach a good outcome.

The "trick 'em" game described here is not something anyone could recommend. Although it appeared to work, imagine what would have happened had a new set of operations officers come into the picture, individuals who did not view Layton as an alarmist but who would take his inflated estimates at face value.

Before we fault Layton, however, let's be aware that a fairly good analog to the situation just described exists broadly throughout modern business. Consider the relationship between a divisional product planner and a corporate review staff during a meeting at which the product planner is making his pitch for a new product. As a dedicated employee, his job is to sell his department's plan to the company for its own good. He is there to act as champion for an idea. In making the pitch, he will not see it as his responsibility to dwell on the risks or other troublesome issues. Others at the table will most likely see these as their responsibility.

The financial officer can generally be counted on to challenge the cost and revenue projections for any new endeavor. And rightly so. A lower revenue forecast, cheaper materials, or a higher price might be mandated to gain her approval. Knowing this in advance, the product planner may have been generous in his original estimate of revenues. The manufacturing manager may argue for a design change so that existing dies and other equipment can be utilized. The materials manager, too, may want design alternatives to make use of existing materials and components, which may or may not be what would please the customer.

There is a certain gamesmanship in this kind of decision-making process. The presenter of the new product may be using Layton's technique of tricking his colleagues into what he perceives to be the right answer. The other managers bring the perspectives of their respective functions to the table, judging the issue in question in terms of their own narrow interests. There is an adversarial feel to the meeting. Much more energy is spent defending and attacking the proposal than is spent enhancing its value. Aspects of the new product may be compromised to achieve agreement and approval. Very little listening takes place. The participants learn little from one another and share less. The situation is more of a contest than a meeting of minds. And decision making is unlikely to lead to products and services that truly satisfy customers. In fact, the interests of customer and community are essentially unrepresented.

Just as the manufacturing process of an enterprise generates a stream of products, one can think of management as a process that produces a stream of decisions. In the context of this analogy, a useful question to ask is: What quality-control mechanism is built into this traditional advocative/adversarial process? Like the manufacturing processes of the 1950s and 1960s, traditional decision-making processes ensure quality through the use of "decision inspectors." Successive levels of management review form an approval chain performing a series of "inspections" in which questions are asked such as: "Did you consider alternative X?" "What about the effect of factor A?" If a proposal passes these inspections (which usually is a function of the presenter's organization agility), then it gets approved. If not, then it is sent back for rework, which often results in delay with no significant improvement in value.

The way you get quality decisions, as the manufacturing world has learned over the past thirty years, is to build it into the process; attempts to inspect it after the fact are largely futile. The question is: How can we build quality into the process of making important resource allocation decisions?

INTEGRATING FUNCTIONAL KNOWLEDGE FOR BETTER DECISIONS

The problematic process of making decisions is not unique to contemporary business. Judging from the following passage, written by Alfred Sloan, it was a problem even in his lifetime. Sloan, however, understood how to deal with it:

> Much of my life in General Motors was devoted to the development, organization, and periodic reorganization of [the] governing groups in central management. This was required because of the paramount importance, in an organization like General Motors, of providing the right framework for decisions. There is a natural tendency to erode that framework unless it is consciously maintained. Group decisions do not always come easily. There is a strong temptation for the leading officers to make

decisions themselves without the sometimes onerous process of discussion, which involves *selling your ideas to others* [emphasis added]. The
group will not always make a better decision than any particular member
would make; there is even the possibility of some averaging down. But in
General Motors I think the record shows that we have averaged up. Essentially this means that, through our form of organization, we have been
able to adapt to the great changes that have taken place in the automobile market in each of the decades since 1920.[2]

The "averaging up" that occurs through the decision-making process
described by Sloan—improving the concept under discussion—is what
we seek to accomplish. This is what I mean by "leading." It is what Layton and his operational colleagues should have been doing. It is what our
hypothetical product planner and his colleagues should have been doing.
What we seek to accomplish in the process of "leading" is to integrate
the special perspectives of different functions (different voices) to create
greater organizational knowledge and to use that knowledge as the basis
for decision making that systematically produces better outcomes. It is
important to point out that we can make what, by decision quality standards, is a great decision that, because of circumstances outside of our
control, results in a bad outcome.

At any point in time, a number of "leading" companies appear to have
mastered this practice of functional integration; they reflect that mastery
through a number of observable marketplace advantages:

- anticipation of market demand with new, innovative projects before competitors;
- product pricing that reflects internal superiority in engineering,
  design, and production;
- greater market share or profitability;
- distribution and promotion that are better "tuned" to customer
  needs; and
- management processes that are recognized as state-of-the-art by
  academics and rival companies.

A number of public measures can be used to gauge business mastery
and leadership. *Fortune* records the progress or failures of major companies in its annual rating. It also features an annual "Most Admired Com-

pany" article. Given the high turnover among the Fortune 500 companies and the tendency of "most admired" companies to lose favor within just a few years, it is natural to conclude that leadership is difficult to sustain. Even Peters and Waterman's list of "excellent" companies was quickly decimated by the scourges of time, recession, and new competition.

Still, a few companies have managed to maintain market leadership year after year. Hewlett-Packard and Procter & Gamble are among them. The sustained leadership of these companies appears to have several common elements:

- systematic listening to the voices of customers and the community, competitors, and the enterprise itself;
- systematic learning about changes in those voices over time and about how to integrate those voices; and
- common business processes that promote systematic listening and learning and fast response to change.

The question is: How can a corporation develop these elements of market leadership? The answer is to create a network of decision making that links the strategic direction of the organization to the allocation of resources and to the many operational decisions that must be made to support that direction.

LEADING THROUGH DECISION MAKING

Managers lead when they make decisions. These decisions determine how capital, information, people, time, and other organizational resources are allocated. Allocations influence the outcomes of value to the enterprise. In this sense, then, decision making is fundamentally about resource allocation.

Two practical implications emerge from defining decisions in terms of resource allocations. First, it facilitates implementation and accountability. The decision to increase market share, for example, must be defined in terms of specific resource allocations to allow price reductions, increase advertising, improve product features, and so forth. If the "decision" is not backed up with adequate allocation of resources, then it is nothing more than a hope. When a decision is defined in terms of resource allocations, managers can be monitored and held accountable for the various actions it implies. They cannot, for instance, reasonably be held accountable for the outcome of increased market share to the extent that outcomes depend on factors (like competitors' actions) over which they have little if any control.

A second practical implication of defining decisions in terms of resource allocations is that it forces decision makers to explicitly resolve associated conflicts. Again, if the decision is to increase market share, resources will be added to some areas and may have to be stripped away from others. Failure to resolve these conflicts up front will plague implementation.

Although few managers give it much thought, every decision is part of a broad network of decisions within the enterprise. We could go as far as to define the enterprise as *a network of decisions*. This network may be tightly knit, or it may be a tattered fabric that barely holds together. The extent to which decisions from the boardroom to the factory floor are logical and internally consistent components of an integrated network determines how well or how poorly the organization functions and how much integrity its products and services evidence in the marketplace.

All of an organization's decisions fall within a nested natural hierarchy, as shown in Figure 7-1. Decisions at lower levels are nested within decisions at higher levels in the sense that they are constrained or preempted by them. For example, a portfolio-level decision concerning whether or not to serve a particular market would preempt decisions concerning the products selected to serve that market.

Achieving a high standard of quality in the decisions made throughout the network requires that resource allocations complement one another both vertically and horizontally—that is, they must work together to move each business unit forward in a unified strategic direction. The silo problem discussed earlier is a major impediment to horizontal coordination of the network. Additionally, in most organizations there is a major impediment to vertical coordination. This is because the decisions made at higher levels are rarely defined clearly with respect to resource allocation. This can result from a failure to understand the precise nature of those higher-level decisions or from a failure to put in place a process that deals clearly and unambiguously with the implications of resource

Figure 7-1. *The Network of Decisions Composing a Strategic Business Unit Fall into a Natural Hierarchy*

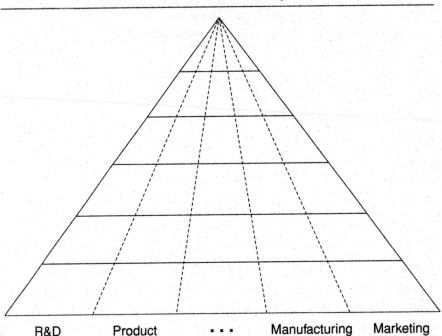

R&D   Product   • • •   Manufacturing   Marketing

allocations. In either case, the resulting ambiguity must be resolved at lower levels, where sooner or later resources must actually be committed.

This lack of clarity at higher levels creates several dysfunctions in the system. First, it is a source of widespread disempowerment when senior management fails to delineate the boundaries for decisions made at lower levels. This failure requires management to micromanage those lower-level decisions to ensure alignment; otherwise the strategic direction of the enterprise is given over to lower levels of management.

Second, micromanagement from the top leads to poor decisions. More lower-level decisions are made than senior management can deal with effectively.

And third, lack of clarity at the top creates instability in the overall network. In a decision-making hierarchy, the appropriate frequency with which decisions should be revisited goes up as you move down in the hierarchy. For example, the decision concerning whether or not to serve a particular market should be revisited less often than would the decisions concerning the product/service features required to meet the needs

Figure 7-2. *A Network of Decisions or Resource Allocations*

Areas of Resource Allocation
($ denotes resource levels)

	Marketing	Technology	Manufacturing	Finance
Business Unit 1	$$$$	$	$	$$$
Business Unit 2	$$$	$$$	$$$	$$$
Business Unit 3	$	$$$$	$$$$	$$$

of the defined market. If the higher-level decisions are only implicitly addressed (and essentially left to the lower levels for clarification), then strategic direction tends to get revisited much more frequently than is appropriate. In a real sense, the (operational) tail wags the (strategic) dog.

Figure 7-1 depicts the hierarchy of decisions for a single strategic business unit (SBU). Most enterprises, however, consist of multiple SBUs. This fact creates an added level of complication because the overall system coordination has both a cross-functional and a cross-business-unit component. This more realistic situation is pictured in Figure 7-2. If this enterprise were to make quality decisions across the whole network, there would be an appropriate rationale for the marketing emphasis of business unit 1 and the technology and manufacturing emphasis of business unit 3. If we look at the columns in this figure, we can clearly see the functional strategies of this enterprise. The capital allocation to each business unit is roughly the same, while the technology strategy emphasizes resource commitments to business unit 3.

Most organizations manage to achieve a reasonably complementary balance among decisions made in one direction, but not in others. When organized by business unit, the decisions that constitute business-unit strategies tend to be more complementary than those that make up func-

tional strategies. When organized by functional activities, the decisions that compose functional strategies tend to be more complementary than the decisions that make up business unit strategies. An effective network of decisions ensures that the decisions made and the resources allocated in both directions—vertical and horizontal—are complementary. As a result, decisions by top management and by lower-level groups are mutually supportive and harmonious. Moreover, decisions at the same level of the hierarchy are cross-functionally integrated—that is, they do not suffer from the silo problem. Enterprises that have sustained market leadership over time seem to have mastered both dimensions of this problem.

THE DIALOGUE DECISION PROCESS

We saw in the previous chapter how individuals create knowledge by passing information through the lens of the learning process. Likewise, functional silos of the business organization were shown to follow the same approach in creating "silo knowledge." What is needed to fulfill the process begun with listening and learning is to create a market-based decision-making process that transforms the organization's abundant but scattered resources into unified, coherent courses of action. At GM we call this the dialogue decision process.

The DDP is a practical tool for functional integration that has been evolving outside of GM over the past quarter century and inside for the past eight years. It can be found under different names (decision and risk analysis, decision analysis, etc.) and in different forms at GM, DuPont, Procter & Gamble, Alcoa, AT&T, Westinghouse, Eastman Kodak, and elsewhere.[3]

The DDP involves a series of structured dialogues between the two groups responsible for reaching a decision and implementing the associated course of action. It also deals explicitly with the uncertainty and ambiguity that go hand in hand with decision making. This process is illustrated in Figure 7-3. The first of the two groups is the set of decision makers who typically represent different functions; what they have in common is their authority to allocate resources: people, capital, materials, time, and equipment. The second group is a team of cross-functional managers and specialists dedicated to the work at hand—those with a

Figure 7-3. *The Dialogue Decision Process*

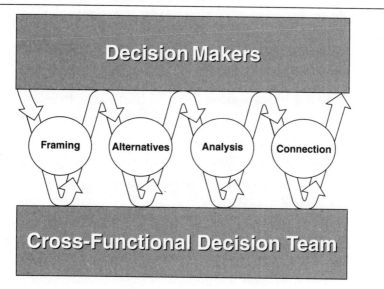

stake in the implementation. They represent design, engineering, manufacturing, marketing, and so forth. As a team drawn from the major functions, they embody the learning of the organization; in working together and sharing their learning, they create the knowledge on which decisions will be based. The interaction, or dialogue, between these two groups, which involves sharing and learning for both, takes place across four sequential, structured stages: framing the problem, developing alternatives, conducting analysis, and establishing connection.

Framing the problem

It is an old saw that a problem poorly defined will never be solved, but a problem well-defined is half solved. This is what the framing stage of the DDP is all about: identifying the problem to be solved, or the decision to be made. It is important to frame the problem in a way that recognizes the multiple perspectives and associated mental models of the relevant decision makers. A common understanding of the definition and scope of the problem must be developed and shared by all concerned. In-depth thinking and clear communication are required to properly frame the problem, to determine which decisions are part of the problem and which are not, to list and evaluate the knowns and unknowns relevant to the solution, and to be clear about the criteria for the decision to be made.

The benefit of this activity is that it puts everyone on the same wavelength right up front before getting too far into the analysis or, what is even more problematic, implementation.

Insufficient attention to framing can lead to bad decisions that leave enormous value on the table. This is one of the reasons why there are no photocopying machines bearing the IBM logo today. In 1958, IBM engaged Arthur D. Little (ADL) to evaluate the market potential of two copiers (Model 813 and Model 914) developed by the Haloid Company (later to be known as the Xerox Corporation). Model 914 was to be a faster, more fully featured machine than competing products. Thus, it would carry a higher price.

The executive summary of ADL's fifty-page final report clearly articulated the "frame" of the problem:

> In considering this course of action IBM hopes to spread present selling costs over two product lines and to exploit more fully the office-equipment market coverage by its ET [electric typewriter] Division salesmen. We understand that selling costs in the division are now disproportionately high in some market territories outside of highly urbanized areas.

In conclusion, the executive summary recommended that the "ET Division terminate considerations of the Haloid-Xerox Model 914 as a new product opportunity for its sales force." Thus, one of the reasons the Model 914 was rejected is that the problem was framed from the perspective of how well IBM's existing electronic typewriter sales force could handle the product. Had the problem been framed from the perspective that copiers represented an entirely new business, the decision might have been different.

There were, of course, other reasons. For example, the copy-volume estimates were based on the existing notion of making copies from an original. They had no idea that considerable volume would be driven by the copying of copies—and so vastly underestimated demand. Another assumption was that customers would want to buy and not rent the machines (much less pay for each copy from a leased machine).

Obviously, that business slipped from IBM's hands into those of others for many reasons. But focusing on the copying business as a way of ex-

Figure 7-4. *The Three Dimensions of the Decision Hierarchy*

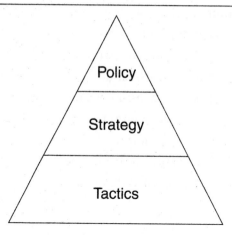

ploiting an existing sales force started the decision-making process on the wrong path.

Framing is most directly related to the notion of systems thinking. It begins by identifying the whole, the scope of the decision, and then moves to systematically identify the set of relationships and their underlying structure and leverage points, which later leads to uncovering the sources of value. In framing, we attempt to:

- capture the different perspectives of each member of the group;
- make sure the underlying assumptions and thinking process of each member of the group are made explicit; and
- formulate and communicate a comprehensive problem description that includes all points of view.

One of the tools used in framing is the decision hierarchy (Figure 7-4), which helps participants determine which decisions are on the table and which aren't. It does this by requiring that all relevant decisions be put into one of three different buckets: policy, strategy, or tactics. *Policy-related decisions* are to be taken as given. They correspond to the resource allocations to which the enterprise is already committed. These decisions establish the boundary conditions for the choice of strategic direction. *Strategic decisions* are to be made. They are at the heart of the issue that the group has been brought together to address. Ensuring that the choices made relative to these decisions result in a coherent allocation of resources will be the focus of the DDP. *Tactical decisions* will be made to implement the strategy. They can be postponed to a later time.

The influence diagram (discussed in Chapter 3, Figure 3-7) is another important tool used in framing. Its purpose is to structure the set of relationships among the relevant issues and uncertainties by bringing to the surface the mental models and assumptions of individual team members. The value of an influence diagram is that it provides discipline and clarity. It provides discipline by requiring that we make a distinction between what we can and cannot control. It provides clarity by facilitating communication among a group of individuals through its simple diagrammatic form.

Developing alternatives

Having clearly established in framing the boundaries of the problem to be addressed, in this next stage we articulate viable potential solutions. Alternative approaches to solving the problem as framed may originate from any of the individual decision makers or cross-functional team members. The only requirement placed on the originator is to describe the alternative's underlying rationale and specify the resources required for implementation. Ideally, the final range of alternatives represent the range of opinion and debate across the organization. In this sense, the DDP is a conflict-surfacing process.[4]

When describing the purpose of alternatives within the DDP at GM, we often use an analogy to the role of test wells in oil exploration (see Figure 7-5). In the early days of oil exploration, the purpose of test wells was to efficiently and systematically collect information about where to place the production well. You would drill relatively inexpensive test wells where you thought the oil might be located. Core samples from these test wells made it possible to draw better inferences as to the location of major pools of oil.

With this oil-well analogy in mind, we can imagine that framing defines the boundaries of the territory over which the search for oil (value) will take place. Alternatives are the specific locations (hypotheses) to be examined during that search. The important thing is to not leave significant amounts of oil undiscovered.

Given the situation depicted in Figure 7-5, a natural question to ask

Figure 7-5. *In the DDP, Alternatives Are Like Test Wells*

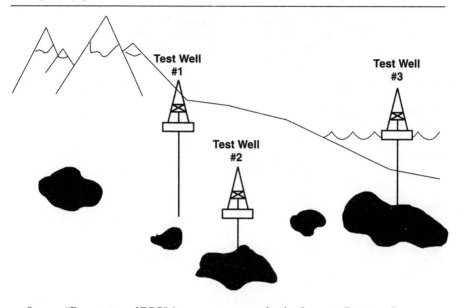

Source: "Description of DDP" (presentation given by the Strategic Decision Center, General Motors Corp., Detroit, Mich.). Reprinted by permission.

is: Why was no test well drilled in the mountains? Whether or not there is a problem with the frame or the alternatives in this situation depends critically on the answer to that question. If drilling for oil in the mountains is a plausible course of action, then the failure to drill a test well there is a significant oversight. Much oil (value) will be left undiscovered because of insufficient creativity in defining the alternatives. But if there is a policy restriction against mountain drilling (owing, say, to an environmental policy of the enterprise or of the community), then the absence of a test well there makes perfect sense. Why waste resources examining a course of action that you know will never be taken? (In the spirit of being open to all points of view, however, this position could be challenged. How much, an individual or group might ask, does the policy against mountain drilling cost the customer, the community, and the enterprise relative to its environmental benefits?)

In defining alternatives in the DDP, we attempt to generate creative *and* achievable paths to our objective. There is an inherent, built-in tension between these two considerations. The alternatives should challenge common perceptions of what is acceptable or what is possible,

Figure 7-6. *Tornado Diagram*

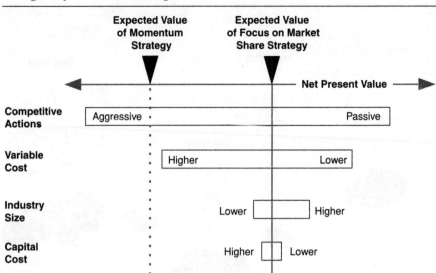

Source: "Description of DDP" (presentation given by the Strategic Decision Center, General Motors Corp., Detroit, Mich.). Reprinted by permission.

while at the same time respecting the predetermined frame. This last point is consistent with Russ Ackoff's observation, quoted at the beginning of the chapter, that we are seeking complete agreement not in principle but in practice—or, in this case, a *feasible* study of alternative actions. The strategy table (discussed in Chapter 3, Tables 3-1 and 3-2) is the tool for defining this feasible set of alternatives.

Conducting the analysis

The purpose of the analysis stage of the DDP is to perform a side-by-side comparison of risk and return for each alternative. The intent is not to pick the best alternative but to develop insight into the value that is embedded in each. That is why this stage can also be referred to as the search for value.

A key tool used in the analysis stage is the tornado diagram (Figure 7-6). The tornado diagram produces a compact visual representation of the impact that each key uncertainty has on the overall value of each alternative course of action. The vertical line in Figure 7-6 labeled "focus on market share" indicates the expected value of that hypothetical strategy assuming all key uncertainties are set at their nominal expected values.

The horizontal bars (competitive actions, variable cost, industry size, and fixed cost) represent the impact each uncertainty will have on the strategy's value from the low end to the high end of its reasonable range (with all other uncertainties being held at their nominal levels). The impacts, assessed by the experts familiar with each factor, are ordered from highest to lowest and plotted on the diagram, creating a tornado-like appearance.

In assessing ranges of uncertainty, three quantities are usually considered: a low, a high, and a nominal value. The low value is a number such that the assessor believes that there is only a one-in-ten chance that the actual outcome will be lower. Correspondingly, the high value is a number such that the assessor believes there to be only a one-in-ten chance that the truth will be higher. Finally, the nominal, or median, value is a number for which the assessor believes it is equally likely that the truth will be higher or lower. When a range is assessed this way, it is often called an 80 percent capture range because the range represents the belief that the true value will lie within it 80 percent of the time. Assessing uncertain factors consistently in this fashion holds the degree of uncertainty constant across factors so that their relative contribution to overall risk can be ascertained without bias.[5]

Tornado diagrams indicate which factors are large and which are small. For example, in Figure 7-6 the potential impact on the expected value owing to the uncertainty around competitive actions is far greater than that associated with capital cost. Tornado diagrams almost always contain surprise. This is because in silo-dominated organizations, information from different parts of the organization is rarely presented in the same place on the same scale for easy inspection by managers.

There is another important benefit of presenting information in tornado-chart form. One can easily determine whether it will be worth the effort to gather additional information to reduce the uncertainty around any factor. In Figure 7-6, this can be seen by examining the width of the bars in reference to the value of another alternative, in this case the current, or "momentum," strategy. For the situation depicted in Figure 7-6, the value of acquiring additional information to reduce any of the uncertainties (except for competitive actions) is zero, because the decision (that is, pursue the market share strategy instead of momentum) would be the same with or without the additional information. In the DDP frame, information that has no effect on the course of action has little value. The value-of-information calculation used in making the determination as to whether new information is needed requires two steps:

1. a consideration of what might be learned about an uncertainty by engaging in additional information gathering; and
2. for each of the things that might be learned (item 1), a consideration of what value would be added by acting on that information.

The (expected) value of information is then the sum of the likelihood of each of the things that might be learned (item 1) multiplied by the value added if it is learned (item 2). This calculation represents the maximum a decision maker should be willing to pay for additional information in the context of a given decision.

The value-of-information calculation has proven to be very insightful in specific decision-making situations because it is usually not intuitively obvious whether or not delaying a decision to gather more information (say, to conduct a market research study) is worth the time or the cost. The most important use of the value of information theory, however, is in guiding organizational learning. By applying the calculation repetitively throughout the organization for a variety of decisions, patterns of things "we do not know" emerge that become a natural focus for organizational learning.[6]

The situation with the uncertainty surrounding competitive actions is different. Uncertainty could enter a range in which we would regret having adopted the market share strategy. Additional information about this factor would have value prior to making the decision because it might affect our course of action. It turns out that the DDP has embedded within it an explicit procedure for inferring exactly what it would be worth to have that additional information. This "value of information" capability of the DDP makes it a powerful tool for guiding investments in new information assets.

The use of tornado diagrams also helps to avoid a common situation that arises out of the traditional adversarial decision-making context. Since the traditional business case is part of a selling process, assumptions tend to be optimistic. If the tornado plot for a traditional business case

Figure 7-7. *Traditional Business Cases Use Optimistic Assumptions*

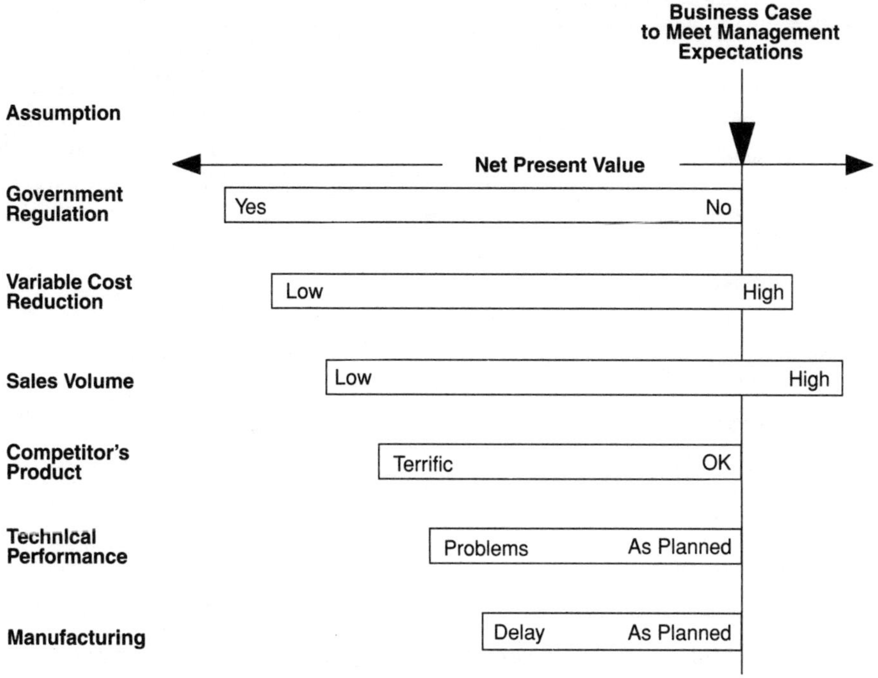

Source: "Description of DDP" (presentation given by the Strategic Decision Center, General Motors Corp., Detroit, Mich.). Reprinted by permission.

were actually shown, it would look something like Figure 7-7—quite damaging to the sales pitch. This is why it is seldom presented by the proposal's advocates. Suppressing the information, however, does nothing to change the underlying reality.

The adversarial approach to decision making provides few incentives for dealing openly with uncertainty and risk. If your role is that of advocate, bringing these to the surface is tantamount to handing ammunition to your adversaries, who will simply use it to point out your proposal's shortcomings. But this scenario is in sharp contrast with what we have been observing at GM after repeated use of the DDP. The nature of the shift is illustrated in Figure 7-8, which is a disguised representation of the tornado chart actually shown in a senior management review of a future product program.

Prior to the management review, a huge debate ensued within the decision team over whether or not to show this chart. The issue revolved

Figure 7-8. *Using the Tornado Diagram to Focus the Dialogue on Issues That Matter*

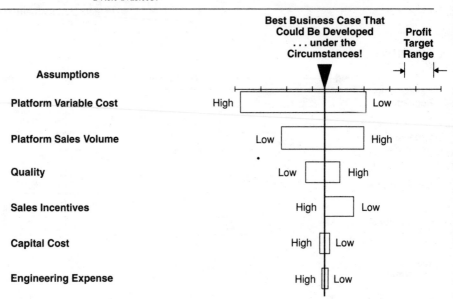

Source: "Description of DDP" (presentation given by the Strategic Decision Center, General Motors Corp., Detroit, Mich.). Reprinted by permission.

around how to handle the operational targets the program had been given by the financial organization. The team was convinced that the targets were at the upper end of their ranges of uncertainty, and they were nervous about surfacing this "bad news" in front of senior management. Some members argued for assuming that the targets would be met. "After all," they said, "these are the targets we have been given. To assume anything else would be in defiance of the management directives." Fortunately, the program manager had considerable experience with both the traditional process as well as the DDP. He argued that it would be dishonest to conceal the full truth of the situation.

The program manager presented this chart as a central part of his message to management, telling them that "based on the best assessments of the future, we do not think we will meet the profitability targets you have set for us in this program." To the surprise of the team (some of whom had expected to be fired or demoted on the spot), an important exchange ensued between senior management and the program manager. Senior

Figure 7-9. *Hybrid Solutions Present New Alternatives*

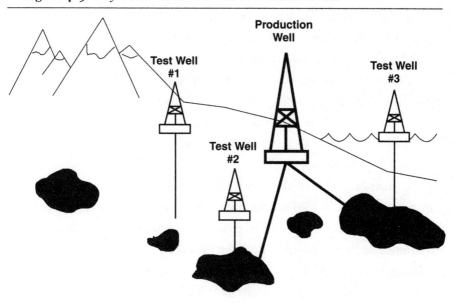

Source: "Description of DDP" (presentation given by the Strategic Decision Center, General Motors Corp., Detroit, Mich.). Reprinted by permission.

management asked him exactly what actions *they* could take to improve the chances of the program meeting its targets. The substance of that discussion is not germane here. What is important is that it took place at all. In an adversarial system, discussions about how to increase the value of a proposed course of action are extremely rare.

By making visible risk and uncertainty, the tornado diagram assists in surfacing the important issues early on and contributes to the organization's ability to focus attention on making improvements where they will do the most good.

Establishing connection

The dialogue that occurs during the connection stage of the DDP is potentially the most powerful. All of the shared insights born of systematic analysis of all the alternatives come together here in the form of two deliverables: (1) a new alternative (referred to at GM as the "hybrid"), which combines the best elements of each of the initial alternatives, and (2) the underlying rationale for the new alternative.

Returning to our oil-well analogy, the hybrid is equivalent to the production well (Figure 7-9). The important point about the production well is that it need not be sunk at any of the test-well locations. In general, insights generated by the test wells lead us to a much more valuable place to locate the expensive production well.

In the DDP, the fact that the hybrid solution is usually a new alternative is important on two accounts. First, the team expects to find a new, better alternative—one that will create a "win-win" situation (as distinct from "win-lose" in the traditional process). This is analogous to what Alfred Sloan referred to years earlier when he and his associates "averaged up."

The business value of these win-win, hybrid courses of action is difficult to overstate. At GM we have used the DDP in more than one hundred major decisions during the past eight years. In this wide range of experience with the process, we have observed GM people use it to systematically identify hybrid courses of action, which, on average, the teams believe will generate hundreds of millions of dollars in shareholder value over the values of the next most attractive alternatives considered. When stacked up against the cost of the resources required to engage in the process, these added-value increments make resources allocated to the DDP an investment with a significant payoff to the prospective bottom line.

The other core deliverable of the connection phase of the DDP, the articulation of the rationale underlying the hybrid, serves two important and related purposes. First and foremost, it serves as a unifying vision, one that integrates the conflicting points of view that exist within the problem frame and the initial alternatives. This rationale can be both simple and compelling. Individuals who come in at the end of the process and hear the rationale will often ask, "Why did it take you so long to come up with something so obvious?" When you hear a statement like this, you know you have nailed the problem: the solution makes intuitive sense to a wide range of individuals with conflicting perspectives on the business. As Russ Ackoff would say, they might not agree in principle, but they all believe this is the right action to take—under the circumstances. The unifying rationale for the hybrid also provides a powerful organizing principle. This approach naturally aligns the thousands of detailed decisions that have to be made in an internally consistent manner during implementation.

The dialogue decision process is an effective methodology when it comes to reaching such a unified vision, especially in the environment of multiple decision makers typical of the large corporation organized by function. It is key to unifying the knowledge that otherwise often gets trapped in various company silos. With the DDP, each function that has a hand in bringing the product to market can claim ownership of the product concept.

Case Study

The nature of the problems that the DDP overcomes is spelled out in the following case study, which represents a composite of several actual GM applications. In this study, the decision board is comparable to the decision makers in Figure 7-3, the management team comparable to the cross-functional decision team.

The chief executive officer of an energy resources enterprise had just called to order the fourth and final meeting of the decision board. The purpose of the meeting, he had been informed by his planning director, was to garner support from top functional corporate officers for a hybrid corporate strategy developed through the framing, alternatives, and analysis meetings in which both decision board and the management team had previously participated. The CEO thought to himself, "I'm impressed with Jones, our corporate planning director. Instead of developing the strategic direction and trying to get my management team to accept it, she's introduced a process that allows the team to develop the strategic direction, using experts from their functional areas. I was prepared to dictate direction, but it doesn't look like I'll have to."

The meeting began with a review of three "test-well" strategy alternatives developed by the management team. All agreed that they covered the full range of possible and realistic strategies:

- *Momentum*: Maintain current investments and allocations of capital over the next three to five years.
- *Strong base business*: Increase investment in the traditional areas of the business—generation and distribution of electricity and the distribution of natural gas.

- *Aggressive diversification:* Reduce investment in traditional, regulated businesses and diversify into similar unregulated ones.

As the alternatives were being reviewed, the CEO mused to himself, "It's amazing how we were able to get everyone's issues out on the table. Considering the alternatives as explorative test wells and not as positions of the various vested interests helped. Even more amazing is that we were able to get on with the strategy development once everyone felt that their views would be given a fair hearing." The CEO also felt good about the fact that each strategy alternative had been defined in terms of the resources and actions required from each functional area, making it easier for him to monitor implementation.

As the meeting progressed, one of the management team members explained that a hybrid strategy drawn from various test well strategies had 50 percent more value than the current momentum strategy. Analysis of the three alternative strategies indicated that no level of capital or resource allocation could make the gas business profitable in the future. The team agreed that reducing investment and perhaps selling the gas business would enhance future profitability. On the other hand, substantial investment increases in the electric generation and distribution business would show substantial returns. Everyone agreed with this analysis. Most important, the team's explanations as to how the expected returns would be achieved made sense to the entire group.

The team named the hybrid strategy "new directions" to highlight the substantial investment increase in the electric business that would be required; funding would come from investments diverted from the gas business or from funds gained by the sale of the regulated business. One of the decision board members who had favored the "strong base business" alternative because of its "stick to your knitting" philosophy interrupted the presentation. "Well, by 'strong base business' we didn't really mean to invest in unprofitable portions of the base business." Another decision board member and a proponent of diversification, in the spirit of the moment, also voiced support for the new directions strategy: "The 'aggressive diversification' alternative was a good 'test well' to gain understanding, but this hybrid seems like a good compromise. I guess it's not really a compromise; it's a superior strategy." "You know, this is really pretty obvious," responded another member of the decision board. "Sell off the parts of the base business that won't be profitable and use that money to diversify into more profitable unregulated businesses that are similar."

Now a management team member introduced a critical issue that had led to a previous conflict between the vice president of electric transmission and distribution and the vice president of customer service, both members of the decision board. The tree trimming that had helped to reduce electrical outages during storms was an enormous expense, but it went a long way toward curbing customer dissatisfaction over interrupted service. The team member pointed out that one element of the strong base business alternative, which was included in the new directions hybrid, was a 20 percent increase in the tree-trimming budget. Prior to this strategy development process, the vice president of customer service had strongly endorsed budget increases because they addressed the large number of outage complaints he dealt with. The vice president of transmission and distribution had argued, just as strongly, that the enterprise already trimmed more often, according to benchmark studies, than other utilities. "Enough is enough!"

The decision team recognized these strongly held points of view and commissioned the market research department to conduct a study to measure customer willingness to pay for outage-free service. The results indicated that, on average, each customer was willing to pay about $10 per year to eliminate all outages. The team had determined that the 20 percent increase in tree trimming would cost about $15 per customer in expenses and still would not eliminate all outages. The vice president of customer service, after hearing from his colleague on the management team that the results of the study could be trusted, commented, "If that's how the customers really feel, we shouldn't increase tree-trimming expenses. I must have been influenced by the fact that I hear only the complaints." He paused a moment and remarked to his colleagues, "You know, at some point we should investigate whether it would be smart to compensate only those customers who experience an outage with a $15 rebate."

At the meeting's conclusion, the decision board members expressed their appreciation to the management team for its work and to planning director Jones for introducing the new decision-making process to the enterprise. The CEO closed the meeting with the following comment: "I con-

Figure 7-10. *The DDP Enables Increases in Individual and Shared Knowledge*

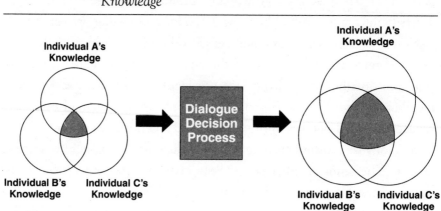

cur. The process has proven useful, but it is only a framework for decision making. It is our people who have improved the value of our business."

ORGANIZATIONAL LEARNING

The dialogue decision process has produced visible improvements in organizational learning leading to corresponding increases in organizational knowledge. As Figure 7-10 illustrates, the DDP is a powerful learning process on both individual and group levels. The increase in shared knowledge at GM, however, is the true source of the value increases we have witnessed. It is the increase in the shared component of knowledge that is breaking down the informational barriers that exist between our silos. The extent to which people in the organization can develop a shared understanding of our business is directly related to their ability to maintain a shared vision of how to coordinate their actions on behalf of the customers, the shareholders, and the community.

The disciplines advocated by Peter Senge are now in greater evidence at GM. The DDP has created, in effect, a microcosm of Senge's learning organization. It addresses Senge's concern that few tools "capture the dynamic complexity that confronts the management team when it seeks to craft new strategies, design new structures and operating policies, or plan significant organizational change."[7] During the years in which it has been practiced, the DDP has repeatedly demonstrated its ability to help teams understand internal contradictions in strategy, discern hidden opportunities, and discover untapped leverage—the desired capabilities of Senge's learning organization. The DDP is also compatible with systems thinking—one of Senge's five disciplines. This systems thinking begins with the dialogue decision process identifying the whole of the issue at hand, the scope of the decision required, and the systematic consideration given to each potential course of action.

The learning organization is, of course, always in a state of "becoming." Since learning must be continual, the learning organization never "arrives." In fact, the enterprise that believes it has arrived at some state of final knowledge is the one you should sell from your investment portfolio; it is only a matter of time before this enterprise finds itself outdated and outflanked by competitors who have continued to learn and develop new concepts.

As a device for ensuring continual learning, the DDP has proven highly effective at GM. Its repeated application in the domain of product development, for example, has enriched our understanding of early product concept decisions. It has also expanded learning about the hierarchy of decisions within the product development process. There is a growing understanding that product development decisions, along with upstream product portfolio decisions and downstream product execution decisions, are all part of a system—a *network* of market-based decisions.

Each application of the DDP helps us to learn more about our business. This learning not only informs the decision at hand but fosters the broad evolution of knowledge throughout the extended enterprise. Through the systematic use of the DDP, we are building the frameworks, mental models, and shared visions around which the larger enterprise can engage in dialogue. This, in effect, is building powerful connections between the separate business silos that GM has built up over the years.

CULTURAL CHANGE

One of the by-products of the repeated application of the DDP at GM has been a noticeable change in the management culture. There has been an observable shift away from a culture of advocative and adversarial interactions toward one that is more open and cooperative (see Figure 7-11).

Figure 7-11. *Contrast between Traditional Decision Making and the DDP*

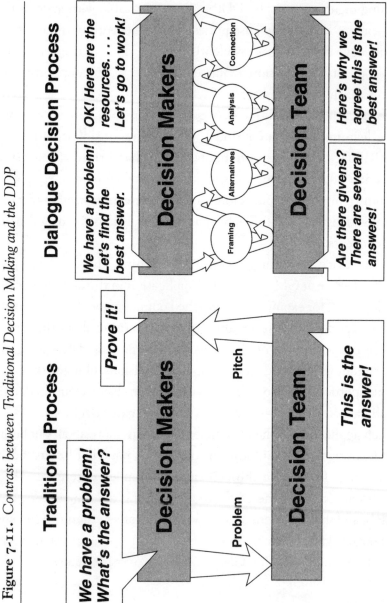

This effect was unexpected. Our objective was to change the way decisions were made, not to change the culture. But we have come to understand how intimately the two are linked. Much of the interpersonal conflict between managers stemmed from conflict over who got what resources and whose ideas were most instrumental in directing the destiny of the enterprise. Traditional, adversarial decision making only encouraged these conflicts. The DDP, on the other hand, encourages a win-win game.

The objective of the DDP is to create a shared vision from the best ideas drawn from diverse points of view. Our experience at GM indicates that this discipline is likely to:

- increase the chance of developing recommendations that will actually be implemented; and
- generate highly favorable benefits relative to the costs of its use.

Avoiding the Hammer-and-Nail Syndrome

Visualize a carpenter walking around a roughed-in house and suddenly noticing a nail not fully hammered down. One quick blow with a hammer and the problem is neatly solved. Since the hammer is in hand, the carpenter looks for more loose nails; after all, if one nail hadn't been fully hammered down, who is to say that others weren't. With a keen loose-nail-seeking sense, the carpenter expertly tracks and pounds many more nails. He becomes quite skilled at spotting loose nails and confident at wielding his hammer. Soon, however, no more loose nails remain. No matter; our carpenter can simply squint his eyes a bit and switch to pounding in loose screws, staples, and other hardware.

The same hammer-and-nail syndrome can plague new decision support tools and decision problems. Far too often, we try to force fit the problem at hand into a proven analytic process or framework. We squint at certain aspects of the problem to the point where we can almost see the answer, only further reinforcing the "correctness" of our analytic approach. The problem with successful analytic processes and frameworks is that we can become so accomplished at and accustomed to using them that we forget to consider whether they are appropriate for addressing the problem at hand. The true power of analytic processes and frameworks comes from our being cognizant of their weaknesses and shortcomings.

In this book, I have described the dialogue decision process and how it has been adapted from traditional decision analysis to its current form as a strategic business learning process. But I do not recommend blindly wielding a decision and risk analysis hammer—particularly during the *analysis* phase. At GM we have found it necessary to embed other analytical techniques, such as multiattribute utility technology (conjoint measurement), system dynamics modeling, linear programming, and so on, into DDP. As in any selection process, when choosing an analytical modeling frame, we must recognize not only what kind of answer that frame might include but just as important, what considerations or possible answers it will likely overlook. A system dynamics modeling approach, for example, will focus on aspects of the problem that vary over time but will be of less help in dealing with uncertainty, whereas a decision and risk-analysis approach will emphasize uncertainty but minimize time dynamics.

Ultimately, understanding the nature of a given problem should determine which analytical approach to take. At GM we are exploring the nature of problems in an organizational setting and how various analytical approaches might map to them. The framework presented in this book should be seen as a thinking tool that reminds us that the tools we select influence outcomes and that we need to consider using new approaches and tools as they are developed.

A FRAMEWORK FOR CONSIDERING ANALYTICAL APPROACHES TO DECISION PROCESSES

When examining a decision, one must consider both its organizational and its technical aspects. Organizational aspects include, but are not necessarily limited to, the number of decision makers (is there a single decision maker, or will multiple stakeholders allocate resources?), organizational complexity (how much cross-functional consideration does the problem entail?), shared vision (to what extent do the stakeholders share a vision of the problem and its linkage to the organization?), and the

Figure 7-12. *Problem-Solving Assessment Tool*

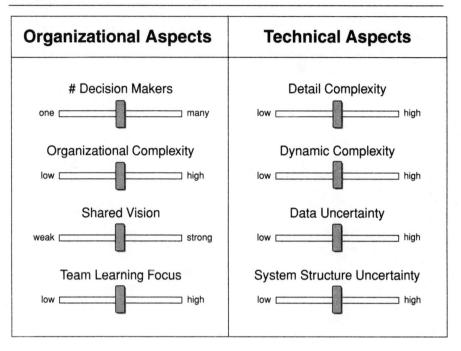

degree of a team-learning focus (is the emphasis solely on generating a solution, or is retaining organizational knowledge also important?). Technical aspects include, but again are not necessarily limited to, detail complexity (how broadly and deeply into the issues of the problem will the analysis probe?), dynamic complexity (how significant is the system behavior over time, and how interdependent are the issues across time and space?), data uncertainty (how much uncertainty exists in the data assessments?), and system structure uncertainty (how much uncertainty exists in the relationships of the problem structure?).

Figure 7-12 shows a problem-solving tool that aids in visualizing the nature of a decision problem.[8] Any problem can be assessed on these dimensions, and the slider positions (all shown in a neutral position here) can help indicate an appropriate decision process and analytical approach. The left panel dimensions (organizational aspects) indicate how formal and structured a decision process (such as DDP) might be necessary to arrive at an organizational solution. The right panel dimensions (technical aspects) indicate which analytical approach would be appropriate. In considering a corporate leasing strategy decision, for example,

Figure 7-13. *Leasing Strategy Problem*

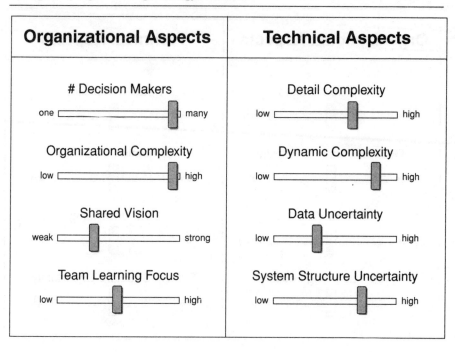

the project manager may assess the nature of the problem as represented in Figure 7-13. From an organizational perspective, the manager determines that many decision makers from a wide range of functional organizations will be involved, all of whom come to the issue with varying points of view. Based on this assessment, she chooses the structured discipline of a full-scale DDP, recognizing that the analytical approach must address the high level of dynamic complexity that would direct the decision team toward a dynamic modeling approach in designing the decision process. To take another example, a vehicle program manager might assess his decision problem as shown in Figure 7-14. Based on these results, the manager requests a customized DDP with emphasis on organizational learning, and a multiattribute utility technology using a conjoint measurements approach is designed into the decision process.

When the organizational aspects vary, GM modifies the DDP to match the needs of the decision team. Thus DDPs span the gamut from large-scale, analysis-intensive, multimonth projects to framing-intensive one-

Figure 7-14. *Vehicle Program Development Problem*

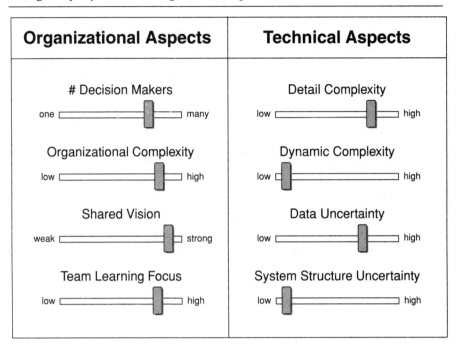

or two-day turbo-DDPs. Regarding the technical aspects, Figure 7-15 shows a starting point for considering analytical alternatives in the design of a decision process. Here, only those dimensions related to the technical aspects of the problem-solving assessment tool are listed. The position of each slider represents an *expected* level of the attribute for that analytic approach. (Although the settings are based on our experience, they are intended to be more illustrative than definitive.)

The systems structure uncertainty dimension attempts to capture the nature of the decision-making group's mental model of variable interrelationships. For example, if the group views the problem from a correlational perspective, it will likely find value in econometric approaches. If instead it sees problems from a probabilistic perspective, it will favor the decision analysis tools. Finally, if the decision makers view the problem as primarily operational, they will tend toward system dynamics modeling approaches.

From an organizational standpoint, the dialogue decision process has been a practical tool for realigning the enterprise on a horizontal basis.

Figure 7-15. *Technical Aspects of Alternative Approaches*

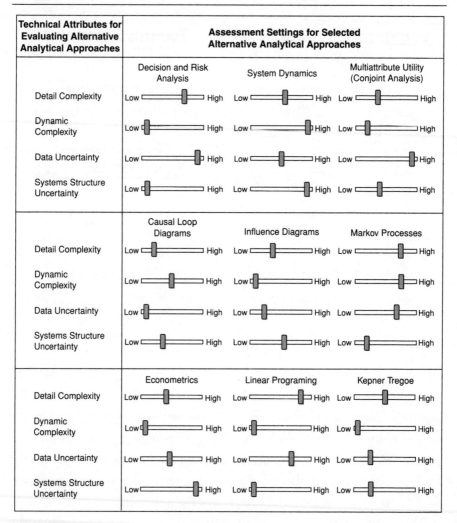

By putting individuals from different functions into project teams, by developing a common framework around which each may contribute, and by taking the best from each to form a new and superior concept, the process delivers many of the benefits of the horizontal organization while maintaining the deep knowledge of the vertically aligned, functional organization.

NOTES

1. Gordon W. Prange, *Miracle at Midway* (New York: McGraw-Hill, 1982).

2. Alfred Sloan, *My Years with General Motors*, ed. John McDonald, with Catherine Stevens (Garden City, N.Y.: Doubleday, 1964), 435.

3. Ronald A. Howard, "The Foundations of Decision Analysis," *IEEE Transactions on Systems Science and Cybernetics* SCC-4, no. 3 (1968): 211–219. See also Michael W. Kusnic and Daniel Owen, "The Unifying Vision Process: Value beyond Traditional Decision Analysis in Multiple-Decision-Maker Environments," *Interfaces* 22, no. 6 (November–December 1992): 150–166.

4. For a deeper understanding on procedures for surfacing and challenging assumptions, see Vincent P. Barabba, "Making Use of Methodologies Developed in Academia: Lessons from One Practitioner's Experience," in *Producing Useful Knowledge for Organizations*, ed. Ralph Kilmann et al. (New York: Praeger Publishers, 1983), 145; Richard O. Mason and Ian I. Mitroff, *Challenging Strategic Planning Assumptions* (New York: John Wiley & Sons, 1981); and Vincent P. Barabba, Richard O. Mason, and Ian I. Mitroff, "Federal Statistics in a Complex Environment: The Case of the 1980 Census," *American Statistician* 37, no. 3 (August 1983): 203.

5. C. S. Spetzler and C. S. Staël von Holstein, "Probability Encoding in Decision Analysis," *Management Science* 22, no. 3 (November 1975): 340–358.

6. Ronald A. Howard, "Information Value Theory," *IEEE Transactions on Systems Science and Cybernetics* SSC-2, no. 1 (August 1966): 22–26.

7. Peter M. Senge, *The Fifth Discipline: The Art and Practice of the Learning Organization* (New York: Doubleday, 1990), 315.

8. Much of the development of this problem-solving assessment tool has been done by Nick Pudar and Pam Pudar of GM.

8

WHAT MANAGEMENT
MUST DO

Without changing our patterns of thought, we will not be able to solve the problems we created with our current patterns of thought.
Albert Einstein

Earlier chapters provided a vision of the market-based enterprise. This chapter revisits that vision and indicates steps managers can take to make it a reality. But before we get into those prescriptions, we should look back briefly at the key ideas just covered—listen, learn, and lead—and consider the challenge they pose to senior management.

Fire! Ready! Aim!

The Western mind has always been concerned with categorizing things. It was, after all, Western science that gave use the taxonomy of animals and plants and Western religion that divided the universe into the clearly bounded spaces of hell, purgatory, earth, and heaven. It should be no surprise, then, that the West gave us a corporate universe of marketing, finance, engineering, and the like.

This same mode of thinking likes to place things in logical sequences. "You have to learn to walk before you run, crawl before you walk." Managers, whose duties include planning, are no less interested in the right order of activities. That is why the title of this section—"Fire! Ready! Aim!"—is anathema to so many. It is the wrong sequence. To a field artillerist, however, it makes plenty of sense. First you fire in the general direction of the target, observe the location of the impact, and adjust the next shot (aim) based on the knowledge gained from the first impact.

The earliest theorist of the quality movement, Walter Shewhart, offered a similar thought in his now-famous "Shewhart Cycle," shown in Figure

Figure 8-1. *The Shewhart Cycle*

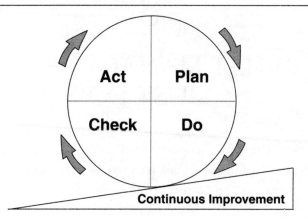

8-1. Here there is a continuing cycle of "plan," "do," "check," and "act"—or, depending where you start, "act," "plan," "do," and "check." Again, the implication is that actions create results from which we learn. And based on that knowledge, we do something else—hopefully something better. Or in Bacon's terms, knowledge gives us the power to make good things happen. This is the basis of continuous improvement. Likewise, there is no strict order to be observed in listening, learning, and leading. Yes, we learn by listening (and observing), and we lead (make decisions) in response to what we've learned. But we also learn from the decisions made in the process of leading and from the results of those decisions.

Managers, then, should not be overly concerned with the order in which things happen but should put their faith in the dynamism of the market-based enterprise and its ability to grow and improve. What managers should be concerned with are the organizational and behavioral constraints on that dynamism. These constraints are the negative aspects of functional silos, barriers to the free flow of information, and the tendency of influential departments or individuals to muzzle the voice of the market. In creating the market-based enterprise, management must create an environment in which these constraints are either eliminated or held at bay.

CONNECT THE SILOS

The corporate makeover that enables an enterprise to listen, learn, and lead through a market-based decision-making network, as described in the last several chapters, may be accomplished via painful restructuring (the "horizontal organization"), knowledge and activity integration, or some combination of these two.

Reshaping the enterprise from vertical to horizontal typically eliminates layers of management and control, allows information to flow more freely, and puts decision making closer to the customer and to the task at hand. As discussed in earlier chapters, however, the jury remains out with respect to this form of reorganization, especially in large industrial firms. Organization by function did not happen by chance, and it has not persisted over the decades because of mindless inertia. The functional organization persists despite obvious shortcomings because each of the various functions provides a space in which the core capabilities of the organization can develop and flourish. These functions encourage and nurture the specialized expertise that all large enterprises require. The challenge of managers is to retain the benefits of functional organization while ameliorating its deficiencies—namely, getting the specialized knowledge out of the silos so that it can be shared by all concerned.

The process of breaking the enterprise apart and putting it back together is fraught with unknowns. Things that look good on paper do not always work out in practice. General Motors, like other enterprises, has gone through two major reshufflings over the last dozen years; in neither case has the outcome produced the intended results. This kind of disappointment with reorganization is more the rule than the exception in modern business. The only certainty is that pain and anxiety will persist during and after the period of reorganization planning and execution. Not that pain and anxiety are entirely bad; they go with change and progress. But during these periods of stress, managers and workers spend less time engaging in activities that create "value" and more time figuring out what will happen to their jobs, who they will work for, how they will fit in, and various other self-protecting behaviors. The 1984 reshuffling at GM had just this effect, and in the end the corporation was not much better off.

In the final analysis, major reorganizations by and large attempt to rationalize functional activities, not to facilitate the listening, learning, and leading activities recommended in this book. Large corporations reorganize to improve manufacturing efficiencies, to consolidate back-office activities, and to lower overhead. So to get to market-based decision making, connecting the silos in terms of communications is the most practical approach. This can be accomplished through activity integration. The dialogue decision process described in Chapter 7 is an important tool management can use to break down the informational barriers between silos. Furthermore, it addresses directly the thorniest issues of implementing the marketing concept of sense and respond:

- achieving synergistic results from the behavior of empowered functional employees, who are intimately involved from the beginning; and
- understanding which market signals can improve the customer value of the enterprise's offerings.

Activity integration and improved information flow can be accomplished in traditionally organized enterprises through the establishment of permanent or shorter-term project teams and the decision-making discipline described in Chapter 7. Indeed, for many established enterprises, a hybrid functional form—one that preserves the strengths of the traditional silo organization and adds those of the horizontal organization— may be the best solution. Here, strong functional groups provide a solid base on which special project teams can be formed. But management must support the relative independence and decision-making power of these teams—something many top managers have trouble doing.

ENSURE THE FREE FLOW OF INFORMATION

The free movement of information between the marketplace and the enterprise—and within the enterprise itself—is the force that sustains the principles of listen, learn, and lead. Like a cardiologist with an angiogram, management must examine the organization to find blockages to the free flow of information. Externally, these blockages may exist in any number of forms:

- inadequate or passive market research capabilities;
- intermediaries that stand between the customer and the entire enterprise;
- lack of direct feedback mechanisms between customers, suppliers, distributors, and the enterprise; and

- information systems that fail to detect and properly classify data coming from the marketplace.

Internally, information blockages are usually found between the functional silos. Silos are much better at designing information systems that serve their own needs than at designing systems that circulate information to other areas.

Most concerns with information naturally circle around the idea of "systems." While systems are important, never forget that people run these systems and that barriers to the free flow of information more often than not involve people. If we recognize that information is a valuable asset, then we should not be surprised that people will want to possess and control it. Among the ancient Mayas, the priesthood controlled information about the changing seasons. They alone knew when it was time to plant and to harvest. Control of this vital information gave them control over the agrarian society in which they lived. Most corporations, too, have information priesthoods, and their control of vital information invests them with status and organizational power. It shouldn't be surprising that some information handlers feel threatened when senior managers go looking for ways to free up the movement of information within the enterprise. As Tom Davenport reminds us, "If information is power and money, people won't share it easily."[1]

Yet this sharing is an absolute requirement of the market-based enterprise, and so management must drive the information priest from the temple, so to speak. Information handlers have an important and honorable place in this enterprise, but they cannot stand between employees and the accumulated information and knowledge of the organization. There can be no keepers of enterprise information. There can be only stewards. Information stewards act as facilitators and as coaches for others in finding and using the right information and in developing enterprise knowledge. They represent the nervous system of knowledge in the enterprise.

PRESERVE THE INDEPENDENCE OF THE "VOICE OF THE MARKET"

If the information handler cannot be allowed to control information and access to it, neither should any single function be the sole owner of the customer and of the marketplace of suppliers and competitors—what we have called the "voice of the market." No single authority should act as the official conduit for the voice of the market or represent it to others in the organization. Every function, team, and individual employee should have access to market information and the ability to develop an independent view of what the market is saying. When this happens, the enterprise develops a richer set of insights about products and services, competitors, pricing, and so forth.

ORCHESTRATE THE MANY VOICES WITHIN THE COMPANY

Management theorists tout the idea that a key function of leadership is to provide a vision that the organization can accept and follow. As generally presented, this idea is incomplete. Taken too seriously, it is downright dangerous in its implication that one person at the top has the vision to guide the organization to the Promised Land. Lao Tsu said it well more than two millennia ago: "To lead the people, walk behind them." Nehru also understood: "I must go now, for there go my people, and I am their leader."

The role of leadership is not to impose a vision or the leader's own "voice" but to draw out the best of the many visions and voices that already exist in scattered parts of the enterprise. This is particularly true in complex, multidivisional enterprises. As we saw in earlier chapters, the enterprise has many competing voices. It is from this rich and sometimes discordant diversity of sound that the truly wise senior executive must orchestrate a harmonious "voice of the enterprise," which is superior to any one of the competing voices. This challenging executive task can be addressed with the assistance of a powerful tool: the dialogue decision process.

CHANGE THE DECISION-MAKING PROCESS AND CULTURAL CHANGE WILL FOLLOW

Today, most senior executives are interested in reengineering, reorganizing, and reshaping the corporate culture as means of improving coordination in customer services. These may be the least efficient and most difficult approaches to solving the problem.

If there is one thing we've learned from managers at other enterprises like Hewlett-Packard and Procter & Gamble, it is that the most effective way to create a market-based enterprise is to institute a market-based decision network. Many corporations make the mistake of altering the organizational chart or of trying to change the corporate culture. In the end, these efforts are expensive, painful, and usually doomed to failure. It is my belief, based on the experiences referenced in this book, that when decision making is considered as a process—which can be improved—decision making can also be considered a core competency. The decision-making process is what really defines the enterprise. Change it by adopting a process that embodies the principles of the dialogue decision process or Senge's five disciplines or Ackoff's circular organization, for instance, and the rest will follow.

In the command-and-control model, decisions are made at the top and passed down for execution. This process defines the rules and relationships—that is, both the shape and the prevailing culture—of the organization. The decision-making process recommended in this book draws the insights of the organization to it like a magnet. It creates an operational link between higher and lower levels and between different functional groups. A much different culture forms around these linkages.

So if you want cultural change to come about—and to stick—stop fiddling with the organizational chart and start changing the decision-making process.

Move the Enterprise from Data to Decisions

The business of gathering information, learning, and creating knowledge is inherently and seductively rewarding, but it creates no value for the enterprise or its customers until that information, learning, and knowledge find their way to decisions that compel action.

A tremendous amount of resources can be expended in gathering data. Some staff people could happily spend their entire careers categorizing and analyzing these data and then writing them up into reports. In the absence of clear orders to the contrary, both things will happen. The job of management is to create a sense of urgency, making it clear that the only point of these data-gathering and learning activities is to provide the intellectual content for effective decision making. For their part, decision makers must understand that every issue has a time line within which action must occur. The enterprise cannot wait until the nth degree of uncertainty is eliminated before making a decision.

Move from Marketing as a Function to Marketing as a State of Mind

Most textbooks describe marketing as *the* communication link between the customer and the company. Given this description, we can almost picture a hand radiant with light reaching down from the corporate cloud and touching the outstretched hand of a customer. Energy passes between them. Miraculously, the company now understands the customer and the customer understands the company thanks to this communication link. And the marketing department makes it all possible.

This may be how some marketing professors would like their students to understand the role of marketing, though they might describe more concrete means of communication, indicating that customers signal their needs in various ways and that companies signal their capabilities in other ways—through products, pricing, various promotional messages, service guarantees, and so on. In either case, these professors identify the communication link as being owned and controlled by marketing. This is a limited and outdated view in one respect. Marketing may be the link, but the marketing *organization* should not control it. Just as war is too important to be left to the generals, marketing is too important and too universal to be left to the marketing organization—indeed, to any single function. The communication link that defines marketing must be seen as everyone's responsibility.

Fred E. Webster, Jr., once wrote that

> From a philosophical point of view, marketing . . . should be a focus for everyone in the organization, not a separate department. Marketing in many companies has been "pushed out" into the operating units of the business, especially in those companies that are consciously "dis-

integrating" their organizations. . . . I think that marketing as a stand-
alone function in the typical organization will become extremely rare.[2]

Webster here echoes what Peter Drucker and other sages of modern business have advocated for years—that marketing must become everyone's
business. Of the many things that "management should do," making marketing everyone's business should be a top priority.

We can rephrase Vince Lombardi's actual quote, referenced in the Introduction, with Drucker's marketing concept as follows: "Marketing activities as a way of doing things isn't everything; marketing as an extended enterprise state of mind that seeks improved customer and
enterprise value is everything. In fact, it's the only thing!"

DEVELOP A KNOWLEDGE-USE NETWORK

Last on our management "to do" list is the creation of a functioning
network for the development and transfer of knowledge both between
the outside world and the enterprise and within the enterprise itself. The
whole point of this development and transfer is to put knowledge to work
in making good things happen for the customer and for the enterprise.

In addition to the opening quote in Chapter 6, C. West Churchman
also wrote, "To conceive of knowledge as a collection of information
seems to rob the concept of all its life. Knowledge is a vital force."[3] This
statement goes to the heart of what we propose in this section. The problem we face in making knowledge a vital force in our decision-making
processes is that most of the information we use is merely an abstraction,
a "reflection" of the reality we hope to know. The statistical data that
most decision making relies on, for example, represent just a small piece
of the reality from which we "infer" a larger picture. When dealers,
customers, and suppliers talk to us, we hear just a few voices in a
larger crowd. In studying our competitors' products, we are examining
historical artifacts—what our competitors' designed and built sometime
in the past, not necessarily what they are designing or building at
this moment.

The problem of "knowing," of differentiating reality from its manifes-
tations, has puzzled thinkers since ancient times. In the *Republic*, Plato
gives us the allegory of the cave, in which human knowledge is likened

to the shadows—reflections of reality—that play on the walls of the cave as people and objects pass between the walls and the light. As Plato tells us through Socrates, "The forms which these people draw or make ... are converted by them into images. But they are really seeking to behold the things themselves, which can only be seen with the eye of the mind."[4]

Modern business decision makers likewise seek to know "the things themselves." But while they strive to move closer to reality, their knowledge is based on the images and reflections they see. The traditional systems that support decision making with information can, like the cave images, provide no more than a reflection of market reality. What decision makers need is a system that allows them to get still closer to reality. The dialogue decision process described in Chapter 7 is an example of a way of thinking and deciding that contributes to such a system.

At General Motors, we have been developing a process to bring the many and varied parts of the organization closer to the reality of the market. What we are creating could be called a knowledge-use network; our purpose is to enhance individual and group capabilities to learn and to generate the knowledge needed to make market-based decisions.[5] A knowledge-use network should be designed and dedicated to the learning process, to the development and distribution of information and knowledge, and to the practice of helping managers move beyond facts and analysis to decision making that incorporates a broader understanding of the market.

To ensure objectivity and the incorporation of broad-ranging interests, the knowledge-use network should be kept organizationally independent. Thus, it cannot be part of the market research department, which is usually an appendage of the marketing organization and its particular interests. Ideally, it should exist as a "nonentity"—as its name implies, a network. As such, it should exist within the appropriate boxes in the organizational chart and in the gray areas between and surrounding them. Networks, as we define them, form connections within and between functional activities, whether they are vertical or horizontal. The knowledge-use network, then, acts as a conduit for the transfer of knowledge from one node of corporate activity to another, facilitating the shared learning described in Chapter 6 and providing decision makers in all areas of the enterprise with the raw materials from which to make market-based decisions.

The development of a knowledge-use network will require new thinking in the information systems community. Fortunately, some of this thinking has already begun. Research conducted by the CSC Index Foundation forecasts a basic shift from domination by applications in today's corporate software portfolio to more effort and development in the enterprise infrastructure (operating systems, data base management, electronic mail facilities, etc.). This will be accomplished by pushing software functionality from the applications to the infrastructure, where it will be readily available for multiple users.[6]

A knowledge-use network, unlike Plato's allegory of the cave, a physical entity with floors, walls, and ceilings, should instead have the thinking and doing dimensions of logic, creativity, and consensus development. Each of these dimensions should be equipped with all the important tools of learning: statistical inference, economic forecasting, and so forth in the *logical dimension*; brainstorming, scenario planning, and envisioning in the *creativity dimension*; and groupware, Delphi, and other tools in the *consensus dimension*. The knowledge-use network should also be the home for processes operating in all three dimensions, such as the influence diagram, the strategy table, and—of course—the continued development and facilitation of processes like the dialogue decision process.

Finally, the knowledge-use network, in whatever form, should act as the binding agent for the activities of listening, learning, and leading—ensuring that each is done well, that each informs the other, and that every operating unit of the enterprise follows these processes in a systematic way.

At this writing, the knowledge-use network at General Motors is in its formative stage, although a broader outline is now emerging. Elements of the network now exist within operating groups and technical centers, providing analytical capabilities and support as well as assisting others in "thinking through" new concepts and strategies using relevant information sets and a range of methodologies, including the dialogue decision process. Eventually, this network will be the vehicle for disseminating practical know-how in the use of the DDP throughout General Motors.

At the core of the network will be a set of principles related to knowledge use. The principles, though not fully articulated at General Motors, might look something like this:

> Only when *data* are put into *context*, to make meaning clear or relevant to the current use, do they become *information*. If we do not know what data mean in context, they are uninformative. All *data* are not incorporated into information; they are incorporated when they are deemed relevant by those who will make decisions.
>
> The manner in which data are put into context will strongly determine the way in which the information can be. The decision team, by drawing *inferences* about how the information relates to a specific issue or decision, can *certify* information as *intelligence*.[7]
>
> To be intelligence the information must be:

- *clear* because it is understandable by those who must use it;
- *timely* because it gets to them when they need it;
- *reliable* because diverse observers using the same procedures should see it in the same way (although they may draw different conclusions);
- *valid* because it is cast in the form of concepts and measures that can capture congruence with established knowledge or independent sources.[8]

It is in the generation of intelligence that policy makers and information providers work jointly to ensure that their inferences from information are shared and that the intelligence has been sufficiently analyzed and reviewed to be certified as a *knowledge state*. To move from intelligence to a knowledge state, all involved decision makers and the information providers warrant the intelligence as certified; it is what they believe to be true from their decision-focused analysis.

Knowledge is then synthesized by the decision-makers and connected through a common set of processes to the broader system and the eventual *wisdom* and *understanding* of the enterprise.[9]

A Benchmarking Parallel

One interesting and successful parallel to the knowledge-use network concept proposed here is the network of benchmarking expertise that is now part of Xerox Corporation.[10] Beginning in the early 1980s, Xerox began developing a systematic approach to benchmarking its business processes and products to those of world-class enterprises in its own and other industries. Over a period of years, a practical methodology was developed by Xerox personnel and outside consultants, and this was codified in a booklet—"The Little Tan Book" as it's called around Xerox—and given to most employees.

Today, although benchmarking is not the only thing done at Xerox, it is one thing that is a fact of life throughout Xerox. All large operating units have personnel dedicated to training and assisting others in benchmarking studies; small units typically have a benchmarking "resource person" who fills the same role as a part-time responsibility. All employees with a strong interest in benchmarking share learning and new methods through periodic meetings and a benchmarking newsletter.

On the Xerox organizational chart, this network of benchmarking know-how and activity is essentially transparent. But it's there just the same, as a vibrant force for keeping the corporation's products and processes competitive with the best in its industry. The goal of this book is to encourage the development of a similarly vibrant and growing network for knowledge use at other enterprises within the next few years.

A core of market knowledge

Xerox provides yet another example of how a knowledge-use network can aid market-based decision making, in this case as a bedrock of core market knowledge on which narrowly focused market studies can be built. When I joined Xerox in 1976, the firm was struggling with the possibility that it would be significantly challenged in the marketplace for the first time. Xerox had literally owned the copier business, but this was changing as new foreign and domestic competitors entered the field. In view of this development, the company needed a much broader understanding of its market and customers.

While Xerox had some of the very best market researchers in the country, its depth of market knowledge was surprisingly shallow. This was essentially a result of the uncoordinated and unrelated studies the researchers were asked to conduct. Researchers were typically directed to answer narrowly construed questions about product features, particular segments, the purchase decision process, and so forth. These provided important bits and pieces of market information, but, like disconnected pieces of a jigsaw puzzle, they failed to form a coherent picture of the total copier market. With no common base of market information to draw from, these studies were both time consuming and expensive. Until 1978, Xerox had never, in fact, measured the entire market. After all, if you believed you *were* the market, why would you spend the resources to learn about anything beyond your own data base, which was created in a relatively inexpensive way from daily company sales transactions. Because Xerox lacked this broader understanding of the entire market, however, it could not gauge the pace of market change or the incursion of competition. Worse, each new study added only a small increment to the company's broader knowledge of its market. Had these been built on a solid base of broad market knowledge, each study would have provided the company with greater knowledge returns.

In 1978, we conducted a study of the entire copier market. Working from this bedrock of market knowledge, subsequent research—even studies that focused narrowly on quality, competitive performance, and individual rivals—incrementally added more information. The company obtained a higher payoff from the time, money, and effort it put into research.

What we learned from this experience at Xerox is that the most effective approach to creating market knowledge is to create a core of organizational knowledge that serves broader, decision-based, information requirements and to build on that base with a series of coordinated studies focused on specific information needs.

Both the benchmarking network and core of market knowledge examples should stimulate our thinking about developing knowledge-use networks. The idea of having a common core of knowledge to serve the requirements of market-based decision making is a powerful idea that is becoming a reality as the Information Age takes shape.

CREATING CHANGE

For the most part, effective management at the top has less to do with handing down directives than with creating and preserving an environment in which the "virtues" that lead to market success can flourish.

Nevertheless, there are occasions when direct and forceful action by top management is critical. One of these occasions is when an important innovation must be introduced and disseminated throughout the enterprise. The market-based decision network described in this book represents this type of innovation, and executive action is required to help it develop and to embed it into the fabric of corporate operations.

Previous experience in three large corporations, a large government agency, and many political campaigns has led me to the belief that there are (at least) seven key questions to answer before attempting to introduce a change or innovation to an organization. The first two are megaquestions:

1. Have top managers agreed on the need for the change?

2. Has a specific person or group been given both the responsibility and the authority to make the change happen?

    A no answer to either of these questions indicates that the change has little chance of successful implementation. Yes answers invite us to proceed.

3. Who has participated in planning for the change and who has not?

    Little will be gained if the parties affected by the change have not been consulted or asked for their input. The change itself may be flawed in that the people closest to the issue were not solicited for their knowledge or insight. Also, not having been consulted, their natural inclination may be to resist the "imposed" change.

4. What, if anything, does the change modify or replace, and how will personnel make the transition from the old to the new?

    Nearly every change implies the discontinuance of some way of thinking and behaving. That is why change is discomforting. Generally, change is from the known to the unknown, causing fear and a desire to hold onto current practices—the same fear that prompted Hamlet to say that we prefer to "accept those ills we have, than fly to others we know not of."

    A change in the software used to analyze and present data, for example, may require changes in how managers access and interpret data. They may have to reduce their reliance on data specialists and do more of their own analysis. The change agent must design ways to assist employees in the transition from prior ways of thought and behavior to the new.

The fifth and sixth questions are two sides of the same coin.

5. Who will benefit immediately from the change and who will benefit in the long term?

6. Who will suffer immediately and who will suffer over the long run?

When change in the status quo creates losers, resistance follows as night follows day. Machiavelli recognized this when he warned that "the reformer has enemies in all who profit by the old order." Some people may suffer initially, but benefit over the longer term. For others, it may be the reverse. For example, when an innovation in the data-tabulating system was introduced to the U.S. Census Bureau, many employees believed it would eventually diminish their status and possibly jeopardize the job security of certain programming managers, even though as trainers in the use of the new system their importance to the organization was initially enhanced.

7. How will the change affect major relationships in the organization?

Changes, both technological and organizational, typically alter job relationships as well as social and informal contacts. Many years ago, Harvard University's Paul Lawrence remarked that the resistance of workers to change was more often motivated by the altered social arrangements that the change would provoke than by the change itself.

The success of the effort to institute change relates to the extent to which you can answer each of the above questions and the way in which you deal with those answers.

THE CHALLENGE OF THE ADOPTION AND DIFFUSION OF AN INNOVATION

Assuming that you can answer and deal effectively with each of the seven questions listed above, you will need to assess the difficulty involved in adopting a market-based decision-making process—or any business improvement initiative. Based on my personal work experiences and on ideas drawn from the works of Everett Rogers, I have developed the following framework for assessing the level of that challenge.

Table 8-1 shows the framework in a modified scenario table. The scenario table identifies two dimensions of concern for the change agent: the *scope of the problem* and the *perceived attributes* of the change that affect its potential for adoption by the enterprise. Let us consider each dimension in turn.

Scope of the problem

Three categories describe the scope of the problem:

1. *Clarity of the problem*: There is a range of clarity as to the problem and the decision makers. On the one extreme is a clearly defined problem with accessible decision makers—those who allocate resources (1); on the other is an ill-defined problem (our "messy" problems again!) and inaccessible decision makers (3). The term *inaccessible* here means that the decision makers will not be personally involved in the problem's solution.

2. *Organizational complexity*: This is a measure of complexity as determined by the number of functional units (silos) affected and the identity of decision makers.

3. *Importance of the decision*: Here the three alternatives range from those having an impact on a single function to those that represent "betting the company."

Perceived attributes

The perceived attributes are those qualities of the change that will have an impact on how readily the proposed change will be adopted by the organization.[11] These include the following:

1. *Relative advantage*: This dimension spells out how the change is perceived in terms of its impact on profitability.

2. *Ease of application*: This dimension asks how easy or difficult the change will be to apply within the organization.

3. *Consistency with existing processes*: Every organization has ways of doing things—processes and procedures. The proposed change

Table 8-1. *Scenario Table for Assessing the Difficulty of Change*

Scope of Problem			Perceived Attributes of Change			
Clarity of the Problem Frame	Organizational Complexity	Importance of Decision	Ability to Demonstrate Relative Advantage	Ability to Demonstrate Ease of Application	Consistency with Existing Processes	Application Perceived as Trial or Commitment to Change
1 Clear alternatives and identified boundary around the problem. Accessible decision makers	1 Clearly within one silo. Clarity as to who decision makers are, who allocates resources	1 Important decision within a silo	1 Low impact	1 Appears easy	1 Appears consistent	1 Definitely a trial
2 Ill-defined problem with accessible decision makers	2 Clearly identified, multiple decision makers	2 Important decision to the company	2 Medium impact	2 Some difficulty	2 Needs modification	2 The beginning of change
3 Ill-defined, "messy" situation. Inaccessible decision makers	3 Problem is across silos. Not clear who decision makers are, who allocates resources	3 "We're betting the company!"	3 Significant impact	3 Appears complex	3 Needs fundamental change	3 A commitment to change

may appear to be either consistent or inconsistent with these existing processes.

4. *Perceived as a trial or a commitment to change*: This category alerts participants as to whether the proposed change is a first, experimental step or a full commitment to a new way of doing things.

With these dimensions understood, we can evaluate the degree of difficulty involved in adopting a change. If the change is to introduce a market-based decision network, the subject of this book, we would consider just what that change would entail for the existing enterprise and how the affected parties would perceive the change. Let's consider an example using this framework.

Table 8-2 depicts this framework as it would apply to a hypothetical case. In this case, assume that you intend to introduce a market-based decision-making process to your company. Because the effort is important and of interest, management is committed to participating. But because the problem cuts across functional boundaries, with little clarity as to where the change begins and where it ends, it is not clear who will allocate the resources necessary to get the job done nor who should participate. Under the "importance of decision" column, we can see that implementing our new decision-making process is not a "bet the company" proposition, but it is an important decision. In essence, we have an important, ill-defined issue with willing and accessible decision makers, but no clear indication as to who should participate.

We have now determined the scope of the problem of introducing a market-based decision network. (*Note*: At this point it would be prudent to discuss with management whether we should continue to develop this effort across silos or whether it might be more appropriate to start out in one department or at most two departments that work well together.)

Given the alternatives identified in the scope of the problem, we must then consider the perceptions that our change initiative will generate among the relevant individuals in the organization. What are the factors that determine whether the change is adopted and diffused or simply stonewalled? First, people will ask: "What is the advantage of this change

Table 8-2. *Case Study on Assessing the Impact of Change*

Scope of Problem			Perceived Attributes of Change			
Clarity of the Problem Frame	Organizational Complexity	Importance of Decision	Ability to Demonstrate Relative Advantage	Ability to Demonstrate Ease of Application	Consistency with Existing Processes	Application Perceived as Trial or Commitment to Change
1 — Clear alternatives and identified boundary around the problem. Accessible decision makers	1 — Clearly within one silo. Clarity as to who decision makers are, who allocates resources	1 — Important decision within a silo	1 — Low impact	1 — Appears easy	1 — Appears consistent	1 — Definitely a trial
2 — Ill-defined problem with accessible decision makers	2 — Clearly identified, multiple decision makers	2 — Important decision to the company	2 — Medium impact	2 — Some difficulty	2 — Needs modification	2 — The beginning of change
3 — Ill-defined, "messy" situation. Inaccessible decision makers	3 — Problem is across silos. Not clear who decision makers are, who allocates resources	3 — "We're betting the company!"	3 — Significant impact	3 — Appears complex	3 — Needs fundamental change	3 — A commitment to change

relative to profits?" In our example, we estimate that it will have a medium impact on profits.

"How easy will it be to apply the proposed change?" is the second question. Here we estimate that the application will be difficult.

"How consistent is the change with existing processes?" is the third question. We determine in this case that the change will be sufficiently inconsistent with current processes and that some modifications will be required.

Finally, we ask if the change will be perceived as a trial, a full-blown commitment, or something in between these extremes. In this instance, given the comprehensiveness of the activity and management's participation, we estimate that the affected individuals will perceive the change as representing a true commitment.

Having defined both the scope of the problem and the way its adoption will be perceived by others in the organization, we are in a much better position to estimate (1) the potential for success in getting our market-based decision network adopted, and (2) the level of resources and management commitment needed for success. If the assessment is made that we do not have adequate resources or that this is a bad time to increase anxiety in the organization, the strategy table offers a visible set of alternative actions to deal with those issues.

Ultimately, the secrets for making change happen have less to do with management and more to do with the timeless craft of leadership. Simply put, leaders provide a vision that others cannot see unaided; leaders help others see how that vision advances their own self-interest; and leaders act in ways that are consistent with that vision. These are things that cannot be taught in the classroom, or even in books like this, but they are nonetheless critical to the change from the traditional enterprise to one in which decisions are based on a deep understanding of internal capability and customer values as well as an appreciation of the uncertainty present in our understanding of both.

CONCLUSION

Years ago, when operating managers asked me to conduct market research on specific subjects, I used to tell them this: "I can get it to you fast, accurate, or cheap—pick any two!" In fact, "accurate and cheap" was not a viable alternative. Working in an environment that lacked a core of broad market knowledge and in which existing knowledge was difficult to share across functions, I came to believe that this response was acceptable—the best that we could expect.

Having had the benefit of working with knowledge users who were willing to invest time and money to anticipate information gaps, I have profoundly changed my point of view. If those who provide information anticipate the needs of their manager-clients through attentive *listening*, if they develop a core of broad market knowledge through *learning* (as in the Xerox example just cited), and if they develop effective business processes for serving their manager-clients (*leading*), then they—like the Pharaoh's carpenter who learned he could make paneled chests that were strong, attractive, and free of cracks—can say more than "pick any two." They can say, "I can give it to you fast enough, accurate enough, and at a price you will value."

Information providers are a microcosm of the market-based enterprise many managers hope to create. We must all follow the injunction to *listen* to both our customers and the community in which they live, we must *learn* to relate that knowledge to what the enterprise is capable of doing and willing to do, and we must then *lead* by ensuring that everyone in the enterprise knows it is his or her job to use both forms of knowledge—"what's going on out there" and "how do we do things around here"[12]—to sense and respond in creating and satisfying more customers better than the competition. The uncertain future we all face demands that those who will be successful develop the ability to listen, learn, and lead as they attempt to bring the customer, the community, and the enterprise to a meeting of the minds.

NOTES

1. Thomas H. Davenport, "Saving IT's Soul: Human-Centered Information Management," *Harvard Business Review*, March–April 1994, 122.

2. Frederick E. Webster, Jr., *It's 1990—Do You Know Where Your Marketing Is?* Report No. 89-123 (Cambridge, Mass.: Marketing Science Institute, December 1989), 6.

3. C. West Churchman, *The Design of Inquiring Organization Systems: Basic Concepts of Systems and Organization* (New York: Basic Books, 1971), 10.

4. Plato, *The Republic*, Book 7, trans. and ed. R. W. Sterling and W. C. Scott (New York: Norton, 1985).

5. The knowledge-use network is a conceptual descendent of the "inquiry center" proposed by Vincent P. Barabba and Gerald Zaltman in *Hearing the Voice of the Market* (Boston: Harvard Business School Press, 1990).

6. According to the CSC report:

> In response to competitive pressures, business executives now seek new forms of information. They need forecasts as well as historic information for techniques such as planning by scenario. They demand external as well as internal information for comparing the organization against market or international trends—and they need access to soft as well as hard data for marketing and planning decisions. In the new information infrastructure, information sources and servers are independent of applications, so new information sources can quickly be added to existing applications. At the same time, the way in which information is integrated from multiple sources, analyzed, and then presented, is very much in the control of the users.

See *Building the New Information Infrastructure: Final Report 91* (Cambridge, Mass.: CSC Index, July 1993), 4–5.

7. Drawn from the combined efforts of Vincent Barabba, Gerald Zaltman, and Stephan Haeckel. Discussed in Barabba and Zaltman, *Hearing the Voice of the Market*, 41–43.

8. Modified from the original found in Harold L. Wilensky, *Organizational Intelligence: Knowledge and Policy in Government and Industry* (New York: Basic Books, 1967), viii–ix.

9. Barabba and Zaltman, *Hearing the Voice of the Market*, 41–46.

10. For a full discussion of the Xerox benchmarking network, see Gregory Watson, *Strategic Benchmarking* (New York: John Wiley & Sons, 1993).

11. This discussion draws heavily on the work of Everett Rogers. See his book, *The Communication of Innovations: A Cross-Cultural Approach* (New York: Free Press, 1971).

12. Stephan H. Haeckel, "Adaptive Enterprise Design: The Sense-and-Respond Model," *Planning Review* 23, no. 3 (May/June 1995): 12.

Index

About the Author

Vincent P. Barabba is general manager of the General Motors Strategic Decision Center and oversees the centers for market data, market information, decision support, and information management as well as corporate strategic planning. Previously at General Motors he was executive in charge of the General Motors Business Decision Center/Corporate Information Management and executive director of market research and planning. Before joining General Motors, Mr. Barabba had been director of market intelligence for the Eastman Kodak Company, manager of market research for Xerox Corporation, twice director of the Bureau of the Census, and co-founder of Decision Making Information (now the Wirthlin Group).

He serves on boards of the American Institutes for Research, the Marketing Science Institute, and the National Opinion Research Center of the University of Chicago. He is a former president of the American Statistical Association, a former vice president of the American Marketing Association, and an elected member of the International Statistical Institute.

Mr. Barabba is the co-author, with Gerald Zaltman, of *Hearing the Voice of the Market: Competitive Advantage through Creative Use of Market Information* (Harvard Business School Press, 1991).